TEACHING HISTORY IN THE NEW EUROPE

Cassell Council of Europe series

This series is the result of a collaboration between the Council of Europe and Cassell. It comprises books on a wide range of educational material, drawn largely from seminars and research which have been initiated and sponsored by the Council of Europe.

TITLES IN THE SERIES

Teaching History in the New Europe

John Slater

CASSELL

This book is dedicated to countless students and pupils from whom I have learnt most that matters.

Cassell
Wellington House
125 Strand
London WC2R 0BB

215 Park Avenue South
New York
NY 10003

First published 1995

British Library Cataloguing in Publication Data
A catalogue record for this book is available from the British Library.

ISBN 0-304-32778-6 (hardback)
    0-304-32777-8 (paperback)

The views expressed in this book are those of the author and do not necessarily reflect those of the Council for Cultural Cooperation of the Council of Europe or its Secretariat.

Typeset by Action Typesetting Limited, Gloucester
Printed and bound in Great Britain by Redwood Books Ltd, Trowbridge, Wiltshire

Contents

PART 1: Past and Present

PART 2: The Future

List of Tables

Acknowledgements

This book would not have been possible, first, without the facilities and help of the staffs in numerous libraries: in London those of the University of London in Senate House and the Institute of Education, the Milicent Fawcett Library at the London Guildhall University, particularly David Dougan, and the libraries of the Science Museum and the Wellcome Institute of Medical Research; in Australia, the Bailleul Library, Law Library and the Library of the Institute of Education at Kew of the University of Melbourne, and the State Library of Victoria. I would also like to thank Caroline Elam, Eric Hoyle, Emilio Lastrucci, Nicola Madge, David Parry, Dennis Shemilt, John Standen, Robert Stradling, David Sylvester and Robert Unwin.

Second, thanks are also due to Peter Lee, my colleague at the University of London Institute of Education, and my patient neighbours Mark and Stuart Gunn, who saved my sanity and taught me to begin to love and use my word processor.

Lastly, thanks to the Council of Europe and its staff, particularly Alison Cardwell and Maitland Stobart, Deputy Director of Education, Culture and Sport, whose hard work and vision have sustained history for so long and whose idea this book was. If protocol allowed, it would be to him that it should be dedicated.

Introduction

History is an unsettling and sometimes uncomfortable subject. It is controversial and often very sensitive. There is some consensus about its importance but much less agreement about what it is *for*.

Is it simply a search for past societies, to understand them in their own terms, to disinter and exhibit the objective truth about them? Or is it a value-laden activity whose priorities and choice of content are inescapably affected by current social, political and personal circumstances? Is it studied, as some would claim, for 'its own sake'? Or are there instrumental aims, outside and beyond its concerns with the past – preparation for national or European citizenship, for liberal democratic societies, for patriotism, for challenging racism? Is history essentially a socializing or a mind-opening subject? Is it concerned with transmitting or examining values? The importance of these questions and our response to them will inevitably guide not only choice of subject matter, but also how we teach and, above all, how school students learn.

But where do the power and influence lie? *Who* influences the selection of content, decides pedagogy, identifies priorities and aims? Is it governments and their ministers of education, or educational administrators and inspectors (and who are *they* and how are they appointed)? Educationalists? University historians? Teachers of history in schools? Pupils and students? Parents and employers? Publishers and the media? Or is it more a matter of inherited, asserted and unexamined tradition? All, somewhere in Europe, play their part.

But where *is* Europe? What do Europeans have in common – a shared history and culture? And what is new about the New Europe? New since when and for whom? What is *significantly* new? Are Europeans citizens or subjects? Of where? Do moves towards European unity complement or conflict with separatism and fragmentation? Like history, these questions are highly controversial and can do little more than suggest lines of enquiry, rather than expect tidy answers.

They also provide the context in which this book was written. It was prompted by the Council of Europe's Symposium on 'The Teaching of History in the New Europe' held in Bruges in December 1991. It draws on the symposium's many predecessors dating back to 1953, on its successors in 1992 and 1993, and on many other Council of Europe initiatives. It is not, however, a report on, or summary of, these occasions, nor is it an apologia for them. It is, in part, a subjective reflection written by an Anglo-Scot who has always believed that we must see our national, cultural and personal roots in their European and world context.

The first chapter of this book examines the geographical, historical and cultural nature of Europe and considers some of the special features of a 'New Europe', particularly those which might be part of the learning of young Europeans. Chapters 2 and 3 describe the long record of support given to history by the Council of Europe, and a number of current initiatives, most of which are associated in some way with the Council of Europe. Chapters 4 and 5 are concerned with the particular circumstances in which curricular change is taking place. Chapter 4 looks at the issue of control; Chapter 5 examines the question of the kind of history learning young Europeans might need as they grow towards the twenty-first century. An appendix lists addresses throughout Europe that are relevant to history education.

PART 1

PAST AND PRESENT

CHAPTER 1

What is Europe? Place, Past or Culture?

History is a questioning subject. History teachers know that different questions not only have different answers, they also have different *functions*: to test factual recall, to question assumptions, to provoke debate and stimulate speculative thinking, to demand attention or maintain class control. But what are the *functions* of the question 'What is Europe?' Clearly it is not a question quite like 'Where is Australia?' or 'What is the Vatican City?' If it were, its repetition throughout the forty years of Council of Europe meetings on aspects of history teaching would have been both wasteful and wilful. It was raised again at the three 1991 Council of Europe conferences concerned with history – by Sean Lang, rapporteur at the Tuusula Conference,[1] in the opening keynote address by Professor Maurice De Vroede at the Bruges Symposium,[2] and, later in the same year, by Professor H. van der Dunk at the 1993 Conference in Leeuwarden.[3]

What linked this question, and others like it – 'Where is Europe?', 'Has Europe a shared past?', 'Has it a common culture?', 'Is Europe unique?' – is that they have been posed by historians to audiences, for the most part, of historians. Historians are crucially concerned with *change* in human affairs. Thus they are, or should be, suspicious of views of the past which prioritize continuity and similarity at the expense of discontinuity and difference, and they are, or should be, suspicious of any easy predictability. Historical conclusions are almost invariably provisional and tentative. Historians also pose questions in a language that is generally accessible and shared. There is no apparent need to acquire tools of translation as in, for example, much mathematical and scientific language; they have codes, which, once cracked, often reveal simple, usable and testable phenomena.

Historians, on the other hand, use non-technical language, often in general circulation, to describe, initially anyway, familiar and easily understood human situations: victories and defeats, 'terrorist' and 'freedom fighter', the 'free world' and 'evil empires', faith and persecution, nations that civilize and those that colonize, or the idea of a common European culture. *But*, and here is the point of thinking historically, behind these simple categories and tidy questions lie complexities, hidden subtleties, contradictions, uncomfortable exceptions. History as a subject moves

3

from the simple to the complex, from certainty to doubt, often from comfortable tidy moral categories to reservations, exceptions and uncertainties. That is the context in which we pose these deceptively simple questions about the location and uniqueness of Europe. Their principal function is to raise doubts, not to provide certainties.

However, the waters have been muddied, because many of us who have attended Council of Europe conferences and seminars and posed these questions have worn two hats: as *historians* whose perceptions of contemporary Europe seen in its historical context must be consistent with available evidence; and as *Europeans*, believers in, say, the vision of a united Europe or the concept of European citizenship. As historians we depend on the past; as Europeans we look to the future. We must not confuse aims that are historical with others that may be social, political, moral and, in the broadest sense, educational. Educational and historical aims may well be complementary, but they are different. 'The conception of European unity is certainly a high ideal, worthy of effort and sacrifice; but it draws its strength from our hopes for the future and not from our interpretation of the past', wrote Geoffrey Barraclough.[4] If we cannot be constantly aware of that distinction, we are in danger of confusing what history in the New Europe *is*, with what history might, potentially anyway, *enable*.

This confusion between an objective attempt to understand the past and our subjective aspirations for the future is revealed in many of the documents and recommendations emerging from Council of Europe meetings since the end of the 1940s. The confusions stem from three related but distinct flaws. The first is a failure to define concepts, usually based on assumptions more often asserted than examined; for example, 'the European idea' (the first Council of Europe conference held in Calw in 1953 was on 'The European Idea in History Teaching'), 'European awareness', 'European culture' – all phrases used in papers submitted to the 1991 Bruges Symposium, although such terms were scrutinized far more sceptically at the Leeuwarden Conference in 1993.

Second, there are statements assuming generalized aspects of the European past. For example, the document on proposed European cultural routes,[5] submitted to the Bruges Symposium, refers to 'European genius as a continuous phenomenon, expressed in various guises at each stage of European civilisation ... [and] the European tradition [which] continues to regard man as the principal object of its activities'. Another paper referred to 'the European cultural heritage'. A delegate to the Tuusula Conference argued that 'if Europe is to find a new identity' it must depend on 'a common ideological and cultural heritage of the past'. Participants at the 1965 Elsinore Conference recommended that 'in the teaching of history a certain number of historical facts which bear witness to the common culture of the peoples of Europe ought to be stressed.' Earlier, the 1954 Oslo Conference on 'The Middle Ages' wanted more emphasis on 'the heritage of Rome and the Greco-Roman world in the formation of Europe and its civilisation'. The 1979 Braunschweig Conference on 'Cooperation in Europe as Presented in the Resources for Teaching History, Geography and Civics in Secondary Schools' described the visit to Chartres Cathedral by the black American writer James Baldwin, who:

entered it at the same time as an old peasant couple. They moved around in the church with a sort of everyday practicality. Baldwin felt they belonged there and that the church was part of their heritage in a way which it could never be of his, in spite of all his intellectual knowledge of history. Consequently he defined a 'European as someone who is able to enter Chartres Cathedral and feel it has something to do with him'.[6]

Perhaps. It is not suggested that all these statements are invalid, merely that we should read them as *historians*, and see them less as statements than as questions to be asked about the past.

The final flaw is that many of the statements about the European past are closely associated, and sometimes confused, with others about the European future or with intended outcomes of learning history. A delegate at Tuusula stated that one of the priorities for the 1990s should be 'a re-awakening of the awareness of a European cultural identity', while one of the final recommendations of the same conference was that history syllabuses should include topics which *'foster'* (author's italics) a 'pan-European approach'. Earlier, the Elsinore Conference saw history as part of education for European and world citizenship, while the 1979 Braunschweig Conference said that teaching about Europe should make pupils aware of 'the common heritage they share as Europeans'.

Collectively, these statements fail to distinguish between historical and educational or more social aims; between what outcomes learning history may *enable* and those it should seek to *guarantee*; and whether at the heart of historical learning is the *transmission* or the *examination* of values. These questions will return in subsequent chapters. None, however, should divert us from continuing to pose the questions at the head of this chapter.

WHERE IS EUROPE?

> Do I contradict myself?
> Very well then I contradict myself,
> I am large, I contain multitudes.[7]

Despite the aspirations of many participants in the Council of Europe's history conferences, in the past it has been easier to define and explain Europe not so much in terms of a common culture as in those of a common adversary. Popular attitudes gave thanks for not being as other non-Europeans were. Metternich said Asia began on the *Landstrasse* (a statement that had just a touch more than metaphorical force); Adenauer is reputed to have said as he crossed the Elbe, 'Now we are in Asia'; the Italians say 'After Rome, Africa'. 'Beyond the pale' lives pejoratively on. Pope Julius II's 'Fuori i barbari!' ('Out with the barbarians!') continues to echo down the centuries. Past Europes were defined negatively, with political frontiers arbitrarily decided by geography or political circumstances – the Oder or the Vistula, the Pripet Marshes, the Carpathians, the Urals, the Alps or the Pyrenees, the Atlas or the Sahara, the Iron Curtain – and by a changing enemy, producing for the most part short-term pragmatic alliances united by little more than fear.[8] A suspicion of foreigners has often given Europe's shifting frontiers a spuriously moral as well as a geographical function.

We cannot expect to find much continuity in our search for Europe's location, nor will we find consistency, logic or tidiness. In May 1992, the London *Observer* published a map of the new Europe of 42 nations.[9] It included the republics of Belarus, Moldova, Georgia, Armenia and Azerbaijan; Yugoslavia was becoming Slovenia, Croatia, Serbia, Bosnia-Herzegovina, Montenegro and Macedonia; Czechoslovakia has now become the separate Czech and Slovak Republics. The accompanying article reminded us that associate arrangements had been reached with the European Union by Poland, Hungary and what was then Czechoslovakia, and that similar arrangements are likely to be negotiated with the Baltic States, Romania, Bulgaria and Albania. The former Soviet Republics in Europe have shown interest in joining the Council of Europe, and some of them participate in the organization's programmes on education and culture. Yugoslavia was a member of these programmes, and when the tragic civil war finally ends the new republics may well apply to join the European Union. Turkey's application to join (it is already a member of the Council of Europe) has been delayed, not because 96 per cent of its territory is in Asia but on economic and political grounds, although Morocco's application in 1987 was rejected as it was not a European power. Three years ago, and 12,000 miles away, the then chairman of the Australian Liberal Party argued the advantages of Australian membership of the European Union.

Two recent publications see the boundaries of Europe rather differently.[10] *Histoire de l'Europe*, published in 1992 with twelve authors drawn from across Europe, gave relatively little attention to Russia and Eastern Europe. Its patron and editor, Frédéric Delouche, sees Russia as a country with 'Asian characteristics' and, in the main, non-European. *European History: Sources and Materials*, published in Munich in 1994, is geographically more comprehensive and includes Russia, and accepts Charles Péguy's Europe as a peninsula of Asia, a continent from the Urals to the Atlantic. It offers a definition of Europe that is clear, all-embracing and historically valid but, as a framework for teaching history, almost unmanageable. Geography alone fails to provide a helpful agenda. So what about history?

HAS EUROPE A SHARED HISTORY?

> The coronation of Charles is not only the central event of the Middle Ages, it is also one of the very few events of which, taking them singly, it may be said if they had not happened, the history of the world would have been different ... On that day as through all the Dark and Middle Ages, two forces were striving for mastery. The one was the instinct of separation, disorder, anarchy, caused by the ungoverned impulses and barbarous ignorance of the great bulk of mankind; the other was that passionate longing of the better minds, for a formal

unity of government, which had its historical basis in the
memories of the old Roman Empire, and its most constant
expression in the devotion to a visible and Catholic Church.[11]

It is clear from statements made at European conferences on the teaching of history,
the content of its syllabuses, and the criteria for their selection (if indeed they are
revealed at all, or even known) that there remains a widely held assumption that
there is *something* unique and shared about Europe's history, and that events and ideas
in its past still affect our ideas and attitudes today. Bryce's eloquently asserted views
remain influential. We remain hypnotized by our classical past. Its legacy is probably
present in the history syllabuses of most young Europeans. From Greece and Rome,
there is an inheritance which is part of, if not a pan-European idea, at least a western
European idea. To Greece, it can be argued, we owe our traditions of liberty and
democracy; to the Romans, our concept of citizenship, urban order and law; the
roots of our intellectual development are Greco-Roman; our spiritual unity stems
from Catholic Rome and was maintained through the universal language of Latin.

After the fall of imperial Rome, continuity with the past was under threat, but
survived in a mix of Roman and Germanic popular culture – providing a key ingre-
dient, of European civilization – and leaving in parts of western Europe a synthesis of
Roman and common tribal law. But the barbarians were still at the gates and the
continuity with Roman order was still threatened. However, it was to be saved in
Aachen, or so it has often been asserted, on Christmas Day AD 800 by Charlemagne's
triumphant coronation, assisted by Pope Leo III. Thus the unity of Europe in its
origins was essentially Carolingian and Catholic, with Latin the medium of its continuity.
Seventy years after Bryce, Christopher Dawson also celebrated the significance of
Carolingian unity, but he added: 'Europe retained its cultural unity, but this was now
based on a common intellectual tradition and a common allegiance to the classical
tradition, rather than on a common faith.'[12] Today, much of this tidy picture remains
familiar. However, it ignores important elements in the Romano-Hellenic tradition
drawn not only from eastern Europe but from Asia. The direct heir of Rome was as
much Byzantium as Aachen, and remained so until 1453. Latin was virtually extinct
in the west by the third century; there was widespread antagonism to Roman traditions, while Christianity struggled against, and often succumbed, to pagan cults
whose links with their past were never broken. Intellectual continuity with the
Greco-Roman past, within which early Christianity was nurtured, was as likely to
be found in north Africa in the cities of Carthage and Alexandria, and in Asia Minor
in Nicea and Cappadocia. Even as late as the seventh and eighth centuries almost half
the popes had been born either in Greece or in Syria. It was not until 1123 that the
first of the great ecumenical church councils was held in Rome (five of its eight
predecessors had been held in Asia Minor, and the remaining three in
Constantinople).

So whatever the strengths of the Carolingian Empire, they coexisted with the
culturally distinct, bureaucratically sophisticated, and generally much more stable
Eastern Empire. Continuity cannot ignore Byzantium, nor indeed its successor,
Moscow, 'the third Rome'. ('Two Romes have fallen, but the third is standing and

there shall be no fourth', wrote Philotheus of Pskov.[13]) The cultural traditions of western Europe not only are a touch frayed at the edges but also have marginalized, even ignored, the cultures not only of Byzantium and Russia, but also of Islam, north Africa and Spain, together with the Scandinavians, Celts and Anglo-Saxons, to say nothing of the Judaic–Christian strands imported from the Asian extremities of the Roman Empire.

Since the Carolingian Empire and the period of high papal power under Innocent III, there have been shared European Bourbon, Napoleonic, Nazi New Order and Marxist proletarian pasts; aristocratic and dynastic pasts; Hanseatic, *Zollverein* and mercantile pasts. All were European, but all less, some much less, than the whole of Europe.

CIVILIZATION, HERITAGE AND CULTURE AS A FRAMEWORK

Civilization, heritage and culture suggest positive qualities and visions about the nature and achievements of a particular 'Europe' which do rather more than set it apart from others 'beyond the pale'. But how do we authenticate their claims? Are they historical realities? If so, there must be evidence of a European past and, further, of its continuity with the present. Or are they myths, metaphors which give a focus for aspirations, since that often appears to be their function? There is nothing wrong with myths and metaphors, provided we all recognize them as such.[14] But we are concerned with young people learning *history*, and this demands different kinds of authentication. So it is perhaps better to see 'culture' and 'heritage' as historical *concepts*, not historical facts. Thus, they do not immediately demand supporting evidence; rather they are tools of analysis which help us organize and apply evidence.

'Civilization' has been exported by Europeans. We have 'civilized' others less fortunate than ourselves, often with an insensitive, sometimes barbaric, certainty of the benefits we have imposed. The idea of European civilization is altogether too smug and complacent, racist even, with its implicit undertones of superiority. Assumed values and proclaimed superiority are uneasy foundations for thinking historically. It is more the task of historians to try and identify values and subsequently to understand them and evaluate them critically.

The concept of 'heritage' also has its problems. 'Heritage' is 'culture' institutionalized into 'foundations', 'trusts', 'museums', 'coffee-table books'. It is something we own; it is *our* heritage. It is often a rag-bag of a hygienic and comfortable past, folk heroes (occasionally heroines) and village fairs, tidily contained within theme parks and carefully mapped heritage walks. Sometimes heritage, confirmed by a manipulated and invented tradition,[15] can have a public and official face in anniversaries, parades and ceremonies. It can have authoritarian overtones, not so much inviting our interest and admiration as demanding our respect and uncritical loyalty. 'Heritage' has too often been the ally of despots.

This is not to suggest that we reject the concept of 'civilization' and 'heritage' but merely to wonder whether they are not treacherous historical guides, inconsistent with the unsettling, sceptical, disquieting functions of history. If we do use these terms, let us see them first as 'cultures' and 'heritages'. The plurals are crucial. Second, let us see them as hypotheses to be tested, *not* as values to be transmitted.

The search for a European culture

What do people who have a common culture *share*? Arguably they share a continuity with a familiar past, a language and means of communication, shared rituals, aspirations and beliefs. Here the term is used in an anthropological sense as in, for example, 'Polynesian' culture, or a sociological sense as in 'working-class' or 'youth' culture. It is often concerned with what is termed 'popular culture'; for example, in the present-day world, with television and the cinema, the tabloid press, strip cartoons and magazines, fashion and popular music, sporting rituals and so on. It is frequently the focus of study of new and expanding departments of 'media studies' or 'cultural studies', in which history, if it is present at all, is one of a federal group of complementary disciplines. It is not an approach that seems, as yet, to have influenced significantly either the content or the methodology of history in European secondary schools.

On the other hand, the tradition of high culture has remained strong – what Ernst Gombrich calls the 'canon'.[16] It demonstrates human achievement in art, architecture, literature and music at its very highest. It is culture, not so much as shared experience as exemplar. It is a tradition which is aristocratic, transcendental and individual, as opposed to being popular, short-term and shared. It is, in the main, how the publications and deliberations of the Council of Europe see culture, perhaps most splendidly exemplified by their great series of art exhibitions, starting with 'Humanist Europe' in Brussels in 1955 (see Chapter 2).

Popular culture is concerned with what is already accessible, familiar, shared and localized. But the study of high culture seeks access to an unfamiliar and apparently elitist world whose aims and values, if not quite universal, demonstrate at least a *European* achievement. Ernest Gellner distinguishes between what he terms 'wild' and 'garden' cultures: 'Wild' cultures are shared and 'reproduce themselves from generation to generation without conscious design, supervision, surveillance or special nutrition ... Garden cultures ... possess a complexity and richness, most usually sustained by literacy and specialised personnel.'[17]

However, the language, rituals, sometimes the prejudices, of 'wild' culture can be exploited and mobilized from above in the cause of a *national* culture, seen less as an exemplar of human achievement than as acceptable social behaviour and a focus for loyalty: positively, as patriotism and a canon of couth social mores; negatively, as conferring a bogus dignity on crude nationalism and xenophobia. But the two cultures are not competitive; one grows out of the other. None of us can escape the 'popular' and 'wild' culture which surrounds and moulds us, but access to 'high culture' and its garden depends on chance, social circumstances, choice, or the guidance of education.

Thus, European culture, whether high or popular, national or class, as a criterion for selecting aspects of European history has some problems. Unlike an all-embracing geographical Europe, culture is essentially *exclusive* and perhaps none the worse for that, if we recognize it as such. However, it can be, and has often been, a self-fulfilling concept, and that is not only unhistorical but terribly dangerous. 'Culture' becomes a form of qualification, an entrée, a testimonial. Those who do not share it are not, or not quite, 'one of us', not wholly 'European'. Their behaviour or their art is seen as aberrant, decadent, or primitive. I hope that most of us would determinedly argue that Europe would have been impoverished, at the least very different, without Jewish achievements in the sciences, psychology, politics, art, literature and the economy, without Islamic contributions to mathematics, medicine and philosophy or Christian ethics, born in the Middle East. All these achievements did not prevent European expulsions and persecutions. 'Culture' can cement groups and proclaim achievement, but there is a dark side of the moon at its celebration which can lead to xenophobia and did lead to Auschwitz.

Europe as a place, with a shared past and culture, seems implicitly to be seeking a commonality, a defined 'Europeanness'. But the quarry remains elusive. It is a search which tells us more about our present political preoccupations and aspirations for the future than it does about history. But it goes further than this. In some of the statements and recommendations quoted earlier in this chapter – 'European genius as a continuous phenomenon', the search for a 'new European identity', 'a European cultural identity' – there is an assumption that not only are there shared, but also *unique*, European characteristics. Even further, perhaps in references to 'European genius', do we not sense that the characteristics are seen as not only unique but superior?

EUROPE, A UNIQUE CONTINENT?

Industry and technology

There is one characteristic that forces itself upon our attention. That is technical progress. If historians, in their relentless search for origins, come to deny beginnings, none can refuse to accept that European technical achievements have no parallel in the past or elsewhere ... what characterises European history is technical knowledge.[18]

Perhaps. Let us extend our time span before nineteenth-century industrialization and look beyond Europe. Joseph Needham, in his epic account of Chinese science and technology,[19] reminds us of their achievements centuries before the European scientific and industrial revolutions. Lynn White's study of medieval technology[20] describes key advances in warfare and agriculture – the stirrup and the water-driven wheel – with their origins in Asia and Asia Minor, although he concedes the development of the three-field system and the plough to western Europe.

Certainly European industrial and scientific advance in the eighteenth and nineteenth centuries was remarkable, but it was largely confined in its origins to north-western Europe. Eastern Europe, southern Italy, the Balkan peninsula and Iberia played relatively minor parts. What about the *second* industrial revolution, associated more with new sources of power, new materials, and in particular the organization and application of industrialization – technocracy rather than technology? Here we must spread our net within and again far beyond Europe. The first oil wells were sunk in 1859 in Ploesti in Romania and, in the same year, in Pennsylvania; the first internal combustion engine was developed in the United States in 1873; the first hydroelectric power plant was on the Niagara, liberating electricity from steam power and coal; celluloid was developed by the Englishman, Alexander Parker, to make artificial billiard balls, but its development and use in photography were due to John Hyatt of New Jersey. And telecommunication cables, road transport and cheap and effective male contraception would hardly have been possible without the vulcanization of rubber in 1843 by Charles Goodyear of Philadelphia. As for the organization of industry, we cannot forget Ford and the assembly line, or the mass capitalist enterprises of Andrew Carnegie, John Pierpont Morgan and, subsequently, the Japanese.

None of this denies some validity to Douglas Johnston's case, but that depends on a geographically limited definition of Europe and has to be stretched to include American and Japanese industrialization and scientific advance, seen as colonized trans-Atlantic/trans-Pacific European salients. But at least we can argue that, during the last two hundred years, and within the frontiers of geographical Europe, there has been a remarkable concentration of scientific and technological progress.

European art

Our appreciation and understanding of European art have often been dominated by three main concerns. In the first place with its *styles*: an ability to relate them to period and give them a chronology; to identify and distinguish between Romanesque and Gothic, early and high Renaissance, Baroque and Neo-Classicism. Further, they have been concerned with *individuality*, not just of styles but of artists, with Giotto and Ghiselbertus, Shakespeare and Tolstoy, Beethoven and Bartok, Fischer von Erlach and Le Corbusier, seen as exemplifying the heights of human achievement. So the final concern has been with *greatness*. Lack of evidence and their contemporary status do not help us identify, let alone celebrate, the individual craft-workers who built Chartres or Durham or St Vitus, or to seek out the lives of the mosaicists of Ravenna or Istanbul.

This emphasis on the evolution of styles and image, and on individual human achievement, has provided us with an agenda which seems peculiarly European and sets us apart from how others look at and *use* the artistic achievements of, for example, Islam, the Maya or Shintoism.

Great art can also distract us with its rhetoric: we may be persuaded by the magnificence of the achievement rather than the credibility of the message. Richard III has not escaped from the clutches of Shakespeare, nor Wallenstein from those of

Schiller. 'The historian has to compete with Holbein and Van Dyck, and he is bound to lose.'[21]

But we have also been distracted by our concern with the visual and decorative aspects of art: art as ornament. It has led to the bleak doctrine of 'art for art's sake', with art galleries, sale rooms and predatory collectors as its memorials. It is a view of art which has only been a feature of European history for the last three or four hundred years, and it has driven a wedge between the artist and society. Style has become divorced from *function*.

For most of recorded history, art had social purposes. Art was less to do with beauty, style and decoration than with power and magic, education and propaganda, worship and politics; less with private collections than with public rituals. Nikolaus Pevsner blames the change on oil on canvas and easel painting, making art portable and separating it from wall painting, and ultimately from architecture, the most socially purposeful of all art forms. He identifies this not just as a minor change in the history of western art, but as a key turning point, arguably a kind of decline, in which artistic 'achievements are torn out of the common ground of life'.[22]

So, in our pursuit of European art, we may too often have been diverted by the relatively minor matter of style, seduced by beauty, dazzled by greatness, and confined to western Europe, and so severed our links from the great mainstream of art as a social, moral and didactic force: sometimes ignored what the frescoes of San Francesco in Arezzo, the limewood sculptures of Tilman Riemenschneider in southern Germany, the Alhambra in Granada, or the mosaics of Monreale and Ravenna, were originally *for*. They share, if not style, something much more fundamental with, say, Buddhist temples in southeast Asia or the Mayan remains or Chichen Itza or Uxmal, and that is a social, political and, almost invariably, a spiritual *function*.

My love and understanding of western European art have been the source of a great lifelong pleasure. But it was as a tourist that I looked and listened. As *historians*, however, we are concerned with pictures and mosaics, buildings and poems, not just as high culture or as the source of aesthetic delight, but as *evidence*. What do they tell us about past cultures, attitudes and societies? Thus historians' questions are less concerned with style, attribution and greatness, and more with social context, argument and function. Consequently we might recognize that the great styles of European art are geographically limited, but that their functions link them with the images, sounds and buildings of a wider world elsewhere.

This is not an argument against high art, and it does not deny that, while some styles developed only within parts of Europe, others permeated most of what we understand as continental Europe. Gothic, particularly Gothic Revival, Baroque, later Neo-Classicism, became some of Europe's most characteristic and successful exports. Those styles and cultures have strong claims to be 'European'.

Gothic, Renaissance, Baroque and Neo-Classical have had both institutional and moral foundations. Until the Reformation, the confessional unity of the Catholic church dominated medieval Europe (perhaps never more united than under the papacy of Innocent III). Its language was Latin, its authority was maintained through the monastic and mendicant orders exercising their educational and disciplinary roles in a way that was truly supranational, and Gothic architecture was its setting. Its spires, pointed arches and ribbed vaults celebrated the faith in much of Europe: in Uppsala and Seville, Cracow and York, Chartres and Cluj.

But by the end of the Middle Ages and among the harbingers of the Reformation, humanism and Renaissance art and architecture drew their inspiration from the classical past of Greece and Rome, proclaiming not only the appropriateness of their styles but the virtues and ethos of their urban cultures. The patrons of this art included not only churchmen but powerful secular princes, bankers and the councils of great cities in Italy and central Europe. Later, the ubiquity of Renaissance architecture evolved and elaborated into Baroque, and was given the institutional and spiritual backing by the Council of Trent, who saw that the dramatic gestures and iconography of Baroque art and the new spaces of its architecture provided a suitably impressive theatre for the preaching of the reformed faith and its rituals. But high Renaissance and Baroque also celebrated the secular achievements and power of the Bourbons and Wittelsbachs, Vasas and Romanovs. Baroque suited Versailles as much as Rome.

Later, the austere Neo-Classical revival proclaimed the virtues of Greece and Rome and saw their achievements as canons against which eighteenth-century art and morality could be measured. Neo-Classicism was disseminated neither by the Council of Trent nor by the armies of Louis XIV, but by the rational ideas of the Enlightenment and, from the end of the seventeenth century, by the new academies of science and art in Italy, Paris and London, followed by others in Berlin, Leiden, Uppsala, Edinburgh and Dublin.

But with the advent of Romanticism we are reminded that a culture and style can turn their back on a shared ethos or on the institutional backing of church or state. The Romantic movement asserted the artist as an individual who creates goals rather than strives for them. To the romantic artist, 'creation is not an attempt to copy some already given, fixed, eternal Platonic pattern. Only craftsmen copy: artists create.'[23] The tidy unitary European worlds of Rome, of classical virtue and of the Enlightenment were shattered by the Romantic movement. An art form complemented the ideas of Fichte, Nietzsche and Carlyle and provided the metaphors, icons and anthems of a continent torn apart by national and cultural rivalries.

Not until the decades after World War I was Europe again to enjoy common cultures, with the advent of the modern movement in painting, design and architecture. The movement had distinguished European exponents, but it was, above all, a pervasive and persuasive import from the United States of America. Most recently and least organized and aggressive, and within the lifetime of many of us, a mid-atlantic youth culture of popular music and colloquial language, fashions and hairstyles, food and lifestyles, disseminated by Hollywood and television, hitch-hiking and charter flights, has ridden roughshod over ideological differences, across state frontiers and generations, and imposed itself on Europe.

When we as *historians* try to understand past societies, our agenda for understanding should have different priorities from those of traditional historians of art, interrogate it with different questions and analyse it with new concepts. To do so will not undermine our sense of wonder at human achievement, which can still increase our understanding of human society. The achievements of the artists and architects who worked within Europe will not be diminished, but we will be reminded that only sometimes were they pan-European, often most significant when most regional; that culture was only sometimes a unifying force; that on occasions, it was an expression of dissent and aggression, often a manifestation of political or spiritual power and one of the tools of conquest and exclusion. On the other hand, a realization of the public function of culture and the arts may give us a conceptual framework which is less self-congratulatory and Eurocentric.

A political tradition

Perhaps we are on more certain ground if we seek a European political tradition. The American historian David Potter argues that democracy depends on a particular combination of an abundance of natural resources and geographical space (Space + Abundance = Democracy).[24] He was writing about the United States, but he offers us a model that can apply to Europe, which has enjoyed an abundance of *usable* natural resources, with science and technocracy able to exploit them. Like the United States, Europe has benefited from space and an expanding frontier: internally to the east towards the Pacific, externally across the Atlantic and into newly acquired colonies in Asia and Africa. Europe has innocently and sometimes arrogantly tried to export democracy to parts of the world without abundance; Potter reminds us that we have not always understood that, in other parts of the world, democracy may seem attainable but not particularly desirable, whereas abundance is most desirable but quite unattainable. Potter's necessary circumstances exist, but have they been sufficient? Has 'democracy' uniquely flourished in Europe?

The emphasis of the question should perhaps be less on 'democracy' as an idea and more on the realities of popular participation in public behaviour. The American historian William McNeill[25] argues that popular participation (at least a symptom of if not a sufficient condition for democracy) in economic, cultural and political life was far greater in *western* Europe than in any other civilization of the world. He reminds us, for example, that the staples of European commerce were not luxury goods, but wool and coarse cloth, herrings, timber; that a wide range of social activities of ordinary people found cultural expression in medieval psalters and the misericordes, gargoyles and roof bosses of Gothic churches. Public art in Europe showed images of shepherds and fishermen as well as princes and kings, of stables and carpenters' shops as well as palaces; a higher proportion of the population participated in war, pikemen recruited from Italian towns and Swiss villages challenging aristocratic knights, the cream of French chivalry defeated by English peasant longbowmen.[26] In politics and public life, the English parliaments, the Estates General of France, the craft guilds of Tuscany, the vertical mobility within the church of Rome all began to challenge the inherited aristocratic monopoly of political power. These institutions were not yet democracies as we understand them, and they were a long way from universal suffrage, but they were already becoming different in kind from the hierarchic and often sacerdotal cultures of medieval Europe, still found in other continents.[27]

Of course, many of these European instruments of popular political participation still had elements of theocracy in common with more hierarchic systems until well into the early modern period, whether papal, Calvinist, Cromwellian or Presbyterian. It was a tradition that died hard. The author of a popular English hymn proclaimed:

> The rich man in his castle,
> The poor man at his gate,
> God made them, high and lowly,
> And ordered their estate.

He died only in 1875.

Social Darwinism invested capitalism and profit with a natural inevitability that enlisted divine approval in its support, or so John D. Rockefeller argued: 'the good Lord gave me the money.'[28] But already, during the preceding centuries, popular participation in political power was beginning slowly to free itself from the magisterial traditions of the established Protestant and Catholic churches. Voltaire may well have been a touch premature and overoptimistic when, in 1760, he termed the eighteenth century 'the age of reason'. But by its end, the theorists of natural law were challenging the ideas of divine right and absolutism, and both the concept of government based on *contract*, and the assertion of the supremacy of reason, were being publicly debated and disseminated.

The influence of these ideas was still limited, both in effect and geographically; their disciples sometimes grievously distorted their ideas ('reason' and 'utopianism' were regularly conscripted by executioners). But, in western Europe at least, a secular and rational political agenda was becoming established. Later, Marx and Engels would supply evidence of the impact of industrial progress on human lives, offering an epic analytical framework of the past and an alternative *secular* route to a visionary future.

Arguably more politically influential in some countries, notably in England, was a non-revolutionary alliance between the traditions of nonconformist Christianity and radical working-class reform movements, assisting at the birth of organized trade unions and the extension of the franchise, and offering at least the possibility of a challenge to the power of employers, and access to parliamentary democracy. Of course, at the end of the nineteenth century absolute monarchies were still the most characteristic form of European government. But the franchise was being extended in many European countries, although this was a result of legislation enacted by men and, until the end of the Great War, exclusively on behalf of men. Equal suffrage between men and women was not achieved in France, Italy and Belgium until after World War II and not until 1972 in Switzerland. A genuinely democratic franchise was pioneered far away from Europe when women for the first time were given the vote in South Australia in 1892. By the end of the last century, alternative visions were slowly becoming available. As a secular morality, the ideals born out of poverty have some claim to being a uniquely European contribution to political behaviour.

But history, as well as our disconcerting present, caution us against sentimentalizing those ideals or exaggerating their acceptance. Ideals offer promises for the future that reality can rarely deliver. Hannah Arendt's pessimistic diagnosis has not, alas, been seriously threatened by events:

> No revolution has ever solved the social question and liberated men from the predicament of want, but all revolutions ... have followed the example of the French Revolution and used and misused the mighty forces of misery and destitution in their struggle against tyranny or oppression.

She invoked the words of Robespierre, who compared the nation to the ocean: 'it was indeed the ocean of misery and the ocean-like sentiments it aroused that combined to drown the foundations of freedom.'[29]

What was uniquely European was not, however, necessarily characteristic. Flourishing alongside liberal parliamentary democracy, revolutionary socialist movements and the old European monarchies was another European strand. It has been called 'Romantic authoritarianism'.[30] It was essentially anti-rationalist and anti-individualist; the state, identified with race, was envisaged as the unit to which total allegiance is owed; it was opposed to economic liberalism and socialism and to government by discussion and dissent; it favoured charismatic leadership; it was not, in one sense, anti-democratic in that it invoked the idea of popular sovereignty. It was born, as Isaiah Berlin reminds us, from a tradition in European history of 'a kind of dialectic between craving for public order and for individual liberty'.[31]

There were elements of Romantic authoritarianism present in some Catholic political thought; it has given us the reality of 'ethnic cleansing'; but its most terrible manifestations have been Fascism, Nazism and Stalinism. This is not the place to argue whether these ideas were distortions of Romantic authoritarianism or inherent symptoms of it; or, for that matter, whether Marxism nurtured the seeds of Stalinism, or was terribly betrayed by it. What cannot be denied is that Fascism, Nazism and Stalinism have also been characteristic, perhaps uniquely so, of twentieth-century Europe.

Assimilating and exporting

McNeill argues another crucial European characteristic − Europe as an *assimilating* continent. 'The ease and eagerness with which [Europeans] appropriated these alien inheritances has perhaps no equal in civilised history';[32] until, we might add, the technological, industrial, cultural and political developments of nineteenth- and twentieth-century Japan. Complementing this last characteristic has been the unique power of Europe to export. This has not just been a matter of trade, of the recycling of primary resources into exported manufactured goods. Ideas were also exported: political, religious and cultural, exemplified in parliamentary procedures, architecture, religious beliefs, military training and uniforms, public pageants and rituals, and popular culture. Europe exported people, too: soldiers and settlers, engineers and academics, missionaries and convicts. The European ability to assimilate and export was the result of an untidy and confusing mix of motives, altruistic and exploitative, sensitive and understanding, arrogant and clumsily innocent. They provide contexts for, and suggest some consequences of, European economic, technological and political developments. They permit us, as Europeans, some cause for pride; they do not acquit us of a measure of guilt and unease.

'Europe' is complex, contradictory, arbitrary and constantly changing. To claim uniqueness or commonality would be to impose on it a coherence that would be artificial, misleading and quite unhistorical. This chapter has not sought to answer the open questions which it posed at the outset. It has sought to avoid dogma and maintain doubt; the questions remain hypotheses that must constantly be reviewed and tested. The enterprise of history will continue to pose these questions, stimulated and inspired not by the expectation of unambiguous and timeless answers, but by the excitement of the chase.

WHAT IS NEW ABOUT THE NEW EUROPE?

We live today in a world different, in almost all its basic preconditions, from the world in which Bismarck lived and died.[33]

The concept of a 'New Europe' was given the imprimatur of the Council of Europe in December 1991 in Bruges, when it convened the most geographically comprehensive and perhaps most remarkable of its symposia: 'History Teaching in the New Europe: Challenges, Problems and Opportunities'. It prompted and provided the context for this book.

But how do we identify not just what *is* 'new' about the 'New Europe', but what is *significantly* new? And how do we decide which of the new factors and circumstances, and which aspects of them, should be part of the learning of history of young Europeans?

Wherein lies this newness? How recent is 'new'? Are we considering circumstances without precedent or forebears? If so, they would provide a poor foundation for the element of continuity in human behaviour, and be unhistorical. Or are they perhaps circumstances which are new within the lifetimes of living Europeans? But this would give 'newness' an uncomfortably narrow, chronological base, sitting on a pinhead, too meagre to sustain historical study, which in any case might too easily distract us with mere novelty, the ephemeral, the insignificant.

'New' circumstances, I suggest, significantly interrupt or disturb continuity with the past. Often they are unanticipated and, to begin with, outside the experience of many living Europeans. They may, on the basis of limited evidence, experience and a measure of anticipatory hunch, suggest a range of possible and significant futures. These circumstances distinguish 'modern' (that is, post-medieval) from contemporary history, which begins, according to Barraclough, *'when the problems which are actual in the world today first take visible shape'*.[34]

The chronology of these problems is untidy. Some developments – in science and technology and the changing balance of power between Europe and Asia and Africa, for example – began to interrupt the continuity between the present and the long

European past well before the end of the nineteenth century; others – developments in information or nuclear technology and space travel – have emerged only since 1945; the collapse of Communist rule in Europe and its effect on the world balance of power and the political aspirations of millions were barely anticipated 10 years ago; while moves for European unity, as well as forces of separatism and fragmentation, can be exemplified from two thousand years of European history.

But how historical is contemporary history? Historians share a broad, if sometimes disputatious, view about, say, the importance of the fall of Constantinople, or the Thirty Years War, or the Napoleonic invasion of Russia. Their ability to claim *significance* for these events is based, in part, on some estimate of their outcomes, on historians' retrospective evaluation of evidence. On the other hand, to claim significance for situations and issues which are not only current but new can only partly be the result of historical analysis. Assertions about the outcomes and significance of the opening of the Berlin Wall, the Treaty of Maastricht, the Earth Summit in Rio, *perestroika*, the civil war in the former Yugoslavia, or space travel are in part predictive. A claim for their significance is speculative, based on limited evidence and on 'guesstimates' about outcomes, conditioned largely by our current personal, social, political and educational priorities. This is particularly so when what we know is based on the evidence of those who have observed and sometimes actively participated in the events they describe. The eyes and cameras of journalists, the experiences of participants, give their views a particular authority which is, nevertheless, limited by location or cultural and political loyalties, which may threaten a wider perspective and the more reflective retrospective interpretations.

But we still have to decide to *which* aspects of Europe we give priority in our syllabuses, write whole chapters on in our textbooks, consign to footnotes, or wholly ignore. If choice is the privilege, the responsibility and sometimes the burden of living in a democratic society, it also lies at the heart of public historical procedures.

To envisage school history syllabuses encompassing the totality of all Europe would be impractical. We need an initial framework for selection. I have already suggested that the criterion of 'the European idea' is too elusive; 'geographical Europe' too vast and unmanageable; a common European past too partial and limited; European 'culture', 'heritage' and 'tradition' too lacking in definition, ambiguous and value-laden. All offer scope, but none gives adequate guidance. They do not prioritize or help us choose. Some too readily assume a consensus about *content* waiting to be discovered. So decision is a matter of ruthless selection.

Clearly, we need a criterion to help us select syllabus content, one which is sharply focused and usable, a framework but not a strait-jacket. One criterion is suggested by the conviction consistently present in Council of Europe documentation, notably in many of the papers submitted to the 1991 Bruges Symposium, that a study of the past helps young people understand the world in which they live, by putting features of it into the historical context of change through time. There are references to a need for 'a critical approach to historical and present day events' and an understanding of 'the present in the context of the past', of 'the present [with] expectations for the future', of the 'processes in the contemporary world' which enable 'pupils to understand the historical context of the society in which they live', and of the 'origins of contemporary economic and political systems'.[35] Such statements were omnipresent throughout the Bruges Symposium. They are based not just on what history *is* but on assumptions of what it is *for*, at least potentially.

Of course, there remain strong arguments for studying the past societies of, say, Rome, Sumer, Byzantium, Renaissance Florence or Biedermeier Vienna for their own sake, although this is a dangerous and evasive personification. But the massed battalions of European history students are aged between 5 and 15. History teaching has a responsibility to contribute to lessening their misunderstanding and diminishing their ignorance of the world in which they live, and in particular, the New Europe.

But *which* features of the New Europe should we teach? They will be themes exemplified *within* Europe without necessarily being characteristic of *all* Europe. While they may be characteristically European, they make no claim to be uniquely European. Some themes may be studied over a long period of time, others will be more chronologically limited. But whatever the time-span, their study should relate *directly* and *explicitly* to the world as we observe and experience it today. The papacy of Innocent III and the Hanseatic League are part of the history of unifying European forces. They are not substitutes for understanding the development of the European Union or support for European federalism. Students on the barricades and Tsarist troops in central Europe in 1848 may present a poignant comparison with Prague in 1968, but they are not the same thing. Nor are the rotation of crops and selective animal breeding, the steam engine, the development of postal systems and Marconi, the Black Death and cholera, substitutes for artificial fertilizers, pesticides and combine harvesters, rocket propulsion and computers, or AIDS. Ancestry must not be confused with explanation.

Any selection of contemporary European themes will only partly use historical criteria, although the methodology of their teaching and learning study must be wholly historical.

SOME KEY THEMES: A PRELIMINARY AGENDA

This section proposes a number of key European themes with some suggested exemplifying detail which could feature in the history syllabuses of all young Europeans. It is no more than a possible framework, a subjective and tentative list, a cautious agenda, with some possible features that might guide their treatment in classrooms. The themes are:

- **technological and scientific change:**
  - *the second industrial revolution* (post *c.* 1860): new sources of power; new materials; new cures; new weapons; new means of travel; new means of storing and communicating information; new forms of organizing industrial production;
  - *some effects of these developments*: a rapid increase in population; new concentrations and distributions of state power; an increased ability to challenge state

power; a new balance between work and leisure; (shorter working weeks, longer holidays, earlier retirement, unemployment, imposed leisure); new moral attitudes and uncertainties (genetic engineering, mass contraception, the pill, antibiotics, AIDS); a different scale and pattern of urbanization; war becoming total; environmental gains and losses;

- **the dwarfing of Europe:**
  - *demographic changes*: global population rise; the redistribution of populations (rural to urban, Europe to Asia, Africa and Latin America; Mediterranean to Atlantic to Pacific);
  - *challenges to European power*: Isandlhwana, Adowa, Tsushima, Pearl Harbor–Singapore–Hong Kong, Vietnam; the end of European empires;
  - *challenges to European economic superiority*;
  - *changes in UN membership*;
- **the arrival of the masses:**
  enfranchisement of males, females; end of property qualifications; enfranchisement but not empowerment; alienation of the masses; trade unions; mass education and literacy; dissemination of knowledge and ideas;
- **the changing status of women:**
  - *women in government and politics*: the vote, influence and pressure groups, ministerial posts; participation and influence in trade unions;
  - *women in education and at work*: access to school and higher education, status as teachers; access to the full range of studies and skills; access to positions of responsibility, equal opportunities and pay;
  - *women in society*: in the home and family and as autonomous individuals; legislation to protect the property of married women against violence in and outside the home and against discrimination; legislation on, and changing attitudes to, family planning, contraception, abortion and single-parent families; impact on domestic life and paid work opportunities of technology (gas cookers, canned food, refrigerators, washing machines, electricity and the typewriter); legislation to protect property and criminalize rape; family allowances;
- **forces for European unity:**
  - *imposed unity*: conquest, conversion;
  - *negotiated and agreed unity*: alliances, the UN, the European Union, NATO, the Council of Europe, the OSCE, the Red Cross, the International Court of Justice, the International Telegraphic Union, the ILO, Socialist Internationals, etc.;
  - *economic unity*: Hanseatic League, EFTA, the European Union, multinational corporations and shops, credit cards and Euro-cheques;
  - *science and technology as unifiers*: roads, railways, navigation, air travel, printing, telephones, faxes and computers, radio and television, etc.;
  - *cultural unity*: the papacy and Catholicism, Gothic, Renaissance, Neo-Classicism, Modernism, popular and youth culture;
  - *cultural dissemination*: by conversion, conquest, persecution; academies of science and art, radio and television, the cinema; educational visits and exchanges;

- **forces for disunity and separatism:**
  - *inherited loyalties: to USA, to ex-colonies; linguistic and cultural loyalties;*
    - nationalism and internal separatism: ethnic and cultural minorities and self-determination;
  - *economic rivalries*: mercantilism, protectionism, trade wars, arms sales;
- **a new multiculturalism:**
  - *people on the move since 1945:* post-colonialism, Third World poverty, migration and immigration, flight from persecution; search for employment;
  - *mutual gains:* the enrichment of Europe cultural, religious diversity;
  - *costs:* discrimination, exploitation, xenophobia and racism;
  - *pluralist and open societies*;
- **Europe in an interdependent world:**
  - *economic and environmental interdependence:* international travel and tourism, international labour markets; the indifference of pollution to frontiers;
  - *educational and cultural links:* educational exchanges and the equivalence of qualifications, the sharing of experiences and their images (achievements, wealth, poverty, bloodshed, natural disasters) through print, transistors, television and film;
  - *international responsibilities*: Médecins sans Frontières, Live Aid, European soldiers and the UN in Cyprus, Cambodia, Somalia, Bosnia;
- **the end of ideology: post-Communist or post-imperial Europe?:**
  The suggested agenda which follows is based on the observations of many who witnessed and participated in the events of the east and central European revolutions:[36]
  - *'Why did they not shoot?'*: With few exceptions, the emancipation of eastern and central Europe remarkably and without precedent one of the most fundamental non-violent changes in European history: subsequent violence largely internal and related to implementation of change;
  - *the absence of the east*: long history in central and east Europe of intervention from Russia and Asia (Goths, Avars, Huns, Tartars); Russian intervention in Poland in eighteenth century, 1939, 1945; in central Europe in 1848, 1945 (with support from the United Kingdom and USA), 1953, 1956 and 1968 – but the 1989 and 1990 revolutions largely home-grown, without Russian intervention;
  - *the role of the west*: the west seen not only as an exemplar of liberal democracy, but as embodying the idea of Europe;[37] the west as source of economic aid (sometimes given with political or ideological strings); the west as a source of economic, managerial, educational, scientific and technological expertise; exchanges, professional contacts and joint learning and teaching with the west – what can, and does, the west learn from the east?;
  - *the environment and green politics*: the Chernobyl explosion of 1986 not just a (then) Soviet problem, but also a European one; part played by environmental issues in the first elections held throughout central and eastern Europe not only as part of the programmes of organized political parties but as a focus for public opinion and protest;[38]

- *the entwined tension between nationalism and democracy*: nationalism and democracy often on opposite sides of the barricades during the last two centuries; both invoked the other in their struggles for recognition; during the Stalinist period, nationalism often exploited by party leaders as a means of central control and a focus for organized popular loyalty – for example, by Husák in what was then Czechoslovakia, Hoxha in Albania, above all by Ceauçescu in Romania; democrats and nationalist as allies and joint celebrants of the revolutions of 1989–91; new alliances between disaffected Communists and ultra-nationalists.[39]

The revolutions of central and eastern Europe dramatically disturbed the continuity of European history. Whether they herald a new Europe or simply revive savage aspects of the old remains to be seen. It may well be that future historians will see the real break with the past less as the end of Communism and rather more as a final chapter in the history of colonialism. What happened in central and eastern Europe was not so much the collapse of a party, but the end of the last European empire. The jury is still out.

CONCLUSION: COPING WITH NEWNESS

> Now what is going to happen to us without barbarians?
> They were, those people, a kind of solution.[40]

The stability of Cold War Europe gave us familiar friends and enemies. It gave us time to adjust, calculate and plan. We no longer have the security of reasonable predictability. Time for anticipation is shorter. The New Europe is a continent not only of new circumstances and aspirations, but of new uncertainties and anxieties. We live in a continent of rapid and unfamiliar *rates of change*. No longer does the length of a generation or a lifespan help us to adjust easily to cycles of innovation, implementation and obsolescence. New freedoms are barely enjoyed before they become threats. Before new moral imperatives have time to become acceptable, they are undermined. New political attitudes, lifestyles, personal relationships, art forms scarcely have time to be revolutionary and shocking before they become routine and domesticated. Our abilities to understand and adapt have to operate within a totally new time-span. 'Education for change' is a cliché, a slogan more often asserted than implemented. It is now a matter of the utmost urgency to establish it as a reality.

The last section of this chapter listed features and events all within the living memory of at least some Europeans. They mark significant breaks with the past. They are, in sum, the New Europe.

NOTES

1 'Teaching about European History and Society in the 1990s', Tuusula, Finland, August 1991.
2 'The Teaching of History in the New Europe', Bruges, Belgium, December 1991.

3 'The European Dimension in the History Curriculum', Leeuwarden, the Netherlands, April 1993.

4 Geoffrey Barraclough (1957), 'The continuity of European tradition', in *History in a Changing World*, Oxford: Blackwell, p. 45.

5 'European Cultural Routes', a Secretariat Memorandum prepared by the Directorate of Education Culture and Sport.

6 Quoted in (1986) *Against Bias and Prejudice: The Council of Europe's Work on History Teaching and History Textbooks*, Strasbourg: Council for Cultural Cooperation.

7 Walt Whitman, 'Song of Myself', in Reeves, J. and Seymour-Smith, M. (eds), *Selected Poems of Walt Whitman*, London: Heinemann.

8 But sometimes with vision as well: 'Resistance to Nazi oppression, which united the people of Europe in the same battle, has created among them a solidarity and a community of aim and interest whose significance and meaning is expressed ... in their hopes and their intentions for the fate of civilisation and peace.' From the Draft Declaration by the European Resistance Movements, July 1944, quoted in U. Kitzinger *The European Common Market and Community*, London: Routledge and Kegan Paul, p. 29.

9 S. Hoggart (1992), 'Mapping out a Europe of 42 Nations', *Observer*, 10 May.

10 Both these publications were introduced to participants on the teachers' course, 'New Approaches to History Teaching in Upper Secondary Education', and are described in greater detail in Chapter 3.

11 J. Bryce (1864), *The Holy Roman Empire*, London, p. 50.

12 C. Dawson (1932), *The Making of Europe*, London: Sheed and Ward, p. 229.

13 Quoted in G. Barraclough 'Continuity of European tradition', p. 41.

14 See, for example, H. van der Dunk, (1993), 'Europe: Historical Reality or Myth', paper read to the Council of Europe Conference at Leeuwarden.

15 See, for example, E. Hobsbawm and T. Ranger (eds) (1983), *The Invention of Tradition*, Cambridge: Cambridge University Press.

16 In, for example, E. Gombrich, (1979), 'Art history and the Social Sciences', in *Ideals and Idols*, Oxford: Phaidon, p. 155ff.

17 E. Gellner (1983), *Nations and Nationalism*, Oxford: Blackwell, p. 50.

18 Douglas Johnston, quoted by R. Wake (1973) in *Trends*, London, Department of Education and Science.

19 J. Needham (1956–95), *Science and Civilization in China*, vols. 1–6, Cambridge: Cambridge University Press.

20 L. White (1962), *Medieval Technology and Social Change*, Oxford: Oxford University Press.

21 This statement is not the author's. He would be grateful for an attribution so that it can be acknowledged.

22 N. Pevsner (1963), *An Outline of European Architecture*, London, Penguin Books, p. 16.

23 I. Berlin (1990), 'European unity and its vicissitudes', in *The Crooked Timber of Humanity*, London: Fontana Press, p. 188.

24 D. Potter (1954), *People of Plenty*, Chicago: University of Chicago Press, esp. chs 5 and 7.

25 William McNeill (1963), *The Rise of the West*, Chicago: Chicago University Press, esp. Chap. 5, pp. 558–9. I am particularly indebted to this remarkable and epic survey for this part of the chapter.

26 M. Harrington (1967), *The Accidental Century*, London: Penguin, p. 75, quotes Schumpeter, who suggests that the 'knight was rendered obsolete by a weapons technology' – by the 'gun which democratised the battlefield and made a peasant or an artisan as lethal as a prince'.

27 McNeill, *The Rise of the West, passim*.

28 In a speech to the University of Chicago, 1906, quoted in J. Abels (1965), *The Rockefeller Millions*, New York: MacMillan Inc., p. 279.

29 H. Arendt (1973), *On Revolution*, Harmondsworth: Penguin, rev. edn, pp. 94, 112.

30 T. E. Utley and Stewart Maclure (1957), *Documents of Modern Political Thought*, Cambridge: Cambridge University Press.

31 Berlin, 'European unity and its vicissitudes', p. 195.

32 McNeill, *The Rise of the West*, p. 558.

33 G. Barraclough (1964), *An Introduction to Contemporary History*, London: Watts.

34 *Ibid.*, p. 12.

35 From papers submitted by delegates respectively from the Flemish Community of Belgium, the then Czechoslovakia, Denmark, Estonia, Luxembourg and Poland.

36 The five headings which are used were identified at a remarkable seminar in Cambridge in December 1989, organized by the Global Security Programme. Papers were read by representatives from the then Czechoslovakia, Hungary, Poland, the United Kingdom, the United States and what were still at that time the German Democratic Republic and the Soviet Union. The seminar papers have been collected and published as G. Prins (ed.), (1990), *Spring in Winter* Manchester: Manchester University Press.

Three other publications were of particular help: Misha Glenny (1990), *The Rebirth of History: Eastern Europe in the Age of Democracy*, London: Penguin; Geoffrey Hosking (1991), *The Awakening of the Soviet Union*, London: Mandarin; Mary Kaldor (ed.) (1991), *Europe from Below*, London: Verso.

37 One slogan of Civic Forum in the Czech elections of 1990 was 'Come Back with Us to Europe!'

38 'In Czechoslovakia, as in much of the rest of Eastern Europe, we have inherited an industrial rust belt and a natural environment ravaged from forty years of scornful and systematic abuse.' J. Urban (1990), in Prins, *Spring in Winter*, pp. 132–3.

39 'The greatest threat to democracy today is no longer Communism either as a political movement or as an ideology. The threat grows instead from a combination of chauvinism, xenophobia, populism, and authoritarianism, all of them connected with the sense of frustration typical of great social upheavals.' A. Michnik (ed. of Solidarity newspaper *Gazeta Wyborcza*) (1991), 'The two faces of Europe', in Kaldor, *Europe from Below*, p. 196.

40 C. P. Cavafy (1989), 'Waiting for the barbarians', in Savidis, G. (ed.), *Collected Poems*, trans. Keeley, E. and Sherrard, P., London: Hogarth Press, p. 15.

CHAPTER 2

The Council of Europe and History

This chapter describes the Council of Europe's activities on history in schools.[1] It also describes the series of great exhibitions organized by the Council of Europe on European culture, and some of the initiatives not specifically concerned with history but having important implications for it, such as political education, the contributions to European culture of Islam and Judaism, and human rights education. Current projects at present under way or still being considered will be described in Chapter 3.

THE CONFERENCES

The first Council of Europe history conference was held in 1953 at Calw in the Black Forest. It was concerned with 'The European Idea in History Teaching'. The most recent (at the time of writing) were in 1993, at Trondheim in Norway on 'The Teaching of Local History in a European Perspective: Approaches and Challenges for the 1990s', and at Visby on the island of Gotland in Sweden on 'The History of the Baltic Sea: A History of Conflicts', and, in 1994, at Delphi on 'History Teaching and European Awareness'. By the end of 1994 some 21 conferences had been held, as well as numerous smaller bilateral meetings and workshops. But perhaps the most comprehensive was at Bruges in 1991 on 'History Teaching in the New Europe'. Overall, the Council has had an impressive record of commitment.

The first conferences focused on textbook content: the Middle Ages (Oslo 1954), the sixteenth century (Rome 1955), the seventeenth and eighteenth centuries (Royaumont 1956), the period from c. 1789 to c. 1871 (Scheveningen 1957), and the period from c. 1870 to c. 1950 (Istanbul and Ankara 1958). Their object was to eradicate bias and prejudice in history textbooks.

The 1960s and the beginning of the 1970s focused more particularly on the place of history in the secondary curriculum: 'History Teaching in Secondary Education' (Elsinore 1965), 'History Teaching in Lower Secondary Education' (Braunschweig 1969), and finally 'History Teaching in Upper Secondary Education' (Strasbourg 1971).

Between 1972 and 1983, three further conferences discussed specific issues: 'Religion in School History Textbooks in Europe' (Leuven 1972), 'Cooperation in Europe as Presented in the Resources for Teaching History, Geography and Civics in Secondary Schools' (Braunschweig 1979), and 'The Portuguese Discoveries and Renaissance Europe' (Lisbon 1983).

In 1973, European ministers of education met in Berne and agreed that 'subjects should be decompartmentalised so as to make the pupils aware of the interpretation of knowledge in everyday life.'[2] As a result, the focus of the Council's work shifted from single subjects to the issue of interdisciplinarity.

At the beginning of the 1990s, there was a revival of interest in history teaching in many European countries, and the Council responded with the organization of three further conferences: 'History and Social Studies – Methodologies of Text Book Analysis' (Braunschweig 1990), 'History Teaching in the New Europe' (Bruges 1991), and 'The Teaching of Europe since 1815 with Special Reference to Changing Frontiers' (Leeuwarden 1993).

In addition, the Council of Europe has hosted various seminars and workshops at the Academy for the In-Service Training of Teachers at Donaueschingen in the Black Forest; for example, in 1979 on 'New Trends in History Teaching in Upper Secondary Education', and in 1991 on 'New Approaches to History Teaching in Upper Secondary Education'.

SOME DEFINITIONS: BIAS, PREJUDICE AND INDOCTRINATION

In the deliberations and recommendations of the conferences, the concepts of 'bias' and 'prejudice' occurred more frequently than they were defined. To avoid engaging on a lengthy semantic goose-chase, the definitions offered here do not expect unqualified acceptance, but attempt to ensure that the readers know where the author stands, and to give any subsequent disagreement at least a common starting point.

'Bias' describes evidence that lacks balance and expresses a partial point of view; the bias may lie principally with the writer of the source, or in the historian's criteria for its selection; the bias may be deliberate or unconscious. It leaves unanswered, for the moment, the question whether any historical source or historian's selection of evidence can ever be unbiased.

'Prejudice' describes an emotional cast of mind producing opinions independent of evidence by either denying, ignoring or suppressing it. Like bias, it can be unconscious or deliberate. It can be argued (see also Chapter 5) that the issue of bias lies at the heart of historical thinking, while prejudice is wholly inconsistent with it; historical content can be deployed objectively, but its selection is certainly biased.

Bias, and particularly prejudice, are often associated with *indoctrination*, but it is distinct from either. Indoctrination is a process by which people attempt to persuade others to accept ideas and attitudes by suppressing evidence, or teaching it so selectively that it deliberately emphasizes or conceals certain aspects. The links between the three words might be summed up by saying that indoctrination is the attempt to generate or perpetuate prejudice by using biased evidence.

In the post-war years, the possibility of a single, unbiased European history textbook was often argued. It is an argument that dies hard, and in 1992, as a result of the initiative of Frédéric Delouche, 12 European historians collaborated to write and publish the *Histoire de l'Europe*[3] (see further Chapter 3).

The Calw conference unequivocally stated that its purpose was 'not to use history as propaganda for European unity, but to try to eliminate traditional mistakes and prejudices and to establish the facts'.[4] The first part of this statement begins helpfully to clarify and define the functions of history; the second part begs important questions about those functions.

During the six textbook conferences, some nine hundred of the two thousand textbooks currently used in western European schools were analysed. Overall, the conclusion was that bias was almost invariably unconscious and not deliberate. In 1972, a conference in Dublin on 'The Problems of Bias and Prejudice in the Teaching of History', organized jointly by the Departments of Education in Dublin and Belfast and Her Majesty's Inspectorate (HMI) in London, reached similar conclusions. Deliberate bias was very rare. Such bias as existed was largely a matter of the use of words, and less a result of what was put into textbooks than of what was left out.

But the emphasis of these early conferences was less on second-order concepts (bias, prejudice, cause, change, etc.) than on first-order ones (feudalism, Renaissance, medieval, liberalism, Europe). The Council of Europe commissioned a group of historians to prepare a glossary of 50 historical terms, which were published in German under the title *Grundbegriffe der Geschichte: 50 Beiträge zum Europäischen Geschichtsbild* (1964), while an expanded version of the entry on 'Europe' by Professor R. J. Sattler was published in 1971 by the International Schoolbook Institute as *Europa: Geschichte und Aktualität des Begriffes*.

Analysis of textbooks also revealed their inadequacy in dealing both with religion in history and with the various attempts to give a legal, juridical basis to international and European communities. These shortcomings prompted the Leuven and Braunschweig conferences of 1972 and 1979. It is perhaps worth commenting that the terms of reference of the Braunschweig Conference on 'European Cooperation' referred to the 'whole process of *non-military* cooperation in Europe since 1945' (author's italics). Thus it considered the European Community, the Nordic Council and the Helsinki Conference, but apparently ignored NATO and the Warsaw Pact. These omissions were not prejudiced; nor were they unbiased.

Context and function

But the Council of Europe was not working entirely alone. Its conferences had been preceded by others organized by UNESCO in the immediate post-war years, and the International Schoolbook Institute, founded in Braunschweig in 1951 by the late Professor Georg Eckert, was already established. In 1965 the Council of Europe invited the Institute to become an official European clearing house for the exchange of information on history and geography textbooks. It not only houses a remarkable and comprehensive collection of textbooks, but is an important centre for research, and it has frequently acted as co-host with the Council of Europe for history and geography conferences and seminars, most recently the 1990 conference on the analysis of history and social studies textbooks. After Professor Eckert's death in 1974 the Institute was renamed the Georg Eckert Institute for International Textbook Research. (See appendix for details.)

The conferences on history textbooks raised many important questions about pedagogy and learning as well as the place of history in the curricula of secondary schools. These prompted the three conferences held between 1965 and 1971 on history teaching in secondary education. The documentation from the 1965 Elsinore Conference provided the base for a book written by E. H. Dance on *The Place of History in Secondary Teaching*. It contained chapters on aims, methods, syllabuses, examinations, and history teaching in the six European schools which had been set up by the European Community.

The Strasbourg Conference on history teaching in the upper years of secondary education (16–18) was part of the joint University of Oxford/Council of Europe 'Study for the Evaluation of the Curriculum and Examinations', during which an examination was made of the aims and objectives, content, teaching methods and assessment of 10 subjects being taught as a preparation for university entrance. The findings on each subject were published by the Council of Europe in its European Curriculum Studies series. That on history was written by E. E. Y. Hales, at that time Staff Inspector with HMI. In his book, Hales examined the issues of the status and prospects for history; the syllabus; methods and approaches; the relation of history to other subjects; prejudice, propaganda and error; and teacher training.

Detailed reports on the deliberations, papers and lectures describe what these conferences did and said. But what were they for? At one level they provided opportunities for personal, professional and organizational links which potentially, and often in practice, initiated joint enterprises or strengthened and disseminated work already in progress. The conferences also, however, made recommendations – but to whom? As most delegates are funded by their governments, it is to them that they are primarily responsible and it is to governments that recommendations are principally directed – to their ministers of education, inspectorates, educational administrators and teachers. The Council of Europe organizes the forum for discussion and acts as one of the channels of its dissemination.

Recommendations are also made to the Council itself. The Council of Europe has limited funding. Its authority is not principally financial, nor is it executive. It lies in the persuasiveness of its recommendations and the practicality of its vision. But its work is backed by the European Cultural Convention signed by all member states and an increasing number of non-member states,[5] and is the basis for the Council's programme for intergovernmental cooperation in the spheres of education, culture, sport and youth education, including the teaching of history.

Some initiatives are directly subsidized by the Council; for example, the In-Service Training Programme of the Council's Council for Cultural Cooperation, which enables many European teachers to attend in-service training courses in other countries. About a thousand bursaries were available during the 1993–4 school year.

The Council of Europe also defines European standards and norms through its conventions and agreements. So far, 155 have been opened for signature, and when they have been ratified by all member states, they may represent the equivalent of 11,935 bilateral agreements.

THE RECOMMENDATIONS

This section does not list or summarize all the recommendations since 1953. It identifies important issues that have appeared regularly during the last forty years, in particular: the status of history; aims and function; bias and prejudice; content; teaching and learning; resources; interdisciplinarity and links; teacher training.

The status of history

The Council of Europe and the delegates at its meetings have not wavered since 1953 in their support for history and in their conviction of its crucial importance in the school curriculum.

In 1965 at Elsinore, delegates saw history as a necessary basis for all the humanities, and expressed fears that history might be replaced by civics. They also recommended that history maintain its distinct and separate role, a view which anticipated the fears expressed 10 years later, by R. A. Wake for example, that the trend in the 1970s towards interdisciplinarity posed a potential threat to the position of history (see also Chapter 5). The Tuusula Conference of 1991 recommended that history should be compulsory for all pupils up to the age of 16, saying that it 'is far too essential to be left to chance ... it is impossible to understand the current situations in the Baltic, in the Soviet Union, in Northern Ireland and Yugoslavia without a grasp of history, which should be every pupil's right.'

Aims and function

Throughout these conferences, two themes have remained constant: that history must be politically and ideologically autonomous, and that it is not morally neutral.

The first conference at Calw (1953) stated that history must 'avoid any interpretation of historical developments which might be used in the particular interest of any one state or might disturb the friendly relations between two peoples'. At Braunschweig in 1979, it was stated that 'tolerance, both with regard to European neighbours and to contacts with the world at large, could be furthered through teaching about cooperation in Europe, provided that this teaching does not limit itself to the presentation of one solution or avoid areas of disagreement and conflict.'

These statements, of course, beg some important questions. Some views of the past may well benefit, or discredit, particular nations; imperial and colonial pasts or Fascist and Stalinist pasts may well discomfort some states; topics such as the development of parliamentary democracy or resistance to Communist rule will redound to the credit of others. Most of us may well support the idea of European cooperation, but we would be, alas, a touch optimistic to believe that merely by studying it as a theme, we will further its cause. And sometimes discussion at these conferences was confused by a failure to distinguish between the nature and function of history, and the political and ethical case for a united Europe.

Nevertheless, at the heart of these statements lie doughty convictions about values and autonomy. But *people*, not abstract concepts like 'history', enjoy autonomy; that is, the professional autonomy of teachers and the autonomous thinking of pupils (see Chapters 4 and 5). Such convictions are of crucial importance to our colleagues from central and east Europe; even those of us who have benefited from parliamentary democracy cannot take those convictions for granted.

Two further functions can be identified in conference recommendations. The first is that history seeks to help young people understand the world and society in which they live (see also Chapters 1 and 5). The second is that history helps define our group and personal identity through our family, community, ethnic and cultural roots.

The eradication of bias and prejudice

'Please miss, when were you discovered?'
(A small black child to her white English teacher)

From the outset, the Council's declared aim has been the eradication of bias and prejudice from textbooks. This was clearly stated at Calw: 'Our purpose is not to use history as propaganda for European unity, but to try to eliminate traditional mistakes and prejudices and to establish the facts.'[6] Three years later, at Royaumont, the delegates recommended that there should be a 'respect for historical objectivity and [avoidance of] the use of derogatory and exaggerated expressions', and, at Ankara in 1958, it was recommended that young people should be 'given a working knowledge, presented with the objectivity that is the hallmark of our traditional methods of education'. The 1965 Elsinore Conference defined history's essential contribution to civics, whose aim 'is not propaganda but rather to enable the pupil to form an opinion of his own'.[7]

These statements seem to imply that 'facts' and 'knowledge' are value-free and that 'objectivity' describes 'content'. This important issue will be considered again in Chapter 5. However, later conferences began to offer a different slant on this issue. The Council's Secretariat commenting on the 1990 Braunschweig conference wrote: 'A good textbook need not necessarily be free of underlying assumptions ... In dealing, for instance, with a multicultural society, a textbook should not just list arguments for or against it, but adopt a clear position.' On the assumption that textbooks cannot be value-free, the same conference argued that their values should be clear and declared.

Peter Szebenyi told the Braunschweig (1990) conference that Hungarian research into textbooks published in 1989 'analyzed textbooks axiologically (that is for their value systems), teleologically (that is for their hidden objectives) as well as instrumentally'. And a paper submitted by E. J. Boerma from the Netherlands argued the need for research to discover whether in fact textbooks can help to limit ethnocentricity or prevent subsequent prejudices emerging in the first place.

But bias and prejudice often lie less in explicit statements than in the very vocabulary of history itself: the 1983 Lisbon Conference on 'Teaching about the Portuguese Discoveries in Secondary Schools in Western Europe' rejected the term 'discoveries' because it implied that 'the rest of the world was a blank before the European voyages of expansion' – 'terra nullius', as Australia was described by its early European settlers, arriving some forty thousand years after the first settlements of its original peoples. The Lisbon conference rejected one unconscious prejudice which lurked deep in the vocabulary of much European history and its syllabuses (in, for example, the 25 themes recommended at Elsinore in 1965 and the syllabuses of the European Schools and the International Schools Association). Lisbon reminded us that European history was often 'chauvinistic and Euro-centred', and that bias and prejudice often lie less in explicit statements and overt judgements than in omissions and language usage.

Content

The early conferences concentrated on content and content-based textbooks. They met at a time when there were frequently shared, but less often examined, assumptions about the security of historical facts and the objectivity of knowledge, leading some to pursue the possibility of a European textbook which would in some sense be 'true', and presumably offend nobody. However, it was a barren pursuit and, despite the publication in 1991 of *Histoire de l'Europe*, different priorities have emerged from the conferences. They can be summarized as the need to:

- teach recent and contemporary history;
- establish the idea of Europe;
- embrace not just political but social, economic, cultural, scientific, technological and spiritual history;
- recognize the importance of local and regional history;
- maintain a balance between local, national, European and world history.

Contemporary history seeks to answer the question: 'How have we got to where we are now?' One of the functions of history identified at the 1991 Bruges Conference, and expressed with particular vigour by delegates from east and central Europe, was to help young people know and understand the world in which they live (see also Chapters 1 and 5). A working group at the 1990 Braunschweig Conference asked the question of history textbooks: 'Does the textbook include a presentation of problems the development and solution of which are likely *to be found during the pupils' lifespan*, e.g. the emancipation of underprivileged groups, rich versus poor, the North-South issue, environmental problems, intercultural understanding, problems of communication in an information society?' The question distinguishes 'recent' from 'contemporary' history (see also Chapter 1). World War II is recent, indeed contemporary as far as the experiences of many older teachers go, but to pupils it may appear as strange and distant, or as exciting, as Robin Hood or Asterix, who, with World War II, feature prominently in comics and television adventure series. But none is part of the world in which 14-year-olds actually live.

Two further aspects of recent history also regularly emerge, both for the first time at Calw. The first is that the contemporary world is more interesting for young people. It is a dubious proposition that argues that certain periods are inherently more interesting or intellectually accessible to young people. Anecdotal evidence suggests that effective and sympathetic teaching may ultimately be a more important motivating factor.

The second recognizes, implicitly, that young people are not ignorant of the contemporary world. In fact, they may know almost too much about it – from television, the press, comics, their peers and the memories of their grandparents or the old people who live down the street. But what young people know is a chaotic mix of myth, prejudice, and religious, personal and political partiality. The task of the history teacher is not just to add to young people's knowledge, but to help them organize, categorize, reflect on and critically evaluate, the knowledge they already have. Thus history has a compensatory and a counteractive function (see also Chapter 5).

The familiarity of the recent and remembered past may well motivate young people because it enables them more actively to participate in its learning and gives them some status in the classroom, but this will depend on teachers being able to listen, and being prepared to abandon over-didactic teaching.

The early conferences emphasized the need to find pan-European themes and issues which reflect the unity of Europe. But are we to suppose that less attention is to be given to those issues which divide? It has been urged that local history is 'the only appropriate framework for the study of certain phenomena which do not coincide with the frontiers of states', that 'international history should not be treated as an extension of national history' and that 'it would be desirable not to introduce into the past contemporary national antagonisms.' The Crusades have been suggested as an example of a unifying theme, although many would now regard this as a wayward interpretation of those melancholy events; more defensibly, it has been suggested that the Ottoman Empire should be studied in its own right and not merely as a factor in great power politics, and that Turkey should not only be seen as a non-European power. (The Turks once complained to the Anglo-Turkish Cultural Commission that their image in British textbooks suggested they did little other than invade and massacre people.) The Elsinore Conference of 1965 proposed that in 'the teaching of history, a certain number of important facts which bear witness to the common culture of the peoples of Europe ought to be stressed … and that as far as possible history should be presented from a European point of view'.

Such a list of facts depends on a more precise definition of a 'European point of view' and a clear recognition that there may have been events of importance that did *not* bear witness to a 'common culture'. Twenty-six years later, the delegates at Tuusula were still recommending that 'syllabuses should include topics which *foster* a pan-European approach' (author's italics). 'Such topics might include the Reformation or the French Revolution, or else themes which affected all of Europe, like poverty, industrialisation, or the study of an ideology.' This all makes good sense. Yet there remains a nagging doubt that, at Elsinore and Tuusula, history was being used to support conclusions the syllabus makers had already reached, and sustain aspirations which depended less on evidence from the past than on hopes for the future.

A further running theme has been the need to counteract the dominance of political, military and, in particular, national and nationalistic history. 'National' history studies and evaluates the evidence of a nation's past. 'Nationalistic' history, often concerned with political and diplomatic achievement and military victories, is essentially celebratory. The former can be concerned with *examining* values; the latter is almost inevitably concerned with transmitting them. Nationalistic history is to do less with examining cause than with attributing blame (an important distinction made in 1958 at Ankara/Istanbul), conferring approval and demanding loyalty. It is the literary equivalent of the public statues and street names found all over Europe.

But the case for more broadly conceived syllabuses has an inherent historical justification. A claim to study a nation or Europe almost entirely on the basis of political and military events is too ruthlessly selective. Human behaviour is far more extensive and diverse. Several conferences recommended that history syllabuses should be syntheses not only of political and military happenings, but also of economic and social issues, cultural history, scientific and technological change, and human spiritual and religious experiences.

A final theme has been the importance of local and regional history, mentioned at the first conference in 1953, again at Tuusula in 1990, and in particular at the Trondheim and Visby conferences in 1993. The 1969 Braunschweig Conference first spelt out its advantages: 'the locality deals with the pupils' own background, provides the best basis for introducing historical methodology and consciousness, offers opportunities for close collaborative work with geography and is a realistic introduction to social and economic issues in their European and world context.' One can add that history is not just a matter of learning about famous dead people, but is also concerned with establishing the worth of pupils' own background and roots. Thus, the locality is a necessary, if not always a sufficient, component in pupils' personal development and their sense of identity. As the 1979 Braunschweig Conference put it:

> The general opinion is that content should be concrete and should deal with problems, which pupils know from their own surroundings and feel to be of immediate interest to them. Abstract notions will be met with polite passivity or rejection.

There is much sense in this, even if it too readily polarizes 'immediate surroundings' and 'the abstract', and too easily forgets that the distant and exotic often excite and motivate. Medieval knights or the Aztecs – and dinosaurs – compete strongly with, and sometimes offer escape routes from, overfamilar high streets and suburbs.

Finally, there are reminders throughout forty years of conferring and recommending, that Europe must be seen in a balanced context of local, regional, national and world history. Without that balance, the case for understanding Europe will be wholly unpersuasive in schools with pupils whose cultural backgrounds may well include, for example, the Caribbean, the Indian subcontinent, north Africa and southeast Asia. A concern for Europe must not challenge intercultural education in an interdependent world.

But a central problem remains untouched. In 1991, the delegates at Bruges looked again at the 25 themes from 1965, and added another 19. (The Elsinore and Bruges themes are listed in the appendix at the end of this chapter.) Time for teaching remains static; money for resources does not increase; only the burden of content grows. Neither Bruges nor Elsinore suggested how that burden might be reduced, or defined any criteria for its selection. So the problem is compounded, not solved.

Teaching and learning

Although the earlier conferences focused on content and textbooks, they were, from the outset, concerned with *how* pupils learned. There were references to the importance of 'a critical attitude and [of] interpretations'; 'a minimum of dates' was recommended, with the suggestion that it was 'important to foster understanding and historical reasoning'. The importance of 'a strong element of the critical appraisal of the past' was stressed; 'encyclopedism and mere erudition' were condemned. The 'investigation and handling of accessible documents ... the active participation, handling and exploitation of documents ... [and the making of] connections and syntheses' were recommended, with the addition that 'local history was the best basis for active methodology' (although surely local history must not be diminished by being seen as a mere pedagogical device?). Clearly the participants at these conferences (Calw, Royaumont and Elsinore) saw history as much a matter of acquiring active ways of thinking about people as one of accumulating inert knowledge about them.

Twenty-six years later, delegates in Braunschweig were still asking whether textbooks helped pupils relate history to personal experience with regard to society, region and nation, and the Council's Secretariat reminded the seminar that textbooks (and the learning of history) 'should not just transmit knowledge but stimulate critical thinking'.

But these recommendations were seen mainly as aims. Overall, little has been said about how teachers should translate them into behavioural objectives, into what teachers and pupils should actually *do*. However, at the 1991 Tuusula conference, where 'all participants stressed the importance of employing a variety of teaching methods', considerable interest was raised by a detailed account, supported by videos of real *pupils* learning in classrooms, of 'cooperative learning'.[8] Its significance was not only that pupils talked and worked collaboratively in groups, as opposed to working, often competitively, as individuals in silence, but that it also altered the traditional relationship between pupils and teacher. In these classes, the teacher was seen not as a monopolist or the sole purveyor of knowledge and learning, but as one of the partners in learning.

Issues of methodology also arose in the previous year at the Braunschweig Conference on the analysis of history and social studies textbooks. Previous conferences had analysed textbooks and sought means of improving them by eradicating unacceptable bias. But at Braunschweig, voices were raised to question whether a dependence on textbooks, no matter what their quality, could ever adequately support autonomous learning.

Resources

Recommendations on resources were concerned either with the ability of resources to stimulate autonomous and critical learning or with increasing their variety. During the first ten years, recommendations were made about the importance of documentary evidence; different kinds of textbook to 'stimulate pupils' own activities by questions and work plans'; the need for collections, perhaps collated and published by the Council, of time-charts, source collections and audio-visual aids; the importance of teachers not only as users but as authors of textbooks; and the importance of resources outside the classroom – historic sites, museums and art galleries, field trips, etc.

The 1990 Braunschweig Conference recognized the key role of textbooks, of the need for their scholarly analysis, and of the importance of the Georg Eckert Institute, but began to question textbooks' status, their use and, in too many schools and educational systems, their centrality. The Conference Report commented that:

> textbooks have long been and are likely to remain a necessary support or crutch which all teachers have at some time needed. But the object of using a crutch is to abandon it as soon as possible. If the medical metaphor can be extended, let us accept textbooks as crutches to be thrown away as soon as possible rather than as drugs which may create permanent dependence.

These comments were a further reminder of the focus of much of the Council's work, concentrating on textbooks rather than on the great diversity of resources and influences which affect children's historical understanding and learning both inside and outside the classroom.

At Bruges, however, delegates were harshly reminded that for many the problem was not just inadequate textbooks, but none at all. Many schools in eastern and central Europe had few resources, and virtually all limited to those so ideologically tainted that their use would be wholly inconsistent with their countries' determination to break with their Communist pasts. The lack is compounded by a shortage of authors with the experience of writing books for schools which encourage a critical examination of the past and describe a variety of interpretations of it.

Interdisciplinarity and links

Interdisciplinarity describes one kind of link between subjects. Delegates at Elsinore recommended that there should be the 'maximum planned co-ordination with the teaching of geography and other relevant subjects', and those at Braunschweig (1979) that 'Europe should be treated as one element in a global approach to the teaching of history, geography and civics.' The Tuusula Conference was impressed by the Baltic Sea Project, which involves some one hundred and fifty schools in all the countries on the Baltic sea coast. The rapporteur described it as follows:

> They [the schools] communicate and cooperate in a number of projects based on the environmental problems of the region. While the project is clearly slanted towards geography and science, it has involved other subject areas, notably English, music and art, and participants recognised that it offers an invaluable model for other initiatives which would make more use of history.

The theme of interdisciplinarity and integration is developed further in Chapter 5, but at this stage three comments are relevant.

First, history's natural ally is assumed to be geography. History is usually seen as a humanity. Many geographers see their natural allies as scientists, although geographers are divided on this issue. Are there not profitable alliances to be made with sociology, language and literature, the creative arts? Is history a 'humanity'? If so, where are the other humanities? With the exception of the important Leuven Conference in 1972 on 'Religion in School History Textbooks', the range of interdisciplinary links which have been examined in any detail remains limited.

Second, there are references to the links between history and 'civics'. Delegates at Calw declared that 'history is an adjunct to civics', an assumption shared by delegates at Braunschweig in 1979. But there is a problem of definition. What is 'civics'? Is it a subject, like history and geography, with its own content and procedures? (See also 'History, political education and citizenship' in Chapter 5.) Fear was expressed that history itself might be displaced by 'civics'. Delegates seemed a touch clearer about what 'civics' was *for* than what it actually *was* (a point taken up later in this chapter). If interdisciplinarity is going to be seen as a pedagogical strategy and not just as an aim, the meaning of terms such as 'civics' and 'social studies' will need to be clarified. Alliances cannot be turned into teaching strategies unless we are clear about the nature and intentions of our possible allies.

Third, regular recommendations that history should synthesize a wider range of human activities suggest that the first priority is to develop the links *within* subjects rather than *between* them. 'History is in itself an integrated subject' (Elsinore, 1965).

Teacher training

None of the conferences has been primarily concerned with the training of teachers. However at two of them – Elsinore (1965) and Braunschweig (1969) – some specific recommendations were made. These can be summarized as follows:

- The teaching of history must be entrusted to history specialists.
- Training should include an introduction to historiography and a critical attitude to historical problems.
- In-service training should help teachers embody the results of the latest university research in their work.
- Emphasis must be placed on the study of economic, sociological, geographical, ethnological and political problems, while links with other disciplines, such as the humanities (*sic*), archaeology, the history of art and thought, literature, technology, etc., must not be neglected.

It is a very comprehensive, ambitious and daunting agenda.

THE EXHIBITIONS

So far this chapter has been solely concerned with the Council of Europe's work on behalf of teaching history in schools. However, the Council has a distinguished record in organizing a series of public exhibitions on European culture. Since 1955, it has organized 22 of these. The first was in Brussels on 'Humanist Europe', and the most recent in 1992 on 'From Viking to Crusader: Scandinavia and Europe 800–1200' held in Berlin, Paris and Copenhagen. The Council writes of these exhibitions:

> To help Europeans better understand and appreciate their heritage, the Council recognised as far back as 1952 the need to give fairly regular public reminders to the cultural values of Europe and chose to organise a series of large scale exhibitions of its artistic treasures. These events demonstrate that, despite innumerable wars and divergences of all kinds, Europe has slowly taken shape as a unity. And, through an awareness that they indeed belong to a common civil-isation, Europeans can readily make choices consistent with the fact.[9]

Most of the great periods of European art have been illustrated during the last forty years: Byzantine, Romanesque, Gothic, humanist, classical, Baroque, rococo, Neo-Classical, Romantic, modern and contemporary. Other exhibitions have focused on people: Charlemagne, Queen Christina of Sweden, the Knights of Malta, the Medici, and King Christian IV of Denmark. Two further exhibitions in the 1980s on 'The Anatolian Civilisations' (1983) and 'The Portuguese Discoveries and Renaissance Europe' (1983), extended the geographical scope of the exhibitions. Political events were recalled in the 1989 Paris exhibition on 'The French Revolution and Europe' and in 'Emblems of Liberty', held in Berne in 1991. An exhibition will be held in London in 1995 on 'Art and Power: Art and Architecture under the Shadow of Totalitarianism'. It will be followed by an exhibition in Vienna in 1996 on 'Historicism'.

The exhibition catalogues, written by distinguished scholars, are important contributions to the literature of European culture. The exhibitions have also provided stimulus for historical, scientific and art-historical research, and have led to the creation of new museums in, for example, Florence, Lisbon and Istanbul.

Until recently the exhibitions have not been specifically linked with the learning of history in schools, although the slide collections associated with many of them have been a rich source, accessible to a wide ability range and age group of young people. However, in 1992, in connection with the exhibition 'From Viking to Crusader: Scandinavia and Europe 800–1200', a well-produced, illustrated booklet was published, aimed at younger pupils. Its text is clear, its illustrations are excellent, and it relates its content to supporting evidence. Suggestions for visits are made and there is a series of questions and tasks for pupils, accompanied by a rationale and some suggestions for teachers.[10]

The host country takes major responsibility for organizing the exhibitions, but technical assistance and advice and the loan of exhibits come from many parts of Europe. The exhibitions not only have provided an epic celebration of European culture, but have been the fruits of European cooperation.

MUSEUMS AND HISTORY OUTSIDE THE CLASSROOM

Most of the work of the Council of Europe has been concerned with history inside the classroom. Apart from some discussion and recommendations made at the 1979 Braunschweig Conference on school visits to other countries, delegates rarely looked out of their classroom windows; the organizers of the 1991 Bruges Conference hoped that the topic would be considered, but it was marginalized by other priorities and anxieties. However, there are two important projects, still in their early stages, 'European Cultural Routes' and 'School Twinning and Local History', which will be described in the next chapter.

If local and regional history are going to be taken seriously, young people will have to walk and look as well as read and write. If they are going to use a greater variety of primary source material, they will find much of it outside the classroom, in buildings, in street and pub names, in field patterns, in the memories of old people and on archaeological digs. Money is limited, sometimes very scarce, but much of the environment is free. The content and methodology of schools history can thriftily, but with great profit, be influenced by what pupils can see from their classroom windows, or walk to and from in the course of an afternoon. Across Europe, museums support and give focus to history outside the classroom; new ones are being opened each year and many are free.

Since 1977, under the auspices of the Council of Europe, the work of museums has been encouraged by two annual awards: the European Museum of the Year Award and the Council of Europe Museum Prize. The first two winners were, respectively, the Ironbridge Gorge Museum Trust in the United Kingdom and the Joan Miró Foundation in Barcelona. The 1994 awards went to the Copenhagen National Museum and the Provincial Museum of Lappland in Rovaniemi, Finland. In the intervening 14 years, awards have been made to museums across Europe. Winners and those specially commended have included museums of wheat and bread, clockmaking, peat, photography, costume, gardeners and wine growers, stained glass, brewing, Guinness and marionettes.

In 1990, the Council of Europe organized a symposium in Salzburg on 'Museums and the European Heritage: Treasures or Tools?'. Its first aim was 'to show how those parts of the historical, cultural, scientific and natural heritage which are in museums and similar institutions may be used as an effective educational tool to promote European identity'.

Apparently the symposium was not of one mind about the term 'education'. Was it tautologous? Museums surely are, *per se*, educational. Could they do anything *but* educate their visitors to some degree? Or was education concerned just with what happened in schools? As it turned out, there was no systematic discussion or recommendations on the role of museums in the school curriculum, but in the course of discussion the following points were made:

- From an educational point of view, museums were a resource underused by schools. (The report does not make it clear whether the museums were accepting or shifting the blame for this state of affairs.)
- Each generation had 'a duty to discover a way of transmitting its culture to its successors ... It was the primary task of museums to ensure that the chain of culture was not broken' (Hélène Ahrweiler, President of the Georges Pompidou Centre in Paris).
- 'Museums are institutions which carry the responsibility of maintaining the collective memories which are a source of our identity' (Ambon Barbel, Director of the Luigi Pecci Centre for Contemporary Art in Prato, Tuscany).
- All curators are educators, but it was asked whether educational work should be part of the work of all the staff or confined to specialist departments.
- Some delegates maintained that the concept of a European identity did not correspond to reality, and museums, with their diversity of functions, should primarily be concerned with regional identities.
- One working group urged close cooperation between museums, teachers and institutions in such matters as training personnel, the development of a taste for museums among young people, and the organization of summer schools for teachers and museum staff.
- From the evidence of seven national reports, it was learnt that in Romania everything has to be built from new foundations and there is a desperate need for contacts with the west; in Norway the immediate task was to introduce Norwegians to the world outside their own borders, while in Iceland it was to bring art into their national life; in Spain museums were seen as rejuvenating forces for whole districts and areas; in Finland cooperation between schools and many local museums still depended on enthusiastic but mainly amateur staff. 'Only in the Castle Museum of York does one find anything close to the textbook concept of how museum education should be run' (from the final report of the General Rapporteur).
- It was assumed that in the majority of instances school pupils visit museums as part of compulsorily organized groups. Was the purpose of museum education to

bring children into the museum so as to develop voluntary museum-going habits when they were young?

• The General Rapporteur commented on the absence of two voices from the symposium: those of the museum-going public and of school pupils.

There remain untapped items for an agenda for a future museum symposium:

• the voices of the public and the pupils;
• the function of the visit: to enjoy museums and galleries, or to stimulate a love of the past, or of pictures, steam engines, costumes – or Guinness;
• the integration of museums into the school curriculum so that museum visits are seen not so much as interruptions, extras or treats, but as integral parts of learning;
• the issue not of children in museums but of artefacts in schools.

HISTORY AND HUMAN RIGHTS EDUCATION

The discovery of others is the discovery of a relationship, not of a barrier.[11]

The Council of Europe has long had a distinguished record in promoting discussion and urging policies on human rights and education; for example, in secondary schools (1978), upper secondary schools (1980) and primary schools (1981), on the promotion of democratic values (1982), on bullying in schools (1987) and yet more on human rights education (each year from 1984 to 1989, including twice in 1986); other seminars have examined the role of the mass media and the arts in a multicultural society. This is described in some detail in Hugh Starkey's companion volume on *The Challenge of Human Rights Education* in this series.

In October 1993, the first Summit of the Heads of State and Government of the Council of Europe's member states was held in Vienna. It stressed that:

the end of the division of Europe offers an historic opportunity to consolidate peace and stability on the continent. All of the countries are committed to pluralist and parliamentary democracy, universality of human rights, the rule of law, and a common cultural heritage enriched by its diversity.

On the other hand, the Summit expressed its alarm at:

the present resurgence of racism, xenophobia and anti-semitism, the development of a climate of intolerance, the increase in acts of violence, notably against migrants and peoples of immigrant origin, and the degrading treatment and discriminatory practices accompanying them.

The Summit also expressed concern at 'the development of aggressive nationalism and ethnocentrism which constitute new expressions of xenophobia'.

As a follow-up to the Vienna Summit, the Council of Europe has launched a European Youth Campaign against racism, xenophobia, antisemitism and intolerance. Its aim is to mobilize young people in favour of a 'European society based on common values, characterised by democracy, tolerance and solidarity'. The campaign culminated in 1995 – the United Nations' International Year of Tolerance.

The concerns are genuine, the aims unchallengeable. The need for action remains depressingly urgent. The ethos of school communities must surely relate to the aims of the Vienna resolutions, just as teaching styles and learning objectives must exemplify them.

In one of the Council of Europe's seminars, its Director of Human Rights quoted the Austrian novelist, Leo Perutz:

> I do not like national consciousness and I do not like patriotism, both are responsible for the evil which has come upon the world during the last 150 years. Things start with national consciousness and end with cholera, dysentery and dictatorship.[12]

But how do we know this is true? Well, we can start by demanding evidence, and testing such statements against it. We can continue by interrogating the evidence in our search for explanations. In other words we can start by thinking historically about human behaviour and attitudes.

The Council of Europe's experts believe that some subjects make a particularly important contribution to human rights education. One of these is history, because, so the Council argues, young people should realize that: 'human rights have had to be won and defended throughout history and that human rights are not static, and new rights emerge as society develops.[13] In 1985, the highest political body of the Council of Europe, the Committee of Ministers, adopted Recommendation R(85)7 on 'Teaching and Learning about Human Rights in Schools'. It identified skills which are central to historical thinking, and 'knowledge' which can only be properly understood by placing it in its historical context of change through time:

> The skills associated with understanding and supporting human rights include:
> *skills involving judgement such as*:
> the collection and examination of material from various sources, including the mass media, and the ability to analyse it and to arrive at fair and balanced conclusions; the identification of bias, prejudice, stereotypes and discrimination.
> *Knowledge to be acquired in the study of human rights includes*:
> people, movements and key events, both successes and failures, in the historical and continuing struggle for human rights.[14]

The seminar was reminded that in:

> the high time of chauvinist propaganda, more tolerant approaches inevitably lose: while intolerance seems to be a self-escalating process that has recourse to more and more simplistic devices, tolerant views are, conversely and by the same development, forced to use more and more sophisticated arguments.[15]

It is a sober warning to those who believe in the inevitable triumph of reason. E. M. Forster reminded us that 'the historian must have some conception of how men who are not historians behave.'[16] Reason is not enough; rational thinking in itself does not build sturdy enough barriers. Neither Hitler nor Stalin lacked reason. Their wickedness stemmed not from their lack of logic, but from premises unsupported by evidence, and their unshakable confidence in the predictability of human behaviour.

However, if in history classes all over Europe there is an unrelenting demand for evidence, if stereotypical thinking and generalized statements about races, cultures and groups are constantly challenged by the questions, 'Where is your evidence?', 'How do I know you are telling me the truth?', 'What was it like to be someone different from me?', then, even though the devil has the best tunes, historical thinking may sometimes, if we are lucky and stubborn enough, have the more powerful weapons. Human rights are not guaranteed by historical knowledge, or by the informed and responsible scepticism which historical thinking engenders, but without them, human rights do not stand much of a chance. Six related questions remain, which, for the moment, must be left hanging in the air.

The first concerns gender and sexuality. As long ago as 1958, the Ankara/Istanbul Conference commented on the neglect of the emancipation of women in history textbooks. Have the battles by women for equal opportunities, educational, legal, occupational and social, been won? All over Europe?

The second is prompted by a Polish speaker at a human rights seminar. He said that 'when Poland was freeing itself from the Communist regime ... a pogrom was carried out against gypsies in 1981 – not a very bloody one but a pogrom all the same – followed by a second one in 1991.' He poses a question that none of us can duck. He refers to the holocaust of gypsies which took place at the same time as that of the Jews:

> [the Holocaust] perhaps explains why people are ashamed to be anti-Semitic or, at least, have difficulty in expressing anti-Semitism because it is shameful; but is it just as obvious, just as easy, just as natural to say that anti-Gypsy sentiments are shameful?'

So here is another question. Homosexuals, wearing a pink triangle, also went with the Jews and gypsies to the gas chambers. Are not anti-gay sentiments shameful? If not, why not? Homosexuals have a history, and an identity. They learn in history classes and teach in history departments all over Europe.

The third question is about what pupils actually *do* as opposed to know and remember in history classrooms. The emphasis of much of the Council's work on history has been on content and textbooks and overall aims. Of course, behavioural objectives and pedagogy have not been ignored, particularly in recent years, but if history is not only going to help people understand human rights but also play its part in implementing and defending them, knowledge and understanding will not be enough. Dictated notes about the European Convention on Human Rights, with a detention if the homework is badly done, is, perhaps, education *about* human rights. It is not education *for* human rights.

Fourth, if history is really going to contribute to human rights, in what kind of school will it need to be learned? Paragraph 4 in the appendix to Recommendation R(85)7 is headed 'The Climate of the School'. It starts: 'Democracy is best learned in a democratic situation.' How do we recognize such a situation when we see it? How do we establish it in the first place? (See also Chapter 5.)

Fifth, does the identification of groups as minorities, with particular needs for human rights, sometimes studied within distinct categories (black history, women's history, gay history), tend to perpetuate a kind of ghettoization, and distract us from a view that society as a whole is a mix of minority interests and cultures? How many minorities do *we* all belong to?

> 'Woman' may well be a massively misunderstood historical being, but she was never – any more than 'man', 'child', 'parent' – a socially isolated being and should not be artificially isolated in textbooks. Probably it will be a long time before textbooks with chapters on *The history of the family, the sexes and their relationship to each other* provide us with an adequate picture of women for our history lessons.[18]

This comment does not query the importance of specialist studies, but it does suggest a revision of strategies in the writing of textbooks and the construction of syllabuses.

Finally, history is a humanity, but does it *humanize*? If it does not, does it matter? (See also Chapter 5.)

HISTORY, CIVICS AND POLITICAL EDUCATION

On several occasions, delegates at history conferences have referred to 'civics'. In 1953 the Calw Conference stated that 'as an adjunct to civics, the study of recent history is invaluable, for, without in any way departing from historical accuracy, it is possible to make the pupil aware of both his rights and his duties as a member of the European community.' The Elsinore Conference in 1965 justified civics with the claim:

> All education of future citizens aims at creating the desire and capacity to understand the problems of the world today and to participate actively in the political, economic, and social life of the community ... [as] the teaching of civics should aim to give pupils norms of social thought and behaviour, respect for fundamental values, love of one's country and the understanding of the community of Europe and of the world ... As the aim of civics is not propaganda, but rather to enable the student to form an opinion of his own, there ought to be no indoctrination.

Delegates were not agreed whether or not civics was 'a special intellectual discipline', although there was acceptance that 'human geography like history is one of the bases of teaching civics.' The assumed alliance between history, geography and civics appeared again at Braunschweig in 1979: 'Europe should be treated as one element in a global approach to the teaching of history, geography and civics.'

All these statements leave some important questions unanswered. First, they are less clear on what 'civics' *is* than what it is *for*. The term is used in concert with history and geography. But they are different in kind: geography and history have their own identifiable procedures and substantive content, at the very least institutionalized by years of practice and academic and curricular organization. But civics is no such creature. It is concerned with living in organized, legally recognized communities whose study depends on an alliance not only of history and geography, but also, at the very least, of economics and politics (another study in search of a discipline). Does the confusion matter? It does to history. If civics is a distinct discipline, it is a competitor for time, and a threat to history. If, however, it is a federal term, dependent on history, it is one of the guarantors of its presence. It also matters because, if the Council of Europe in the future intends to analyse civics textbooks and evaluate the pedagogy of civics, a decision will have to be taken whether it is one subject or several.

Second, is civics essentially a socializing or a mind-opening study? Looking again at the Elsinore statement, 'to give pupils norms of social thought and behaviour, respect for fundamental values, love of one's country and the understanding of the community of Europe and of the world' suggests the former. 'The aim of civics is ... to enable the student to form an opinion of his own' suggests the latter. In any case, in an open society just *who* defines 'norms of social behaviour' and 'fundamental values'? Ministers? Inspectors? Parents? School principals? Are society's values necessarily valuable? Nazism and apartheid were never short of values. Further, if civics encourages citizens to 'participate actively in the political ... life of the community', on behalf of whom and which beliefs is one to be active? And should we not feel a touch uneasy if civics is *committed* to a love of one's country? Perhaps not, but, at the very least, only if we can distinguish between love of one's country and loyalty to one's state. Even if there is an *educational* and *social* case for seeking norms, values and love, is it consistent with the study of history?

In the late 1970s, the Council of Europe used the term 'political education'. In 1976, it held a conference on 'The Development of Democratic Institutions in Europe', at which Professor Ian Lister read a paper on 'Aims and Methods of Political Education in Schools'. This was followed by a conference in 1977 at Tützing on 'Political Socialisation and Political Education'. In 1979, the Council for Cultural Cooperation published *Political Education for Teenagers: Aims, Contents and Methods*, by Willem Langeveld of the University of Amsterdam. The issue of history's contribution to political education, civics and education for citizenship, and to the teaching of controversial issues, will be considered further in Chapter 5. Suffice it to say here that the thinking which emerged from these conferences and publications not only widened the agenda but made it more precise by making the following points:

- The political attitudes of teenagers are formed not just in the classroom but also by the media, peer groups and family attitudes.
- Political education within the school is affected not just by what goes on in civics or history classrooms but by what the 1985 Recommendation called 'the climate of the school', and whether lessons – history, mathematics, music or whatever – are taught in what Crick and Porter called 'the tolerant classroom'.[19]

- Political education is concerned not just with political machinery and ideas, but with public *issues* over which there is disagreement.
- These issues can be nationally, locally or institutionally public, including those in the school, or classroom.
- Political issues are thus not limited to *party* political differences.
- Political education is an important part of helping young people understand their identity.

Langeveld and Lister also made important contributions to relating the aims of political education to curricular planning and pedagogy.

THE CONTRIBUTION OF JUDAISM AND ISLAM TO EUROPEAN CULTURE

In 1987 and 1991, three events of importance for the understanding of European history were held. The first, in Toledo in October 1987, was a symposium on 'The Jewish Sephardi and European Culture'; the second, a colloquy on 'The Contribution of Islamic Civilisation to European Culture', was held in Paris in May 1991; and the third, held in Strasbourg in November of that year, was a seminar on 'Euro–Arab Understanding and Cultural Exchange'. The first two were organized by the Committee on Culture and Education of the Parliamentary Assembly of the Council of Europe, while the third was convened by the organization's Secretary General.

These occasions assumed that Judaism and Islam were European cultures that were too often either ignored or misunderstood, subjects of negative stereotypes and invented images: Jews as victims, or the wielders of covert power and influence; Muslims as adversaries or, in the invention of European orientalists, as exemplifying a mysterious and exotic east.

The collected papers from these occasions provide a rich source for all of us who need to revise our perceptions and extend our knowledge. (They deserve to be rescued and distributed more widely.) A comment made at Toledo was that Judaism – and this applies equally to Islam – should be seen 'as both an historical phenomenon and a present-day reality'. Part of that reality is xenophobia and prejudice, and a sober realization that the end of tyrannous states has not meant the end of tyrannizing of minorities. Anti-semitism is acquiring once again a public and pseudo-respectable voice.

The attitude of the non-Jewish world to Judaism can never be the same after the *Endlösung* – the final solution. Calm historical analysis is still inhibited by horror, shame and guilt, and sometimes, disconcertingly, by the prurient fascination of the young. It is not just that we have to be told not to forget the Holocaust; there is a desperate need to discover a pedagogy to teach it.

Nothing quite as dreadful in the Islamic world has embedded itself into European history, but three recent circumstances have affected our perceptions. First, events such as the American hostage crisis in Iran, the Gulf War and the Salman Rushdie *fatwah* have reinforced images of an aggressive, expansionist Islamic fundamentalism, often accepted in western Europe as characteristic rather than aberrant. Second, many Muslims have sought work and settlement in north and west Europe. Finally, the revolutions of 1989 and 1990 have opened eastern Europe and its Islamic cultures to the west: at the moment Bosnia, with a Muslim population of more than 44 per cent is still being torn apart by civil war; Turkey wants to be a member of the European Union; Albania is a member of the Council of Europe, and raised at the Bruges Seminar the educational implications and needs of Albanian children living in the diaspora within other nations and cultures; some of the Asian republics in what was the Soviet Union wait in the wings.

There are clear messages for the content of textbooks and the balance within existing European history syllabuses. But will knowing more about Judaism and Islam be enough to help us think differently about them?

'THERE IS A WORLD ELSEWHERE'[20]

... what the people of the Third World are going to have to do today is stop accepting the definitions imposed on them by the West ... The first one is that history books tell you that nothing happens until a white man comes along. If you ask any white person who discovered America, they'll tell you 'Christopher Columbus.' And if you ask them who discovered China, they'll tell you 'Marco Polo.' ... as I used to be told in the West Indies, I was not discovered until Sir Walter Raleigh needed pitch lake for his ship, and he came along and said 'Whup – I have discovered you.' And my history began.[21]

The work of the Council of Europe represents and supports the interests of European states, but it has not ignored Europe's place in a wider world. In 1978 the Council began a new phase in its work on education for international understanding when it began to consider the teaching of the north–south divide, together with the problems of global and development education, and to examine the ways in which other parts of the world were taught in secondary schools in Europe.

The Council of Europe's Council for Cultural Cooperation (CDCC) responded to the concern expressed by the Parliamentary Assembly of the Council of Europe at the lack of support for north–south cooperation by organizing, often with UNICEF, five seminars on development education in primary and secondary schools. Development education is in the main the concern of geographers, economists and environmentalists. But the rest of the world has its history, and an understanding of the priorities and concerns of development education can be strengthened with a historical perspective.

The Council of Europe's Second Medium-term Plan, from 1981 to 1986, stressed the importance of facilitating and strengthening 'possibilities and dialogue and mutual understanding with other parts of the world'. So a series of CDCC seminars for teachers were held on how other parts of the world were presented in European classrooms, in particular on Africa south of the Sahara, Asia, Brazil, Canada (two seminars), China, Japan, Spanish-speaking Latin America, and the United States (two seminars). They complemented the 1983 seminars on the Portuguese voyages of expansion and the Council's art exhibition on 'The Portuguese Discoveries and Renaissance Europe'. In the same year, as a follow-up to the seminar on Japan, the International Society for Educational Information in Tokyo invited a group of European educators to take part in a three-week study tour of Japan.

Nor has the work of the Georg Eckert Institute for International Textbook Research been limited to the history of Europe. Since its foundation, the Institute has made studies of the content and treatment in European history textbooks of Israel, India, Indonesia, Tunisia, Japan and the United States. Some of the studies have been bilateral, examining the images of Europe and of the partner country in each other's textbooks. These consultations have been followed by recommendations on how best to remove misunderstandings and misleading emphases. After a study of the image of African people and cultures in geography textbooks from five European countries, the Institute is now analysing the geography textbooks of 37 African states and their images of Germany and the European Union. History teachers and text-book writers would obviously benefit from a similar analysis of history textbooks.

The case for knowing and understanding something of Asia, Africa and the Americas is strong. The alternative to this knowledge is not so much ignorance as prejudice and myth, the enemies of historical evidence. At a simple level, we are all disadvantaged and enfeebled by our ignorance if we know nothing of the history and culture of the rest of the world.

Some of the practical teaching implications of this important issue were explored at the 1986 London seminar, 'Asia in the European Classroom'. It was part of the Council of Europe's programme, started in 1978, on education for international understanding (see also Chapter 3). The seminar was not specifically concerned with the teaching of history, but its final report contains a section on 'A less ethnocentric approach to history'.[22] It identifies some of the recent developments in the teaching of history (see Chapter 5) as particularly applicable to the study of Asia.

Our own pasts help us towards understanding our own cultural and national identities. This understanding becomes deeper and more critically perceptive if we can set it against the different ways of thinking and of creating, the different beliefs and histories of other cultures and nations.

> To me this process of self-evaluation in relation to others, though it may be resisted by both the narrow traditionalist and the activist rebel, represents the natural growth of the great tradition of liberal education in the new age of world community we have entered.[23]

Further, the histories and cultures of Africa and Asia belong also to many European citizens and to their children learning history in classrooms all over Europe. This must mean an end to other cultures being 'discovered' by European textbooks and a recognition that the history of the rest of the world did not begin when Europeans first stumbled across it.

Of course Europeans can be tolerant of other cultures, indeed can like the people of other races; benevolent slave-owners often did both. But without knowledge of, and some empathy with, the cultural and scientific achievements of pre-European societies, of our subsequent intertwined histories with their achievements as well as their terrible errors, our tolerance will be blinkered and patronizing.

History does not explicitly seek to create a multicultural society or to argue an informed acceptance of it. But, without an informed understanding of the historical context of the experiences, attitudes and beliefs of other cultures, some necessary, if not sufficient, conditions for the existence of multicultural societies will not exist.

CONCLUSION

This chapter has described some of the considerable achievements of the Council of Europe on behalf of history over forty years. The work of the Council continues to help us identify a future agenda not only for the Council of Europe but for all of us who have a passionate belief in the importance of history in the schools of the New Europe.

APPENDIX

Recommendations on content made by the Elsinore Symposium (1965) and the Bruges Symposium (1991) are listed below.

Elsinore proposed these topics:

- what Europe owes to civilizations past and present, notably Greek, Roman and Byzantine; to Judaism, Christianity, Islam, etc.;
- the Great Migrations, in so far as they concern the history of Europe;
- feudalism;
- the church;
- rural conditions and towns in the Middle Ages;
- the Crusades;
- representative institutions and legal principles;
- medieval thought and art;
- humanism: the Renaissance;
- the religious reform movements;
- the voyages of discovery and expansion overseas;
- the development of capitalism;
- the rise of modern states;
- absolute government and representative government;
- classicism and the Baroque;
- the Age of Enlightenment;
- the industrial and agricultural revolutions;
- the revolutions of the eighteenth and nineteenth centuries: liberalism and nationalism;
- socialism;

- intellectual and artistic, scientific and technical developments in the nineteenth and twentieth centuries;
- European expansion in the world and the formation of colonial empires;
- the two world wars;
- democracy, Communism and Fascism;
- Europe in the world today;
- trends towards European unity in the different periods of European history.

Bruges proposed the following additions:

- the three orders of feudal society;
- medieval towns, their development and local law;
- the birth of parliaments (differences and common problems);
- trade between European regions (the Vikings, the Hanse, Italy);
- the role of the church in written language and material culture;
- central Europe: the birth of the nations;
- central Europe: the dual influence of Rome and Byzantium;
- biographies of leading intellectuals;
- science and humanism in Europe in the sixteenth and seventeenth centuries;
- the wars of religion and efforts at toleration;
- constituents of national consciousness during the Renaissance;
- the Enlightenment in political and material life;
- liberalism and nationalism in Europe;
- the industrial revolution;
- Europe between two totalitarian systems: the reaction of states and parties;
- resistance movements during World War II;
- Fascism and its forms in Europe;
- Yalta as seen by both sides;
- Europe as seen by others.

NOTES

1 This chapter draws heavily and sometimes directly on the reports of the Council of Europe history conferences and on the invaluable summary of them, *Against Bias and Prejudice: The Council of Europe's Work on History Teaching and History Textbooks'*, Strasbourg: *Council for Cultural Cooperation*. A bibliography is given in Appendix 1. Since the text of this book was completed the Council of Europe has organized conferences on 'The Reform of History Teaching in Schools in European Countries in Democratic Transition' (Graz, 1994) and 'The Learning of History in Europe' (Paris, 1994).

2 R. Wake, V. Marbeau, and A. Peterson (1979), *Innovation in Secondary Education in Europe*, Strasbourg: Council for Cultural Cooperation, p. 8.

3 J. Aldebert, J. Bender, J. Grusa *et al.* (1992), *Histoire de l'Europe*, Paris: Hachette. At the time of writing, editions in Italian, Polish, Japanese and English (Weidenfeld and Nicolson, 1993) have been published. Other language translations are planned.

4 *Against Bias and Prejudice*, p. 101.

5 By 1995, 43 states had acceded to the Convention: the 36 member states of the Council of Europe and Belarus, Bosnia-Herzegovina, Croatia, the Holy See, Monaco, the Russian Federation and the Ukraine.

6 *Against Bias and Prejudice*, p. 101.

7 The same conference commended 'A list of prejudices that all history teachers should be made aware of', compiled by the late L. T. Maes, Inspector of History and Sociology with the Ministry of Education, Brussels.

8 In a session led by Dr Taina Huuhtanen.

9 (n.d.) *Art Exhibitions*, Strasbourg: Council of Europe, Directorate of Education, Culture and Sport.

10 S. Kaland and A.-T. Langørgen (1992), *The Vikings and their World*, Strasbourg: Council of Europe.

11 Quoted in A. Perotti (1971), *Action to Combat Intolerance and Xenophobia*, Strasbourg: Council for Cultural Cooperation, p. 7.

12 P. Leuprecht (1991), at the Council of Europe Seminar, 'Intercultural Learning for Human Rights', Klagenfurt.

13 M. Stobart (1986) in Council for Cultural Cooperation, *Against Bias and Prejudice*.

14 Recommendation No. R(85)7 of the Committee of Ministers to Member States on Teaching and Learning about Human Rights in Schools.

15 R. Mocnik (1991), at the Council of Europe Seminar, 'Intercultural Learning for Human Rights', Klagenfurt.

16 E. M. Forster (1940), 'Captain Edward Gibbon' in *Abinger Harvest*, London: Edward Arnold, p. 218.

17 'Intercultural Learning for Human Rights'.

18 E. Hinrichs, (1992), 'Subject matter adequacy', in Bourdillon, H. (ed.), *History and Social Studies – Methodologies of Textbook Analysis*, Amsterdam: Swets and Zeitlinger, p. 47.

19 B. Crick and A. Porter (1978), *Political Education and Political Literacy*, London: Longman.

20 W. Shakespeare, *Coriolanus*, Act III, sc. iii, l. 133.

21 S. Carmichael (1968), 'Black Power', in D. Cooper, (ed.), *The Dialectics of Liberation*, Harmondsworth: Penguin, pp. 153–4. The title of this section is taken from *Coriolanus*, Act III, sc. iii, l. 133.

22 P. Bahree (1986), *Asia in the European Classroom*, Strasbourg: Council of Europe, pp. 33–4.

23 W .T. de Bary (1972), 'The liberal arts amid a culture in crisis', *Liberal Education* **LVIII**, 1, quoted in Bahree *Asia in the European Classroom*, p. 9.

CHAPTER 3

Recent Initiatives and Prospects

This chapter describes, mainly in their own words, some of the current and recent projects which support the teaching of history across Europe. Most, but not all, are associated with, or supported by, the Council of Europe. Not all are specifically concerned with the teaching of history. Some are well established, others are being piloted or are newly started, while others are no more than serious and strongly supported proposals for the future. The list cannot claim to be exhaustive. One problem regularly identified at Council of Europe conferences is the urgent need for a central data bank, storing and disseminating information on transnational organizations and links, current research, syllabuses and curricular developments, projects and teaching materials. We are wastefully and dangerously unaware of the richness and quality of much that is taking place in Europe. There are still dramatic differences of wealth and educational resources within Europe, but all of us, in our different ways, are threatened with inadequate knowledge and impoverished perceptions.

COUNCIL OF EUROPE INITIATIVES

The broad context of many of the Council's initiatives has been a series of recommendations and resolutions of the Parliamentary Assembly of the Council of Europe and the Standing Conference of the European Ministers of Education. A constant theme has been the invitation of member states to encourage and implement in school curricula what has been variously termed a European 'consciousness', a European 'awareness' or a European 'dimension'. Recommendations by Council of Europe bodies include those on:

- educational visits and pupil exchanges between European countries (1980);
- the promotion of an awareness of Europe in secondary schools (1983);
- European cultural identity (1985);
- the European dimension in education (1989);
- the promotion of school links and exchanges in Europe (1994).

In 1991, the Council of Europe's Council for Cultural Cooperation (CDCC) wrote:

> Over the last few years, the European dimension in education has come to occupy an increasingly important place in the concerns of the teaching world.
>
> Whatever the problems and uncertainties in European construction at the level of its institutions, the environment in which those young people at school today live will be as much European as national.
>
> Young people should, thus, be given the knowledge, know-how and attitudes they need to face the major challenges of European society (mobility, cultural diversity etc.) and help them become aware of their common cultural heritage.[1]

Consequently, the CDCC initiated a project called 'A Secondary Education for Europe', which will last until 1996. Its programme consisted of:

- *a permanent forum.* Throughout the project, annual symposia will allow an exchange of ideas, concerns and proposals on the major problems of secondary education in Europe: aims, means, methods, structures, certification and evaluation, and teacher training.
- *a Guide to European Education Systems.* The great diversity of the more than forty education systems is a fact. The Guide will be a simple, brief, descriptive tool. Each system will be described on a fact sheet contained within a reasonably sized volume.
- *pedagogical guides and case studies.* A series of booklets will present possible activities resulting from pilot projects, seminars or workshops taking place within schools both in the classroom and outside (for example, European clubs, school exchanges, multidisciplinary projects).
- *school exchanges: a vade mecum and a network.* (See below for details.)
- *central and eastern Europe.* Specific action will be undertaken to support the immense efforts being made to face considerable tasks and resource shortages by the new partners from east and central Europe in European educational cooperation.

European Dimension Pedagogical Materials Programme

This Programme is an important part of the project 'A Secondary Education for Europe', whose programme aims to support the development of education *for* Europe by promoting education *on* Europe and developing strategies to deal with secondary education *in* Europe'.

These Pedagogical Materials, due to be published in 1996, are intended to be used across the whole secondary curriculum. They are envisaged as a flexible series, or bank, of dossiers, which can easily be updated, rather than once-and-for-all single publication. They will contain not only maps but relevant documents and other source material, pictures, tables and graphs, some explanatory text, and guides for classroom use. A list of topics includes: frontiers, cultural identity, ethnicity and migration, minorities, notions of citizenship, political power and legitimacy, cultural and individual identity, population movements, economic developments, conflicts in Europe, nationalism, the industrial revolution, human rights, Greco-Latin civilization, the European institutions, Europe and the rest of the world.

Clearly, this material offers exciting potential support for the introduction of the European dimension in secondary schools in Europe.

In-Service Training Programme for Teachers

The Council of Europe operates a programme to help teachers attend short in-service training courses in another member State. They can, thus, broaden their professional experience by exchanging good practice, ideas and teaching resources with colleagues from other countries. One thousand bursaries are available annually at present, and the programme is being expanded to cater for more teachers from central and eastern Europe. Some thirty seminars on history have been organized within the framework of this programme, and they have dealt both with questions of methodology and with the content of history teaching, such as important encounters of peoples or ideas in the history in Europe. A new series of seminars is in preparation. Some of them will be linked to the European Cultural Routes.

School Twinning and Local History

In March 1990 the Conference of Local and Regional Authorities of Europe (CLRAE) set up a new committee to deal with questions concerning culture, education and the media.[2] Among its resolutions was a proposed programme of school twinnings involving the study of the history of the schools' own regions and localities, and aimed particularly at pupils in the 9–13 age group. (Some twinnings involve pupils up to the age of 16.) Consequently the CLRAE established a pilot programme, 'School Twinning and Local History', for the years 1991–2. The CLRAE was persuaded by the following considerations, as identified by its rapporteur, Josephine Farrington:

- the need to update the teaching of European history in the wake of the political upheavals of recent months and the desirability of dealing with often-neglected topics such as the history of ethnic and cultural minorities in local communities, the emancipation of women, the daily lives of children, relations with other local communities in Europe and the situation of migrant children;
- the possibility of extending this project at no great cost to a large number of schools in Western, Central and Eastern Europe, including those in the most outlying or deprived regions, and to the most disadvantaged cultural groups;
- the possibility of using widely diversified teaching materials (photographs, computers, videos etc.) and a variety of teaching methods (cooperation with museums and libraries, interviews with individuals etc.);

- the possibility of enhancing the European cultural identity based on intercultural relations and the acceptance of diversity;
- through an exchange of pupils' studies between localities, [providing] an excellent preparation of personal exchanges and [stimulating] the learning of European languages.

Since this report was published, its recommendations have been endorsed by the Standing Conference of the European Ministers of Education, and it has received widespread support throughout Europe.

The Pilot Programme originally involved twelve school-twinning pairs involving twelve member states of the Council of Europe – the then Czechoslovakia, Denmark, Finland, Greece, Hungary, Iceland, Ireland, Italy, the Netherlands, Portugal, Sweden and the United Kingdom – as well as two non-member states with special observer status, Bulgaria and Russia; subsequent participants were the Federal Republic of Germany, Austria, France and Lithuania. There have been some language difficulties but, in the main, either pupils' writing has been translated into the appropriate language or English has been used as a lingua franca. The Council's Secretariat reports that, in pairing schools, efforts have been made in order to:

- 'help build up East–West relations'; for example, a school in Hungary has been twinned with a British school;
- 'reduce the North–South divide'; for example, an Italian school was paired with a Danish one, a Greek school with a British one.

In a few cases, specific requests have been taken into account; for example, a Finnish school was paired with one in Russia, and a Dutch school with one in Germany. The current and expanded list of twinnings is impressive and geographically comprehensive.[3]

However, the project is only a pilot study. If it is to be launched on a wider scale, the staff resources of CLRAE are inadequate. The project has been evaluated and a meeting of teachers involved in it has taken place in Strasbourg. At the last meeting of CLRAE, the Committee agreed to think further about ways and means of launching the scheme on a wider basis for older pupils. This scheme is imaginative, and not only excitingly supports the development of a European understanding but also adds an important and crucial dimension to the learning of history. It deserves to succeed.

TEMPUS and SOCRATES

The Trans-European Cooperation Scheme for Higher Education (TEMPUS) was adopted, initially as a three-year pilot project, by the Council of Ministers of the European Community in May 1990. It was extended in April 1993 for a second four-year phase commencing with the academic year 1994–95.

TEMPUS is the European Union's instrument for the development and restructuring of higher education in Central and Eastern Europe and in the newly independent states of the former Soviet Union as well as in Mongolia.

The main aims of the TEMPUS Scheme are to:

- promote the quality and support the development and renewal of higher education in the eligible Phare and Tacis countries;
- encourage their growing interaction and as balanced a cooperation as possible with partners in the European Union, through joint activities and relevant mobility.

History and the humanities are *priorities* for the TEMPUS programme in the former Soviet Union (Tempus-Tacis). As for TEMPUS in central and eastern Europe (Tempus-Phare), history and the humanities may be included as priorities on a country-by-country basis.

SOCRATES is the European Community action programme for cooperation in the field of education adopted in March 1995 and spanning the period until the end of 1999. It is applicable to the 15 member states of the European Union as well as to Iceland, Liechtenstein and Norway in the framework of the European Economic Area. It embraces all types and levels of education within one single programme for European Cooperation.

SOCRATES is to be seen in the broader context of promoting lifelong learning in response to the challenge of addressing the constantly evolving educational needs resulting from technological change, quickening obsolescence of knowledge, and the role of education in enabling people to fulfill their individual potential.

European Cultural Routes

From the 1960s the Council of Europe's CDCC has concerned itself with cultural tourism, and in 1964 it produced a report called *Collective Awareness of European Cultural Highlights and their Incorporation into the Leisure Culture*. The report commented on 'new centres of civilisation' in Europe, the 'product of demographic and scientific discoveries, whose existence is often more important to non-Europeans than to Europeans themselves'. These contemporary centres are:

> evidence of the constant renewal of European civilisation ... Each era of European civilisation has thus experienced a 'modern' phase. Awareness of the vitality of civilisation, both in the present and in comparison with its own past, means tracing its achievements in a continuous line from the civilisation of the ancient Greeks ... Thus, European genius is a continuous phenomenon, expressed in various guises at each stage of European civilisation and, whether Christian or rationalist, a European tradition continues to regard man as the principal object of its concerns and activities.

To give their views some concrete and comprehensible form the authors of the report identified three aims:

- to increase public awareness of European culture through travel;
- to study the relation between the cultural geography of Europe and the scope for establishing tourist networks;
- to develop the major centres and crossroads of European civilization with a view to tourism.

Thus, in 1987, the CDCC initiated a series of pilot projects to investigate the possible development of a number of 'European Cultural Routes'. In the words of the CDCC's preliminary report, it was seeking 'to signpost those thematic networks where the European identity dominates spiritually speaking ... following a route which indicates the continuity of European thought and behaviour patterns'.

Such aspirations need to be clarified with some concrete examples. There are already numerous local and regional historic itineraries, including town and city trails. But what are *Council of Europe* cultural routes? The working party suggested that they can be: 'transnational', that is, taking in several countries; 'transregional', irrespective of whether or not they cross frontiers; or 'regional', based within one region but with cultural, historical, artistic and social interest going beyond the boundaries of the region or state concerned. The themes selected as examples were seen not only as a series of monuments, but also as recognizing events and periods in European history shared by a number of countries. Proposed routes are:

- an epoch in *the history of culture and art*: Baroque;
- *the history and influence of a people*: the Vikings, Celts or Lombards;
- a *product* of exceptional significance: silk;
- a *geographical situation* with a precise socio-economic features: a rural habitat;
- a phenomenon that was *religious but also cultural* and artistic: the Santiago de Compostella pilgrimage routes, or the monastic orders;
- a successful example of *interrelation* among a group of cities: the Hanseatic League.

In addition, the preliminary report published by the Council of Europe included a route centred on the *life and achievements of one man* – the Mozart routes, linked to the centenary of the composer's death in 1991.

Travelling a cultural route will be a contemporary experience linking the traveller to the past and its continuing impact on the present. For the traveller, culture will not be confined within galleries and museums and ancient monuments, textbooks and classrooms, but seen and experienced as something living: buildings still in use, Baroque altar pieces still objects of veneration for present-day congregations, Renaissance frescoes still celebrating civic pride, war memorials commemorating the unforgotten dead, landscapes and field patterns, festivals and memories, cuisines, political attitudes and religious faith.

The Council of Europe Cultural Routes are for a world-wide public of all ages. Their development in the tourist field will have to concern itself with such mundane essentials as publicity, maps, signposts and guides, the problems of queuing and crowding, of adequate toilets and car parks, and of places to eat and sleep and camp. Delicate paths have to be trodden by the planners in advance of the cultural pilgrims. How do we avoid places along the routes exploiting the past, like medieval barons or Baltic fortresses extracting excessive tolls from innocent travellers, or, on the other hand, being occupied and ravaged by cultural raiders, wielding not swords but the whirrs and flashes of countless international cameras?

A Council of Europe itinerary may be implemented not only in the tourist field, but also in those of heritage and scientific research, or the creative arts. The cultural routes offer potentially rich and very exciting opportunities in the field of education, too, for young people to experience history outside their classrooms. The Bruges Symposium expressed strong, sometimes vehement views that priority must be given to schools with limited budgets and backpacking students on inadequate grants, enabling them to eat and sleep within their means while discovering Europe's culture.

School Links and Exchanges in Europe

Both the Council of Europe and the European Union have drawn the attention of member states to the importance of educational visits and exchanges, and of their crucial contribution to developing a European awareness in young people.[4] Thus, the publication of *School Links and Exchanges in Europe: A Practical Guide* fulfils one of the aims of the 'Secondary Education for Europe' programme, and gives practical guidance for the implementation of the Council of Europe's recommendations. It contains not only advice on the organization of visits and exchanges, but some case studies, information from 29 member states, and summaries of current initiatives by the Council of Europe, the European Union and the Nordic Council of Ministers.

Work is now under way on the preparation of modules or units for use in teacher training.

Guide to School Links and Exchanges

A report on school exchanges based on questionnaires sent to local education authorities was published in 1992 by the Standing Conference of Local and Regional Authorities.[5] The report analyses 588 responses from all over Europe.

Of the exchanges 78 per cent were between twinned schools, the vast majority (73 per cent) of which were based on town twinning arrangements. The strongest support for town and school twinning came from the United Kingdom, followed by Scandinavia. Trans-frontier exchanges had considerable support in the responses from Luxembourg, Austria, Sweden, the Czech and Slovak Republics, Hungary and what was at that time Yugoslavia. About 30 per cent of links are with countries in eastern and central Europe, and 92 per cent of all correspondents expressed an interest in developing links.

Authorities were also asked to identify the main advantages of school exchanges. The most common responses are shown in Table 1.

Table 1 Main advantages of school exchanges

Response	%
Helping foreign language competence	63
Personal and social development	61
Development of a European identity and awareness	43
Improving community understanding	18
Breaking down barriers	14
Learning about other educational systems	6

History is not explicitly mentioned in Table 1, but it is not implicitly excluded either. Determined and enterprising history departments can organize exchanges based on joint class work and fieldwork on historical topics. However, when asked what types of exchange ought to be developed in the future, the importance of history emerged more explicitly (see Table 2).

Table 2 Types of exchange to be developed in future

Type of exchange	%
Language learning	86
Environmental education	68
Heritage	64
History	59
Art education	44
Music	39
Sport	29
Work experience	27
Media studies	26
Political education	26
Science	26
Social education	25

Of course, the categories shown in Table 2 are not distinct. Heritage and history are unavoidable allies, and they are not excluded by either language learning or environmental education.

The report contains interesting national variations in the responses to these last two questions. Why, for example, was there particularly strong support for environmental education and history from Austria, less interest in heritage matters in France and the Netherlands, and stronger support for political education and work experience in the United Kingdom?

There remain considerable logistical and financial difficulties in organizing school visits and exchanges. Obstacles listed are shown in Table 3.

Table 3 Obstacles to school visits and exchanges

Obstacle	%
Financial	62
Establishing partners and contacts	27
Lack of interest or time among teachers	16
Difficulty accommodating pupils	15
Mismatch of pupils	8

The pole star by which we should steer our policies, however, is that such visits and exchanges should surely be seen no longer as interruptions, extras and treats for a minority, but as part of the curriculum entitlement for all young Europeans during their years of compulsory schooling. Without such experiences, it will be difficult to transform a class-bound European dimension into something that can justifiably claim to be a European *awareness*. European awareness without a historical perspective will be half-blind.

The European Centre for Global Interdependence and Solidarity

In 1988, the Council of Europe in cooperation with the European Communities organized a European Campaign for North–South Interdependence and Solidarity. The campaign sought to raise public awareness of the complex, mutual relationship between north and south, which affects the daily lives of all Europeans; it involved grass-roots activities, seminars, public debates and cultural events. As a follow-up, the European Centre for Global Interdependence and Solidarity, known as the North–South Centre, was founded.

Thanks to the Council of Europe, the Centre has the potential to become the first all-European body to deal with global interdependence issues from the perspectives of a New Europe. Its concerns are public information and relations with the media, education and training, and the establishment of contacts. Particular emphasis is given to links with youth organizations and the raising of awareness not only of but by young people. Since its foundation, the Centre has organized a series of international meetings:

- an East–West–South Encounter was held in Budapest (1990), with a follow-up in The Hague (1991) on 'The Effects of Europe's Transformation on North–South Cooperation'.
- a 'Latin America/Caribbean–Europe Encounter' was held in Santiago de Chile (1991).
- a 'North–South Colloquy on Democracy and the Protection of Human Rights' was held in Lisbon (1991).

Other activities include programmes on north–south youth links, and an education and training programme for global interdependence. The Centre has also worked closely with television and broadcasting and, as a sequel to the One World Week of 1990, a further series of television programmes was broadcast in the spring of 1992 in advance of the Rio Earth Summit.

None of these activities is specifically concerned with history, but if history teachers need to understand the historical context of an interdependent world and the nature of north–south relations, then the work of the Centre has relevance. It may well have a part to play in any future Council of Europe history symposia concerned with the global context of European history.

At the time of writing, some two-thirds of member states of the Council of Europe are members of the Centre.

THE UNESCO ASSOCIATED SCHOOLS PROJECT

The UNESCO Constitution of 1946 states that its purpose is to:

> contribute to peace and security by promoting collaboration among nations through education and science and culture in order to further universal respect for the rule of law and human rights and fundamental freedoms which are affirmed of the peoples of the world, without the distinction of race, sex, language or religion.

To give these high ideals some reality in schools and classrooms, the Associated Schools Project (ASP) was founded in 1953. It established national and international networks of schools, initially with 33 secondary schools in 15 member states. Subsequently, its terms of reference widened to include primary schools, teacher training institutions and universities. In 1993, there were some 2,960 associated institutions in 116 member countries.

The project seeks to promote education for international understanding, with publications, seminars, student and teacher exchanges as well as, through the ASP networks, by the sharing, disseminating and exchanging of resources and classroom experiences, and, above all, by the development of good practice in classrooms. The project was externally assessed in 1979 and 1980 by an independent team led by a Canadian and a Tanzanian, and individual member institutions are given guidance on and encouraged to make regular assessments and evaluations of their own work. In 1993, an international symposium at Soest in Germany published a review on the progress of the project on its fortieth anniversary.

'Education for international understanding' generalizes many activities and goals; it is easier to applaud than to define, or to turn into classroom practice. School programmes have been generally based on four related and more focused themes:

- world problems and the role of the United Nations in solving them;
- human rights;
- other countries and cultures;
- people and their environment.

Help is given to schools by UNESCO publications such as: *World Concerns and the United Nations: Model Teaching Units for Primary, Secondary and Teacher Education* (1983), *Innovative Methods in the Associated Schools Project* (1988), *Approaches to Human Rights Education* (1989), *Environmental Education for Our Common Future* (1991), and a series of books produced within member states under the general heading of 'Come Visit Our Country'.

School networks are often linked to particular projects – for example, fund-raising to subsidize exchanges or attendance at seminars or, more specifically, to help rebuild schools damaged in the Guatemalan earthquake of 1976; to occasions such as International Literacy Year, or the observance of international days; with local campaigns – for example, against vandalism or for the protection of wildlife, helping with old people's welfare or with programmes of urban renewal, and the organizing of summer language camps. The focus of many such activities has been the formation of UNESCO clubs. The project's environmental agenda has developed important regional programmes such as the Baltic Sea Project, the Blue Danube River Project and the Mediterranean Project.

Since 1953, nearly 50 seminars, conferences and workshops have been organized in 36 different countries on 4 continents, involving teachers and sometimes students from schools and higher education.

Institutions wishing to participate in the ASP are assumed to have some planned commitment to education for international understanding, apply to UNESCO. They complete a form asking them to describe the goals and the nature of the activities they intend to undertake, and give an assurance that they will participate in the project for a minimum of two years.

INDEPENDENT PROJECTS

The European Studies Project

The European Studies Project was established in 1986 by the Ministry of Education in the Republic of Ireland, the Department of Education Northern Ireland, and the Department of Education and Science in London. It has now been extended and involves some three hundred schools not only in Ireland, Northern Ireland and England but in Belgium, Denmark, Finland, France, Germany, the Netherlands, Scotland and Spain. At the time of writing there is the possibility of the involvement of a school in Greece.

The project seeks to give young people the opportunity of working together as young Europeans, and using modern information technology to reach a better understanding of each other's views and ideas. Within it there are three programmes, outlined below.

1 The 11–14/12–15 Programme was extensively trialled in the Republic of Ireland, Northern Ireland and England. Schools were selected to include non-denominational and church ones, including Catholic and Protestant schools in Northern Ireland. Pupils study relations between England and Ireland in a European context. The selected themes are: 'The Normans', 'Water', 'Plantation in the Seventeenth Century' (that is, English and Scottish settlement in Ireland), 'Attitudes to Conflict: 1914–21' and 'Migration'. The project deliberately chose themes that give young people opportunities to work on sensitive issues which challenge stereotypical attitudes and values.

Each class constructs individual and group profiles of its members and prepares information about the school and its locality. This information, which may be supplemented by audio- and/or video-tapes, is sent by surface or electronic mail to linked schools. Pupils have an opportunity of examining evidence and exchanging their ideas on the sources they have studied in a variety of ways. The units also give pupils opportunities to promote and exchange experiences of group work, role play, simulations and pupil evaluation. Residential courses enable them to meet and get to know each other and extend the links beyond the limits of postal systems and electronic mail.

2 The 16–18 Programme is one of two schemes run by the project for older pupils in schools not only in what we must non-politically call 'the north western European archipelago', but also across Europe. It is not specifically subject-based and involves research into a range of contemporary, economic, cultural and social issues in Europe. Once again, schools and colleges work as linked partners, using electronic mail and video-conferencing to exchange reports.

The success of the residential courses in the 11–16 programme encouraged the establishing of a six-day residential course for teachers and students in the 16–18 programme. These courses have been held at the Irish Institute of European Affairs in Leuven, Belgium, and at other centres in Ireland and the United Kingdom.

3 A related programme called 'Language, Industry and Trade' differs from the others in that it concentrates on enterprise and economic awareness in Europe, and uses FAX alongside electronic mailing.

Many of the schools and colleges carry out their work in the 16–18 Programme as part of a one-year course leading to a Certificate in Contemporary European Studies, which was set up by the project and the Associated English Examining Board.

None of these programmes is cost-free. Although the formal period of funding for the first programme has ended, the authorities in Dublin and Belfast are continuing to support the project with limited budgets. Unfortunately, English priorities are different, and while partner schools in England are determined to maintain their links, they alone will have to do so without any financial support from the government.

The evaluation of the project shows substantial benefits in terms of knowledge and skills and in the enthusiastic support of students and teachers. Dr Roger Austin, its founding director from 1986–1992, writes: 'Taken together, the programmes offer a substantial structure that helps young people achieve a deeper understanding of relationships between Britain and Ireland and a preparation for citizenship in Europe.' The project originated in a part of Europe known to outsiders for its violence and its bitter sectarian and political divisions. But its achievements transcend these divides and offer not only one model for other collaborative projects elsewhere, but also an optimistic message for all of Europe.

The Young Historian Scheme

This scheme was launched by the Historical Association in the United Kingdom and is funded by educational trusts and some private companies. Its overall purpose is to encourage and facilitate the study of history in schools. It seeks to help history pupils and their teachers throughout the school system to become more confident of the value of studying history as a school subject; to extend the opportunities available for involvement in activities which makes history more enjoyable and stimulating; to develop new ways of making contact between history students and the world of work; to generate among the public a better appreciation of the importance of history in the education of children; and to disseminate good practice in the teaching of history.

An important part of the scheme is the establishment of regional and local centres so that teachers can get in touch with each other, and share and disseminate their work. Some work is developed within single schools, but much involves groups of schools; for example, secondary schools working with primary schools, or with higher education institutes, local museums and archives. The scheme also publishes curriculum material in pamphlet form. These are practical guides to teaching and learning, containing source material, detailed bibliographies, and suggested teaching and assessment strategies. Recent themes have included: a study of a local engineering firm and its history, so linking history with the world of work; a 'change in shopping' project; old age in its historical context; and, focusing on a controversial and recently sensitive issue, the Brighton Bomb.[6] The pamphlets and the school projects all involve pupils in their writing, implementation and evaluation.

Other activities include an annual 'History Day' at which four groups of prizes and awards are made for achievements in history. They are: the Royal Historical Society Young Historians' Prizes for pupils aged 14–16; the Wolfson Young Historian Prizes for pupils of all ages (4–19); Past Times Young Historians' Prizes for pupils aged 4–19; and the English Heritage Young Historian Prize for 5–16-year-olds. The Wolfson awards are for work on named topics, which are 'Work and the Local Community', 'Cultural Links with Europe' and 'The World beyond Europe'. One of the prizewinners in 1992 was based on one student's work with twinned schools in Finland and what was then Czechoslovakia.

The Young Historian Scheme offers one model for stimulating the learning of history. Clearly, it has potential for working with schools in other European countries and might well link with the CLRAE project, 'School Twinning and Local History.' The scheme gained the interest of the Council of Europe, and its first coordinator was invited to Strasbourg to discuss its aims and progress. The CDCC is kept fully informed by the Young Historian's publications, reports and thrice-yearly newsletter.

The scheme's motto is 'Local, relevant, detailed and active'. Local it often is, but never parochial or inward-looking. This project surely has a wider function, not only as a model, but as part of a network of similar initiatives across the nations of a New Europe.

History syllabuses in international schools

The dissemination of information and resources and the exchange of experiences between national systems is a matter not only of great importance but, in some cases, of desperate urgency. It has been argued that history syllabuses in the Europe of the twenty-first century must be sensitive to local needs and cannot ignore the particular political and historical circumstances in which they are taught. There are, however, three syllabuses which are designed specifically to be taught in international schools. They offer relevant models and pertinent experience from which all national systems might benefit. They are: the history syllabuses taught in the European Schools of the European Union; the recommended syllabus of the International Schools Association; and the International Baccalaureate. These three represent carefully considered and distinct strategies. All have been taught, assessed and studied by teachers and countless groups of young people all over the world. We can all profit from their experience.

The *European Schools* educate the children of European Union officials and employees. Their syllabuses are centrally defined and are agreed by all member states. History is a core element throughout secondary education. For the first three years, it is taught by one teacher as part of a 'human sciences' course, in close association with geography and social studies. Thereafter, history is taught as a separate subject by specialist teachers. For the first two years of secondary education, 'human sciences' are learned in the pupils' mother tongue. From then on, classes are conducted in the first foreign language of all pupils. Thus, European awareness is developed not just in the content of the syllabus but in the languages in which it is learned.

Aims which run throughout the course include:

- the discovery of personal identity as a means to understanding the present day;
- the development of critical faculties, including a respect for evidence;
- the ability to use and interpret a wide range of source material;
- tolerance (a recognition of the right of others to be different);
- the development of leisure interests.

The course in the first three years also emphasizes the different characteristics and aims of the contributory disciplines.

The content is broadly chronological, starting in the first three years with a study of the environment and early people, going on to the development of agriculture, trade and architecture, and ending with the civilization of the ancient world and the Middle Ages, with special emphasis on the Mediterranean region. During the fourth and fifth years, pupils study Islam and other non-European civilizations (although the rest of the world is still being 'discovered'), and with an emphasis on European history up to the outbreak of World War I. In the final two years, they study a series of key themes in European and world history:

- society and state in the late nineteenth and early twentieth centuries;
- imperialism;
- World War I;
- the Russian Revolution;
- economic consequences of the War;
- society and state between the wars;

- international relations up to 1945;
- international relations after 1945;
- society and state since 1945;
- economic and social changes after 1945;
- the individual in society;
- towards post-industrial society: trends and perspectives.

The content is mainly Euro-centred, although attention is given to Islam and to non-European civilizations and, in Year 7, to such themes as 'decolonialization', 'the north–south conflict', 'Third World developments in India, China and Africa' and 'the Islamic world'.

The members of the *International Schools Association* (ISA) are, in the main, independent and private international schools throughout the world. The ISA-recommended history syllabus is described in the 'Humanities ISA Curriculum Programme' published in 1989. It too assumes that the principal and sole ally of history is geography, although the two subjects are seen as distinct disciplines. The new syllabus is designed for pupils ages 11–16 and has in mind particularly those who will go on to study the International Baccalaureate. The syllabus addresses the particular problems of teaching history to nationally heterogeneous classes. The authors of the syllabus, Malcolm Davis and Caroline Ellwood, write:

> Selling a particular point of view, political philosophy or series of facts, has given way to hermeneutics, at the heart of the critical debate, as the most useful skill. This is especially appropriate in the international school where 'cultures' and 'ideologies' must not be manipulated for particular ends. As international teachers, our business is to develop the mental capacities of all our students. We must create a sense of the world as a place where no one people have or have had a monopoly of greatness; where no one environment is better than another.[7]

Thus, the emphasis of the syllabus is on skills and concepts rather than prescribed content.

Throughout the five years of the syllabus, the fundamental historical concepts of 'time', 'continuity and change', 'similarity and difference' and 'causation' are developed. An interesting feature is that the four age levels are associated with what the syllabus calls 'four basic notions'. They are, successively:

- origins;
- society/technology;
- turmoil;
- dynamism.

Course aims include:

- empathy;
- the detection of bias;

- an understanding of the present through the past;
- an appreciation of human interaction and change in the past – critical thinking and historical imagination through working with and understanding the fragmentary evidence of the past.

The 'basic notions' are exemplified at each stage by a list of historical concepts and ideas. Examples include:

- *origins*: food supplies, population growth, temples, architecture, archaeology, slavery;
- *society and technology*: jihad, serfdom, Gothic art, Confucianism, myth, tribe, division of labour, siege;
- *turmoil*: treason, heresy, sovereignty, citizenship, nation state, democracy;
- *dynamism*: terror, coalition, constitution, imperialism, racism, Marxism, ghetto, propaganda, ideology.

Recommended content is included only as an appendix to the syllabus.

This syllabus, together with the International Baccalaureate, represents a coherent history education for 11–18-year-olds in multinational schools, and strives to give meaning and learning objectives to 'education for international understanding'. The 11–16 syllabus is now administered by the International Baccalaureate office in the United Kingdom.

The *International Baccalaureate* (IB) is studied by 16–18-year-old students in the international or internationally minded schools in some forty-eight countries on all five continents. The IB course is a complete, broadly based, multidisciplinary syllabus. Its aims, based on the pattern of no single country, state that 'it represents the desire of the founders to provide students of different linguistic, cultural and educational backgrounds with the intellectual, social and critical perspectives necessary for the adult world which lies ahead of them.'

The course is divided into six groups of subjects; candidates must select one subject from each group. These are:

- Language A (a first language);
- Language B;
- the study of people in society;
- experimental sciences;
- mathematics;
- one of the following from two groups of options: art/design, music, Latin, classical Greek, computing studies; or an approved school-based and designed syllabus.

In addition, students must follow a course in the theory of knowledge.

History is contained within the 'study of "man" in society' group, which in addition includes geography, economics, philosophy, psychology, social anthropology, and organizational studies. The 'theory of knowledge' contains sections directly or closely related to historical study. The sections of this important course are:

- the role of language and thought;
- the requirements, of logical rigour for knowledge;
- systems of knowledge:
- mathematics;
- natural sciences;
- human sciences;
- history;
- value judgements and knowledge:
- moral judgement;
- political judgement;
- aesthetic judgement;
- knowledge and truth.

The aims of the history syllabus are contained less in its preamble than in its assessment targets and grade descriptions; for example, to achieve top grades, students must be able to construct 'coherent and convincing arguments ... [and show] a confidence and assurance in the handling of evidence as well as a developed and critical sense of historical judgement'.

Content is defined first in ten world history topics, which present a syllabus that is both conceptually precise and globally relevant:

- causes, practices and effects of wars;
- nationalist and independence movements, decolonization, and the emergence and problems of new nations;
- economic developments in the twentieth century;
- social change in the twentieth century;
- the artist and society;
- the rise and fall of single-party states;
- the establishment and work of international organizations;
- religion and politics;
- east–west relations after 1945;
- minorities in the modern state system.

Second, these themes are contained in a document-based paper on defined themes; for example in 1989 and 1990, they were: 'causes of World War II', and 'nationalism and the struggle for independence in the Indian subcontinent'.

Finally, there is one area study selected from: Africa; the Americas; Europe, including Russia; west and south Asia, including India and north Africa; and east and southeast Asia and Australia.

SOME CURRENT RESEARCH INITIATIVES

CIDREE

CIDREE (Consortium of Institutions for Development and Research in Education in Europe) was founded in December 1990. Its aims are:

> to enhance cooperation among development and research institutions in Europe in the broad field of education, by setting up collaborative activities, information exchange and contribution to professional development of staff. Methods of work will include: workshops; correspondence; joint publications; study visits etc.

There were already in 1993 member institutions in Belgium, Denmark, England, Finland, France, Germany, the Netherlands, Northern Ireland, Scotland, Spain, Sweden, Switzerland and Wales; there are associated members in the Czech and Slovak Republics and Norway.

The first stage of CIDREE's programme was the planning of a series of collaborative workshops in important cross-curricular themes. Those with a particular bearing on the learning of history included: 'Values in Education', 'Learning to Think: Developing Students' Thinking Skills', 'The Image of Europe in Schoolbooks and Curricular Materials' and 'European Cultural Unity in Diversity'.

In December 1991, CIDREE embarked on a collaborative project on the core curriculum for 12–16-year-olds in two areas: cross-curricular themes, and history. The intention was to develop a source of detailed information on history in secondary schools on, for example, research findings on learning outcomes, teaching strategies including curricular guidelines and attainment targets, examination programmes and textbooks. Such information was envisaged as of value not only to members of CIDREE, but in helping establish professional contacts, exchanges and collaborative projects. The project proposal stressed the importance of keeping under review certain key issues, such as principles of curricular development and choice, the criteria for choice of aims, objectives and content in national curricula, and the implications of the variations of time allocation for history between national systems.

A report by Dr Robert Stradling of the NFER (National Foundation for Educational Research) in England reviewed history curricula in over fifty educational authorities in northern and western Europe.[8] In his task, Stradling has worked closely with the Council of Europe. This initial report is a feasibility study and may lead to larger, cross-national curricular studies and research programmes. It includes suggestions for collaborative research on, for example, educational systems which have adopted similar types of history curricular guidance, and an assessment of the relative effectiveness of different types of curricular guidance on common problems. Stradling is particularly concerned with outcomes. What difference do all these curricular strategies and national guidelines make to *pupils*? The report draws attention to the need for research that, for example, tells us how, and indeed whether, the aims and objectives in curricular guidelines actually affect pupil motivation and learning; or that informs us of the relative impact of school history on pupils' under-standing compared with other sources of historical information, such as films, television, historical fiction and newspapers. Stradling asks whether history teaching really does develop 'a sense of identity' or arouse pupils' interest. 'Are pupils able to apply the skills and ways of thinking which are integral to the methodology of history to the events or phenomena which have not been covered in the curriculum?[9]

Other topics for collaborative research, Stradling suggests, need to question whether 'active methods of learning', espoused in many European countries, are seriously threatened by such practical problems as lack of suitable source material, poor access to audiovisual equipment, class size, inadequate funding, or practical and financial constraints in developing work outside the classroom. He speculates that 'even where resources are available there is a suspicion that only the more innovative teachers actually make use of such active learning methods.'[10] He also argues the case for a collaborative research programme on the initial training of history teachers.

The report finally deploys a persuasive rationale for collaborative research in the teaching and learning of history in order to:

- find out what is typical (and not just what is required by law) and why particular objectives and principles have been adopted, abandoned, rejected, planned or developed;
- compare systems according to an agreed set of criteria;
- identify useful curricular patterns, and teaching and learning strategies which might be 'exported';
- identify common problems and evaluate the effectiveness of different solutions;
- test fundamental assumptions;
- add to the stock of knowledge about the teaching of history; for example, whether or not it is immediately useful to decision makers.[11]

These research objectives, argues the report, would widen the perspectives of policy makers, whose interests have often been limited to broad principles underpinning curricular reform rather than hard evidence on their classroom outcomes. Practice from other countries has often been selectively approved and uncritically imported with little attempt to evaluate its success in its own country, or to identify the particular local circumstances which may explain either its success or its failure. However, Stradling counsels caution about collaborative and transnational research projects on history. The research experience of the International Association for the Evaluation of Educational Achievement (IEA) has been, in the main, limited to subjects like mathematics, science, civics and English as a foreign language, where there is broad agreement on 'what should be learnt, why, when and in what sequence and on what would constitute evidence of achievement at different ages'.[12] There remains considerable diversity of views in history teaching on such issues as objectives, content, skills, sequence and structure.

The CIDREE report is a persuasive and perceptive document. The questions it raises are important, the strategies it suggests realistic. But it will need the support of member states if it is going to be part of a *working* agenda for CIDREE and the Council of Europe.

History Teaching in Secondary Schools in Italy

However, other research projects into student attitudes to history are under way. One of the most extensive was undertaken in Italy by Professor Emilio Lastrucci of La Sapienza University in Rome,[13] who sent detailed questionnaires to 2,000 students drawn from 60 upper secondary schools; a similar questionnaire was sent to teachers of history. Information is being processed on such issues as: aspects of learning which students found most difficult; students' interests and expectations (ideological, political, recreational, cultural, etc.); newspaper and journal reading; attention to radio and TV programmes; and the reading of books with a historical content.

The research has produced some encouraging results.[14] For example, 76.5 per cent of the responses described history as either very interesting or 'interesting enough'; and in a distribution of preferences of the responses which prioritized the inherent interest of subjects, history was placed second after Italian. This was using responses not just from specialist students of history and other humanities, but also from science and technology specialists.

A majority, however, found history textbooks 'barely interesting' (50.4 per cent), although only 2.5 per cent dismissed them 'as not interesting at all'. These figures relate to others: 72.7 per cent found the language of history textbooks difficult, with 13.9 per cent of the total 'too difficult'. It is, therefore, not surprising to learn that the most popular means of assessment was 'oral examinations' (43.5 per cent), followed by 'individual research projects' (23.7 per cent), with 'written essays' as the least popular (8.7 per cent).

More than half the students expressed no preference for learning strategies, but among those who did, the most favoured was 'the use of film and videos' (17.2 per cent) followed by personal and group research (7.6 per cent), with 'quantitative and graphical' work least popular (1.3 per cent).

Of periods and themes, the French Revolution was most popular, chosen by 53.5 per cent of the students, followed by the industrial revolution (18.9 per cent), the Reformation (10.4 per cent) and the Enlightenment (7.6 per cent). Contemporary history was the favourite period of study, but with support from only 33.1 per cent, followed by ancient (classical) history with 17.1 per cent. Interest, in Italy at least, in periods does not follow a tidy chronological pattern. Philosophy and the social sciences seem to have influenced the choice of aspects of the past. Leading with 35.4 per cent, was 'social history and the history of mentalities',[15] followed by the history of ideas and culture (26.9 per cent), the history of science and technology (20 per cent), and economic history (13.5 per cent). Political, diplomatic and military history, long the firm backbone of many syllabuses, was chosen by only 14.2 per cent. These priorities are of interest, and challenge some assumptions about what involves young people.

Responses from teachers show a preponderance of men over women (59.6 per cent to 40.4 per cent), with only 3.4 per cent of history graduates; 10 per cent of the total submitted graduate theses on historical topics; 15.4 per cent have had some experience with historiographical research.[16]

Fifty per cent of teaching time was spent on didactic class teaching and assessment, followed by debates and discussion (14.4 per cent), the reading and analysis of historical documents (11.0 per cent), textbook reading and analysis (5.4 per cent), excursions (5 per cent), films and videos (3.2 per cent) and research (2.5 per cent). Well over 60 per cent of the responses declared the dominance of didactic exposition largely based on textbooks.

Teachers were also asked to prioritize their aims in teaching history. Equal first – at 38.8 per cent – were the 'development of civic and political awareness' and 'the understanding of the problems of contemporary society', followed by the development of critical faculties (20.4 per cent), 'the understanding of cultural and social identities' (18.4 per cent), 'personal values' (16.3 per cent), 'adding to knowledge' (6.1 per cent), and the 'development of moral awareness' (4.1 per cent).

The research constructed its own tests of achievement, based on the Italian national curriculum. There was little correlation between the results of the research-based tests and those administered by teachers. Student achievement related to responses on the accessibility of language and content of textbooks, but there was no clear correlation between student results and particular teaching methods, the specialist degrees of teachers or their experience. Overall, the results suggest that, when allowances have been made for difference in economic and social circumstances, variations in student achievement and attitudes depend more on the personality and professional competence of the teachers than on different teaching methods, learning environments or resources.

Despite some gloomy comments on pupils' attitudes to history emanating from some countries at the Bruges Symposium, Italian responses on the popularity of history were modestly encouraging. They tally with the results of a French survey of university history students published in *Le Monde*, 20 June 1990, which accorded history first place as a subject of interest and in its ability to challenge assumptions, develop ways of thinking and strengthen young people's understanding of the contemporary world.

The 'Youth and History' Project

Since 1988, scholars from Hamburg University and Bergen College of Education in Norway have been researching historical consciousness among teenagers in Germany and Norway. A more extensive pilot study was carried out in 1992 in nine European countries. As a result, a project group from five European regions has been established,[17] and some thousand 15-year-olds are due to be surveyed in up to twenty countries from all European regions.

The aim of 'Youth and History: The Comparative European Project on Historical Consciousness among Teenagers' is to survey the attitudes of young people to history and to history-related political issues such as identity, nationalism, democracy and immigration. Particular questions which the project team identifies are:

• What is 'historical consciousness'? How is it related to collective identity? Does it change on entering a larger national unit such as a federal state; or on leaving an empire when, for example, autonomy is regained?

- Is there a correlation between historical consciousness, national identity and scientific historical research?
- Are there real differences between historical socialization in different countries?
- Is there a trend towards a united, or at least a coordinated, European historical consciousness?

The project does not claim to be value-free; it is based on assertions of human and civic rights, which include a 'commitment to tolerance and non-violence ... [and to] cultural diversity and authenticity'.

CHATA

CHATA (Concepts of History and Teaching Approaches at Key Stages 2 and 3 – that is, pupils aged 7–14) is directed by Alaric Dickinson and Peter Lee of the University of London Institute of Education. The emphasis is less on children's attitudes to history than on their understanding of key concepts of historical understanding and enquiry. In the second phase of the project, the researchers will concentrate on categorizing teaching approaches in history in order to explore the relationship between these approaches, curriculum contexts (whether, for example, history is or is not taught as a separate subject), and learning outcomes. Much of this research will be based on direct classroom observation and testing. The project team provisionally intends to send their tests to a group of countries drawn from north, south and eastern Europe, to be used in their schools as a basis for transnational comparisons.

TRANSNATIONAL LINKS

European Association of Young Historians

The European Association of Young Historians is an association of national young historians, that is, those under the age of 40; it is targeted principally at historians working in universities throughout Europe. Its main aims are to facilitate and disseminate research and exchange ideas throughout Europe. The Association addresses two problems: the isolation of historical research and 'the lack of attention given to cultural matters in the process of European unification'[18] within the Union and throughout Europe. The Association publishes a review which concentrates on the comparative history of Europe from the classical period to the present day, with an emphasis on comparisons between national histories and historiographies. It also publishes information on archives and research institutions, for which it will be able to provide personal contacts for those travelling abroad. A feature will be reviews written by historians from a different country to that of the books' authors. An editorial board represents 11 different countries all over Europe.[19] The Association also intends to create a Europe-wide index of theses and research in progress, and to further contacts between historians by a programme of conferences and seminars. Its intention is to encourage contact between historians across Europe, in terms of both ideas and practical help. The first issue of its journal was published in spring 1994.[20]

The emphasis is on young historians partly because this will be of more help for those at the start of their careers, and partly because the *Review* hopes to encourage new directions in European history.

EUROCLIO

Representatives of 15 national and regional associations of history teachers, meeting in Strasbourg in November 1992, decided to found EUROCLIO (the European Standing Conference of History Teachers' Associations). This initiative was encouraged by support for such an association at the Council of Europe symposium on 'The Teaching of History in the New Europe', held in Bruges in December 1991. The Strasbourg meeting owed much to the initiative of the associations of Belgium and the Netherlands, and to the Council of Europe, whose financial support made these first steps possible.

EUROCLIO met officially for the first time in April 1993, at Leeuwarden in the Netherlands, at a symposium, organized jointly by the Council of Europe and the Netherlands Ministry of Education, on 'The Teaching of History since 1815 with Special Reference to Changing Borders'. More than twenty-five European states are now members of EUROCLIO, representing almost forty thousand history teachers.

The Standing Conference is an association without political, philosophical or religious affiliations. Its aims are to:

- strengthen the position of history in the curricula of schools in Europe, and the intellectual freedom of teachers;
- promote the European dimension in historical education and teaching in member countries without neglecting global, national and regional dimensions;
- encourage greater European awareness through the medium of history teaching;
- study the position of Europe and its relations with the rest of the world;
- disseminate information on history teaching in Europe through national and international publications and other relevant materials;
- promote the setting up of European Information and Documentation Centres for history teaching in Europe;
- form working groups to engage in joint projects concerned with the teaching of history in Europe;
- centralize and disseminate to member associations information about each other's activities through the exchange of publications, dates of major conferences, seminars, etc.;
- promote the development of associations of history teachers in countries where none exists;

- provide a forum for the discussion of matters of common interest to history teachers in Europe.

Membership is open to associations of history teachers of all levels of education in the member states of the CDCC. The Standing Conference may decide to admit as members associations from other countries.

EUROCLIO held its first general conference at Bruges in March 1994. Provisional suggestions for future conferences and activities indicate the possible scope of the Standing Conference's activities. They include conferences on:

- the situation of history teaching in Europe, the mapping of teaching time for history, and the problems and possibilities in history teaching in different countries;
- history teaching, a key to democracy?
- European conferences in Vienna (1815), Paris (1919) and Yalta/Potsdam (1945) in history teaching;
- assistance in the forming of history teachers' associations in eastern and central Europe.

(A quite separate recommendation for the organization of a European Association of Inspectors of History also received general support at the 1991 Bruges Seminar but, at the time of writing, no further action has been taken.)

The International Students of History Association

The International Students of History Association (ISHA) was founded in Budapest in May 1990. It is an academic, non-political, non-profit-making association of students interested in history and related subjects. The Association seeks to bridge the gap between east and west and to encourage international cooperation and understanding through a more objective and tolerant study of history. It organizes and coordinates joint projects and exchange programmes between history students and young people of all cultures. It has a regular *International Students of History Association Newsletter*. The Bruges Symposium recommended that the Association should be formally linked with the work of the Council of Europe.

The International Society for History Didactics

The International Society for History Didactics, founded in 1980, is committed to scholarship and international cooperation in the field of history education. The Society lists its particular fields of interest as: textbooks; the training of history teachers; curriculum at the primary, secondary and post-secondary levels; popular historiography; history in the mass media and in the public arena; and the general question of historical consciousness.

The Society holds regular international meetings, normally in the autumn of each year. The 1993 meeting took place in Tützing, and the 1995 meeting is planned for Montreal. The Society has participated in meetings of the International Congress of Historical Sciences in Stuttgart (1985) and Madrid (1990). The Society's journal, now in its thirteenth volume, is *Informations/Mitteilungen/Communications*; it contains articles in English, German and French. Membership is by election and open to professionals involved in the field of history education. Currently there are members from 25 countries on five continents.

RESOURCES AND PUBLICATIONS

Reference has been made in the previous chapter to the *Histoire de l'Europe* published in 1992 and intended mainly for students aged 16–18. The authors, from Belgium, the then Czechoslovakia, Denmark, France, Germany, Greece, Ireland, Italy, the Netherlands, Portugal, Spain and the United Kingdom, worked as a team and were jointly responsible for the whole book. Its introduction makes clear that it is not history written on behalf of European unity, and stresses that nationalism and murderous rivalries are as much part of the European past as reciprocal benefits and shared interests. The authors, supported by well-produced maps and illustrations (although surely in a history book they should all have been dated and carefully attributed?),[21] have, with great skill, written a comprehensive, detailed, fair-minded book which is neither bland nor unduly deferential to national sensitivities.

Within the limits of its 381 pages, it is inevitably highly selective. Culture is emphasized, but the impact of science and technology, the changing status of women, a multicultural Europe, and the histories and cultures of eastern Europe are scantily dealt with. Its editor, Frédéric Delouche, apparently perceives Russia as a country with 'Asian' characteristics, and he waits for it either to declare itself 'part of the world of European values', especially democracy, or to persist with 'autocracy and totalitarianism'.[22] These criteria are, arguably, more political and ethical than historical.

Nevertheless, these comments may do less than justice to the aims and achievements of this book and, in spite of critical comments, voices from east and central Europe hoped not only that the 'History of Europe' would widen their field of vision but also stated that they intended to introduce it in the teaching of history in their secondary schools.

A rather different approach, but with similar aims, is represented by *European History: Sources and Materials*, compiled by Hagen Schulze and Ina Ulrike Paul of Munich. This is less a narrative of European history than a collection of thematic source material exemplifying 'comparison and contrast'.[23] The emphasis is explicitly on political issues and the history of ideas; economic and social history may be the subjects of further volumes. Sources are mainly literary but will include some visual material. They expand Delouche's concept of Europe, with geographical limits from the Atlantic to the Urals, and just attention is given to eastern and central Europe and to the cultural and political influences of Byzantium and the Orthodox church.

Its chronological limits start with the classical past and end with contemporary Europe; the origins of Europe are extended beyond classical Rome and Greece to include, for example, the Celts.

The collection is divided into nine themes, each covering the whole chronological span of the book. They are:

- myth, geography and Europeans;
- hegemony and balance (from the Greek city states to the breakup of the Soviet Empire and the events of 1989 and 1990);
- plans and visions (of European unity);
- freedom and despotism;
- humanitarianism and progress;
- faith and reason;
- the familiar and the unfamiliar (for example, imaginary enemies – heretics, Jews, witches, Jesuits, freemasons; historic adversaries – Mongols, Tartars, Turks, etc.);
- Europe outside Europe;
- unity in spite of diversity?

At present the book is only published in German; translations into other languages are planned for a paperback edition. The collection supports the teaching of the history of Europe firmly placed in a world context, although seen mainly through European eyes.

The *International Yearbook for History Teacher Education*[24] is not primarily concerned with curriculum developments in Europe. It seeks contributions from all continents and is establishing a world-wide network of editorial consultants. The first issue appeared in 1995.

The general policy of the yearbook is to encourage rigorous exploration of philosophical, psychological, sociological and historical perspectives upon history in education and, where appropriate, of their relation to practice. The Yearbook will not be publishing material on day-to-day classroom practice, or describing particular schemes of work. It will include reports of regional developments together with relevant research and conferences.

Broad content areas will include issues such as: the role of history in contemporary and past thought and culture, including what is often called 'historical consciousness'; the social and political control of history curricular and syllabuses; children's understanding of history; empirical work on teaching strategies and programmes; analytical work on assumptions and presuppositions; examinations and recent developments in assessment, etc.

Possible themes for early issues include: 'History – prescribed or open?', 'History education in east and central Europe', 'History in post-compulsory education' and 'National consciousness and history'. The first issue will contain contributions from Australia, China, Denmark, Finland, South Africa, Spain and the United Kingdom, and its focus will be 'Centralization and decentralization'.

A CHARTER FOR EUROPEAN TEACHERS OF HISTORY

It was clear at the Bruges Symposium that there was concern about who controls and who should control the history curriculum and its teaching. The impact of this control, in both its source and its extent, profoundly affects the professional autonomy of teachers.

On occasions, the status and autonomy of teachers can be defined and supported by a measure of outside control, but too often those in control misunderstand, ignore, or purposefully undermine teachers' professionalism. What is at stake is not just bruised professional pride or lack of public esteem, but effective curricular development, zest and enthusiasm for teaching and, ultimately, the learning of pupils. Also at stake is the public accountability of teachers and the need for a publicly acknowledged code of professional conduct pre-eminently concerned with the clients' interests, or, as one delegate at Bruges suggested, 'a teaching equivalent of the Hippocratic Oath'.

It was also clear at the Symposium that 'history' as a school subject had different forms, priorities and aims, not just in authoritarian and ideologically led societies, but also in open, democratic societies. Voices from all over Europe were raised in support of a history curriculum consistent with open societies and the needs of democratic states. Among the most passionate arguments were those from east and central Europe. This book argues a possible agenda for the implementation of such a curriculum (see in particular Chapters 4 and 5).

At the final session of the Bruges Symposium, delegates examined closely and strongly endorsed the proposal for a 'charter', which would not only make a public declaration on the integrity of history and the professional standards required of its teachers, but offer a rationale for history teaching and curriculum design. Such a declaration would help guard against political and ideological interference.

It was proposed that a 'charter' should give attention to:

Historical Perspectives
It is important that history curricula should include local, national, European and global perspectives in a sensible balance. Minorities should have the right to study their own history but not to the exclusion of broader perspectives ...
It is recognised that the balance of local, national, European and global history might differ according to the ages and abilities of the students.

Due recognition should be given in the syllabuses to political, economic, social and cultural history. There should not be a predominance of political history. Gender and minority issues must be carefully borne in mind.

History as a Process of Knowledge, Interpretation and Understanding
All good history teaching seeks to develop students' factual knowledge. However, good teaching also seeks to develop students' ability to interpret and critically analyze and thus to improve understanding. One cannot exist without the other. The development of students' critical abilities is an essential safeguard against the misuse of history. Such qualities will often be encouraged by the presentation to students of a range of sources and interpretations.

History should cooperate with other subjects in developing cross-curricular approaches where these are appropriate. However, care must be taken to ensure that the specificity of historical content and methodology is recognised and preserved.

Respect for the Professionalism of Good History Teachers

The skills and experience of good teachers are often undervalued. The opinions of good history teachers, who are sensitive to the issues covered in this Charter and have demonstrated their abilities in the classroom, deserve particular attention in curriculum design, the more so since it is teachers who have to implement the curriculum.

Some autonomy will be necessary for teachers. Firstly, this is so that they can more readily meet the needs of students. Secondly, because lack of 'ownership' of the curriculum can lead to boring and uninspiring teaching. At the same time, all history teachers will welcome full external evaluation.

The principles embodied in this Charter should be respected by others while history teachers should not be expected to transgress them.

Care should be exercised to ensure that history is taught by competent, qualified history specialists.

These suggestions are quoted from the final report of the final session at the Bruges Symposium. They were preliminary and provisional, but they commanded considerable support. Together with some criteria for the general professionalism of teachers (see Chapter 4), and others for defining the functions of history and selecting its content (see Chapter 5), they can be seen as a possible rationale and basis for a charter of European history teachers.

Chapter 4 looks in greater detail at the issues of professionalism and the control of the learning of history.

CONCLUSION

This chapter has described an impressive and diverse series of current initiatives within and between European countries. They not only represent the vision of many individuals, but provide a rich and very practical resource of experience for us all.

NOTES

1 From a Council of Europe working document announcing the programme 'A Secondary education for Europe', 1991–5.

2 J. Farrington (1991), *Report on the Contribution of Local and Regional Authorities to European Educational Policy,* Strasbourg: Council of Europe.

3 The list of twinnings is: Austria (Vienna) with Bulgaria; Bulgaria (Vratsa) with Austria and France; the Czech and Slovak Republics (Brno and Liptovsky Mikulás) with the Netherlands, France and the United Kingdom; Denmark (Herning and Malling) with France and Italy; Finland (Varkaus) with France, Russia and the United Kingdom; France (Montbrison) with Bulgaria, the Czech and Slovak Republics, Denmark and Finland;

Germany (Kleve) with the Netherlands; Greece (Návpaktos) with the United Kingdom; Hungary (Hatvan and Miskolc) with the United Kingdom; Iceland (Hveragerdi) with the United Kingdom; Ireland (Irim) with Portugal; Italy (Viareggio) with Denmark; the Netherlands (Almere and Nijmegen) with the Czech and Slovak Republics and Germany; Portugal (Torres Vedras) with Ireland; Russia (Petroskoi) with Finland; Sweden (Stockholm) with Lithuania; United Kingdom (Preston, Glasgow, Croydon and Cheam) with the Czech and Slovak Republics, Finland, Greece, Hungary, Iceland and Lithuania.

4 R. Savage (ed.) (1992), *School Links and Exchanges in Europe*, Strasbourg: Council for Cultural Cooperation, School and Out of School Education Section.

5 R. Savage (1992), *School Exchanges: The Role of Local and Regional Authorities*, a study completed by CLRAE with the collaboration of CDCC, Strasbourg: Council of Europe.

6 This refers to the attempt by the IRA to kill Margaret Thatcher and her Cabinet in the Grand Hotel Brighton during the Conservative Party Conference in October 1984.

7. M. Davis and C. Ellwood (1991), 'International curricula in International Schools – a background', in P. Jonietz (ed.), *The Yearbook of Education*, London: Kogan Page.

8 R. Stradling (1993), *History in the Core Curriculum 12–16: A Feasibility Study for Comparative Research in Europe*, Scottish Consultative Council on the Curriculum. Dundee. I am particularly grateful to Robert Stradling for allowing me to read an early draft of this report.

9 *Ibid.*, p. 40.

10 *Ibid.*, p. 40.

11 *Ibid.*, pp. 41–2.

12 *Ibid.*, p. 43. A recent study of civic education by the IEA may produce evidence more applicable to history.

13 The information which follows is drawn from papers submitted by Dr Lastrucci to the Bruges Symposium.

14 Some respondents listed items co-equally, therefore some totals reach more than 100.

15 'L'histoire des mentalités' has as yet no English equivalent. It is cultural history in the anthropological rather than art-historical sense. It attempts to apply the concepts and procedures used, for example, to study the totems and taboos of Amazonian Indians to eighteenth-century France or Renaissance Florence.

16 Dr Lastrucci points out that only very few Italian universities offer degree courses in history. Most teachers of history in upper secondary schools are likely to be teaching other humanities subjects.

17 The group is led by Magne Angvik from Bergen, Bodo von Borries from Hamburg and Laszlo Keri from Budapest.

18 The European Association of Young Historians (1993), 'Proposals for an association' in The Bulletin of the British Association of Young Historians, No. 1, March.

19 Albania, Belgium, Denmark, France, Germany, Greece, Italy, the Netherlands, Poland, Switzerland and the United Kingdom.

20 By the Carfax Publishing Company, Abingdon, Berkshire, United Kingdom.

21 The country of origin, when it was identifiable, and subject matter of the illustrations are varied and interestingly distributed: 112 are French, 64 Italian, 51 each from Germany and from the United Kingdom, 35 Greek, 21 Spanish, 18 Belgium/Flemish, 15 Portuguese, 12 Russian, 11 Dutch, 9 Irish, 7 Austrian, 4 from the Czech and Slovak Republics, Denmark and Poland, 3 from Sweden and Switzerland, 2 from Hungary and what was then Yugoslavia, and one each from Romania and Bulgaria.

22 See, for example, the (1992) report on Delouche's contribution to the Council of Europe's Seminar on 'New Approaches to History Teaching in Upper Secondary Education', Donaueschingen, November 1991 – Strasbourg: Council for Cultural Cooperation.

23 H. Schutze and V. Paul (1994), *Europa: Dokumente und Materialen*, Munich: Bayerischer Schulbuch-Verlag.

24 The journal is edited by Alaric Dickenson, Peter Lee and John Slater, from the University of London Institute of Education.

CHAPTER 4

The Issue of Control: Power or Partnership?

To control the past is to master the present, to legitimize dominion and justify legal claims. It is the dominant powers – states, churches, political parties, private interests – which own or finance the media or means of reproduction, whether it be school-books or strip cartoons, films or television programmes. Increasingly, they are abandoning us all to a uniform past. Revolt comes from those to whom history is forbidden.[1]

Those responsible for education and curriculum development are concerned to meet the country's medium, if not long term, cultural and scientific needs.[2]

What is to become of the poor student … if their notions of history are to sway this way and that, according to majorities in the House of Commons.[3]

History is what historians select to write. Their criteria for selection will be predominantly intrinsic to history. What pupils have to learn is frequently selected by non-historians. Their criteria for selection may often be extrinsic to history: political, moral, social and perhaps, only incidentally, historical.

This chapter will address two main questions. What do those who control history actually control? Who does the controlling? The questions are concerned with the curriculum and its syllabuses, resources, assessment and pedagogy, teachers, parents, future employers and pupils.

WHY DO WE HAVE CENTRALLY DEFINED SYLLABUSES AND NATIONAL CURRICULA?

Compulsory education is the most bossy and interventionist arm of the state. Governments tell parents how their children, from the age of 5 or 6 until 15 or 16 have to spend many of their waking hours for two-thirds of the year. Military conscription at least justifies itself with national emergencies, involves young adults, and does not last for 11 years. So it is not unreasonable to expect governments to guarantee by law what young people are entitled to gain from this period of compulsory education, Nor is it unreasonable to expect governments to make resources available, including teachers, to deliver centrally defined curricula effectively. And those who pay for these resources, and who use the products of national curricula – parents, employers, people involved in higher education, and tax-payers – are entitled to expect comprehensible and usable evidence of what they are getting from the educational system. But ultimately the justification of national curricula is that they should *help pupils learn*. Children should not be unnecessarily confused or disconcerted by changes in context or levels of demand as they move up through the educational system, from infant to primary school, from primary to secondary and upper school, or as their parents in increasingly mobile societies change jobs and move home. National curricula may not only help establish the coherence and planned progression of *learning* within an educational system, but also endorse the status of subjects, such as history. National curricula are variously concerned with statements of entitlement, procedures of public accountability, planned coherence and progression of learning and declarations of status.

At this point two provisos must be made. A national curriculum is a public statement of intent and entitlement, but in itself it tells us little about outcomes. It can establish a coherent content; it may help the standardization and comparability of educational standards; but whether it *raises* standards or is actually *learned* is another matter. Second, an agreed national or even a European curriculum need not necessarily mean a uniform or a single syllabus.

Until very recently, the educational system in England and Wales was autonomous. History was not a compulsory subject. In many primary schools (5–11) it barely existed. What, how and for how long it was taught, or indeed whether it was taught at all, were matters for decision by the schools, or by their history departments. By contrast, in many European countries history syllabuses and often resources for their teaching were defined and licensed centrally.

Now all is changing. Over much of Europe, the trend is to decentralize, whereas England and Wales now have, for the first time, a centrally prescribed syllabus. Prescription and autonomy both have virtues. Autonomy recognizes the professionalism of teachers, while a centrally defined curriculum may recognize the status of history. Of course the boundaries between gain and loss are blurred, and not sharply or tidily distributed. This chapter is not setting out to defend either centralization or autonomy. Much good, and plenty of very bad, history learning has taken place under both banners. Autonomous teachers can be enterprising and innovative. They can also be isolated and bewildered.

At present, virtually all European educational systems retain some degree of centralization, although there is great variety in patterns and levels of prescription. Sometimes there is considerable regional and community devolution: in Germany, the *Länder* have their own ministries of education and curricula; in Belgium, there are separate educational systems for each of the three language groups (French-, Flemish- and German-speaking); in Spain, more than half of the 17 autonomous communities have significant and distinct powers over education; in Switzerland cantons enjoy considerable autonomy; within the United Kingdom, there are three distinct educational systems and curricula – in England and Wales, Northern Ireland, and Scotland.

In many countries, centrally defined syllabuses are frameworks which contain a wide range of options, sometimes grouped round a compulsory core. Many countries require a balance of national, European and world history. Overall the trend in almost all countries is to loosen the bonds of central control or, which is not always the same thing, ideological control.[4]

In some countries, only minimum knowledge, concepts and skills are centrally defined, leaving considerable scope for teachers to select content and teaching methods appropriate to the particular circumstances of their schools and the abilities of their pupils (in, for example, Austria, Belgium, the Netherlands and Sweden). Sometimes content is defined only under broad thematic or conceptual headings, as in Denmark and Poland. Even in those countries where centrally defined syllabuses are more detailed, they are seen more as proposed than prescriptive frameworks (as in Portugal).

In Estonia, the history syllabus is based in the first place not on content but on aims related to the Universal Declaration of Human Rights of the United Nations (1948) and the Helsinki Final Act (1975). In France, where the curriculum was formerly seen by many as typical of ministerial detail and prescription, the syllabus for secondary pupils rejects a general survey of national history and focuses on the period from the French Revolution to the twentieth century, defined by the key themes of imperialism, socialism and the world economy. The syllabus is not predominantly political or diplomatic, and there is a strong emphasis on economic, social, cultural and intellectual history. It emphasizes different perspectives on French history – on, for example, how the rest of Europe perceived the French Revolution. There is also an emphasis on comparative approaches to demonstrate that certain historical phenomena are essentially European, such as the industrial revolution. Neither detailed content nor pedagogy is prescribed. It is an interesting example of a syllabus with a declared rationale leaving room for professional autonomy. It contrasts with many European history syllabuses taught in the recent past.

In almost all countries, teachers of history in schools are part of the consultative and advisory processes set up by central governments. The general guidance given in Luxembourg stresses the importance of 'the liberty of professional action' and the Greek statement refers to teachers as 'the guardians of the curriculum'. In most countries, professional associations of history teachers and teachers' unions nominate their own representatives, thus retaining some degree of professional control over the membership of advisory groups (for example, in France, Finland, Ireland, most of the German *Länder*, Luxembourg and Portugal). More rare is the appointment of teachers as individuals rather than representatives (as in the United Kingdom), giving greater ministerial control over the composition of the groups.

England and Wales: intervention's high tide?

In England and Wales, a centralized national curriculum began to be introduced in 1988. Its principal components were 10 foundation subjects, which were compulsory for all pupils between the ages of 5 and 16. History was one of these subjects. Concern was expressed at their total weight and extent, not only because of their impact on teaching methods but because of the loss of other curricular areas, such as careers and general social and personal education. The government commissioned a report to make recommendations in the light of these concerns.[5] As part of slimming down the demands of the national curriculum, the report recommends that history should no longer be a compulsory subject for 14–16-year-olds and should be taught either as an optional alternative to geography, or as part of a joint history–geography course. At the time of writing, these proposals are subject to consultations with interested parties. However, the report unambiguously and considerably diminishes the status of history, and perpetuates the assumption that geography remains history's natural ally.

Subsequently, detailed proposals for history were published in a consultative document which will form the basis of a new, centrally defined curriculum for pupils aged 5–14.[6] Among its aims are to:

- ensure a predominant emphasis on British history;
- provide opportunities to study classical history and aspects of local, European and world history;
- provide increased opportunities for pupils to study twentieth-century history;
- clarify, in ten 'Level Descriptions', what constitutes progression in history throughout the age group;
- define the key elements of history to be used in summarizing pupils' progress;
- extend access to history to pupils of all abilities, including those with special educational needs.

The content of the curriculum is contained within a series of compulsory 'core units', related to the chronological ages of pupils (for pupils aged 7–11, the units include 'Romans, Anglo-Saxons and Vikings in Britain', 'Britain since 1930' and 'Ancient Greece'; and, for pupils aged 11–14, 'Medieval Realms – Britain 1066 to 1500' and 'The Twentieth Century World'). In addition, there is a series of complementary and extension studies, within which there is limited choice. They include a local study; a study of a particular theme – to be selected by the school – over a long period of time; a key turning point in European history (such as the Crusades, the Italian Renaissance, the French Revolution, German or Italian unification); and the pasts of two non-European cultures. In total there are 15 study units (14 to be studied), of which 8 (possibly 9) are concerned with British history, 2 (possibly 3) with European history, 1 with world history treated Eurocentrically, and 2 with the non-European cultures; one study through time of a single theme, e.g. energy, medicine, farming and agriculture, ships and seafarers could be given a European or world context. None is concerned with the recent past of non-European countries, unless they qualified as British colonies, and the history of post-1945 Europe is not specifically identified. Each study unit is accompanied by details of required and suggested content.

Throughout, there is emphasis on the relation of knowledge to understanding, the use of source material, the variety of interpretations of the past, and what the discussion document terms the 'reasons for, and results of, historical events'.

A comparison with Hungary

The draft Hungarian syllabus was influenced in part by the English and Welsh curriculum. But there are some significant differences. The Hungarian curriculum is divided not into subjects but into 'cultural domains': mother tongue; foreign languages; mathematics; visual and mass communications; design technology; arts; life conduct, family and home economics; physical education; the individual and society. Each of these domains is subdivided into several cultural blocks. That on the individual and society contains history, together with geography, economics, sociology and anthropology. This arrangement allows considerable scope for schools to select and interpret.

In the English and Welsh curriculum, there is a single 'Attainment Target' called 'history', which emphasizes the interrelatedness of the various elements of historical knowledge, understanding and skills; but the Hungarians relate their Attainment Targets not to one subject, but to a whole cultural block. In the 'individual and society' domain they are: 'acquisition and adoption of knowledge', 'orientation in time', 'orientation in space and geographical environment' and 'self-knowledge and empathy'. Unlike the ten statements of Attainment in the English and Welsh syllabus within each of four Key Stages, the Hungarian defines only two levels, 'elementary' and 'advanced', each divided into four stages, or years. The distribution of content between the two syllabuses is comparable, but there are some significant differences in the amount of political history (50 per cent in Hungary, 28 per cent in England and Wales); social history (18 per cent in Hungary, 36 per cent in England and Wales) and national history (45 per cent in Hungary, 61 per cent in England and Wales).[7]

This book is not the place to analyse the massive Anglo-Welsh undertaking. In many ways, the national history curriculum is an impressive and considered document and its 114 pages contain much sound and helpful advice. But, unlike many of the curriculum documents being implemented in other European countries, it was not piloted first in a limited group of schools. In Austria, for example, proposals for a national curriculum were trialled in a restricted group of experimental schools. Curricular reform in Spain is the fruit of a period of trialling and evaluation since the mid-1980s. 'School participation in this process has been voluntary. Schools could opt in, if their participation was on a whole school curriculum basis. As a result these schools became the testbed for innovation.'

Compared with these strategies, the English and Welsh curriculum was perhaps too prematurely confident, and there have been signs of strain and growing teacher resistance under the weight of its own untested hypotheses. It was certainly content-heavy, and its Statements of Attainment were often ambiguous, sometimes failed to define general progression, and contained within some single targets, a variety of levels of achievement.

Throughout Europe, patterns and the extent of central guidance vary considerably, as do the strategies for their implementation and evaluation. Nevertheless, the CIDREE (Consortium of Institutions for Development and Research in Education in Europe) Report on *History in the Core Curriculum*, described in Chapter 3, identified certain features in common. They all:

- seek 'to a greater or lesser degree, to change the status quo in history teaching';
- seek, 'to a greater or lesser degree, to influence the way teachers approach the curriculum content, even if they do not prescribe teaching methods to be used;
- reflect the same concern about how to improve curriculum continuity and learning progression ...;
- make fundamental assumptions about teaching and learning processes;
- reveal concern about pupils' access to a core body of knowledge, skills and processes while allowing for different abilities, interests and destinations, i.e. academic study or professional and vocational education and training.[8]

THE ROLE OF GOVERNMENT AND THE ISSUE OF POLITICAL CONTROL

A government's educational policy need not necessarily be politically partial, nor need centrally defined syllabuses to be ideologically led. Towards the end of World War II, the 1944 Education Act for England and Wales was produced by the wartime coalition government. The Act, which was only peripherally concerned with the curriculum, was a bipartisan policy, but its successor, the 1988 Education Reform Act, was passed in a very different atmosphere. Political priorities were determined to break with the policies of previous governments and the power of what was termed 'the educational establishment'. The government was suspicious, sometimes dismissive, of consensus, and of those who were openly described as 'so-called educational experts'. The 1944 Act legislated for local and professional autonomy and was bipartisan. Its successor in 1988, as far as the school curriculum was concerned, legislated for centralization, was more partisan and was, arguably, more ideologically driven.

The distinction between the Scottish and the English and Welsh educational systems is illustrated by their strategies for introducing their respective national curricula. In England and Wales, the curriculum was introduced without prior testing, with limited consultation, and with considerable, and continuing, public controversy. The Scottish Education Department and schools had agreed to work within the new curricula, partly because of a well-established tradition of partnership between the teaching profession and the Department, resulting in a lengthy and thorough period of consultation before and during the period of implementation.

These comments are not concerned with the worth of the proposed changes, or with the issue of centrally legislated curricula. They merely suggest that the effectiveness and *acceptability* of change depends to a large degree on the existence of a genuine partnership between legislators and teachers, not only in prior discussions, but in the preliminary piloting and subsequent evaluation of new policies.

Curricula are not value-free documents, any more than the content of history is value-free (this issue is discussed more fully in the next chapter). How then do we distinguish between acceptable values and those that are politically or ideologically driven? The assumption here is that we do not want our history syllabuses to be politically or ideologically led; but the distinction is not always clear.

First, we cannot avoid the content and aims of a history syllabus being, in the broadest sense, political, in that they are controversial and can always be a matter for public debate. What we must avoid is allowing the teaching of history to become the plaything or tool of a particular party or pressure group. If history is unavoidably, in one sense, political, it must not be *partisan*. Of course the threat of partisanship in a democratic society is not as profound or as potentially permanent as the threat of a centrally imposed party ideology. (Elections offer at least the prospect of changing parties.) Partisanship can undermine professional autonomy, but ideologies can be threats to the very nature of history itself. Unlike ideology, history is not primarily concerned with patterns, or for that matter with the unique; it is more concerned with the particular than with the recurrent. Historians may use evidence to *discover* patterns, not to invent or confirm them; to examine values and ideologies, not to transmit them.

But all of us, including those of us lucky enough to live in countries with established parliamentary democracies, need to keep a wary eye open. In open societies, political influences are not always declared; sometimes they lurk below the surface, more often the products of tradition and established practice than of deliberate and planned partiality. Open societies do not always have open governments, and their politicians can be disingenuous. So we need to have an agenda of questions which help us detect threats to the integrity of history. They are questions which, not only as historians but also as tax-payers and voters, all Europeans should be entitled to ask:

- Are the assumptions on which a curriculum is built public, explicit and openly discussed?
- Does the curriculum include among its aims the critical evaluation of evidence and the understanding of different interpretations?
- Is the range of interpretations solely dictated by the curriculum, or are there opportunities for teachers and pupils to add to it?
- Does the curriculum oblige pupils to opt for one interpretation? (Much Marxist history introduced its students to both Marxist and capitalist interpretations of the past, but ideology and the party limited the agenda and pre-selected the choice.)
- Is there machinery for not only teaching the curriculum but evaluating and, when appropriate, amending it?
- *Who*, in government plans, implements, evaluates and amends the curriculum? Is government control direct or delegated?

- *What* is being controlled and defined? If it is syllabus content, assessment or resources, then it is the teaching profession that is being controlled. If, as in Sweden, control guarantees teaching *time*, then *status* is being protected.

When governments are authoritarian and ideology-led, then at least the criteria are clear, and there is a certain grim predictability about curriculum development. But, in an open, parliamentary system, particularly when the direction of curriculum development and educational priorities becomes a matter of party difference, vulnerable to partisan influences and susceptible to election results, the criteria may be less clear. On the other hand, a bipartisan educational policy may be less subject to changes in public opinion and the ballot box. It may produce a consensus, which can be beguilingly comfortable, and the danger is that public debate and the challenging of underlying assumptions and values will be avoided.

Before the English and Welsh national history curriculum was published in 1991, an advisory working group established by the minister published a final report. In its recommendations it made two statements which gave important guidance to those who are jealous of the integrity of history in schools. The first was concerned with the use of the word 'heritage', particularly '*common* heritage':

> We have been careful to minimise the use of the word 'heritage' because it has various meanings and is in danger of becoming unhelpfully vague. For historical purposes the word 'inheritance' may be more precise in its meaning, implying 'that which the past has bequeathed to us' – and which it is for *individual people to interpret*, employing the knowledge and skills of history. While all British people partake to a greater or lesser extent of a shared 'inheritance', *they also have their own individual, group, family etc. 'inheritances'* which are interrelated. The study of history should *respect and make clear this pattern of 'inheritances'*,[9] (author's italics).

That final plural is crucial. In any country where regional identity, the issue of political autonomy, and the status of cultural minorities are live political issues, it embodies an important statement of intent.

The second statement concerned 'interpretations of history', one of the original Attainment Targets in the new curriculum, and is about propaganda and political interference:

> Many people have expressed deep concern that school history will be used as propaganda; that governments of one political hue or another will try to subvert it for the purposes of indoctrination or social engineering. In some other societies, the integrity of teaching history has been distorted by such objectives, and there will always be those who seek to impose a partial view of society through an interpretation of history ... The best possible safeguard is an education which instils a respect for evidence ... Pupils should come to understand that historical theories and interpretations are there constantly to be re-examined; that there is no final answer to any historical question and that there are no monopolies of truth.[10]

All of us anxious to preserve the integrity of history and keep partisan and ideological intervention at bay should have these statements hanging above our desks and omnipresent in our classrooms.

CONTROL BY RESOURCES: THE TEXTBOOK ISSUE

At the Council of Europe Research Workshop held in Braunschweig in September 1990,[11] on the analysis of history and social studies textbooks, a key issue which emerged was the textbook as a means of central control.

Textbooks remain the principal resource for teaching history in European schools. But what is a textbook? The Braunschweig workshop agreed that it is a book specifically written for school use to support a particular course or syllabus. If those syllabuses or courses are centrally defined and prescribed, then a textbook becomes an instrument of central policy and control. But patterns vary. In England and Wales, despite the detailed and centrally defined curriculum, no resources are prescribed or recommended. In some other countries, there are centrally defined syllabuses as well as prescribed textbooks. In Greece, textbooks are prescribed by the Ministry of Education but are written by teachers. In Spain, textbooks 'still remain fixed to a classical pattern: "one book, one pupil, one year, one subject"'; in Norway, the influence on textbooks by the sanctioning authorities is among the strongest in Europe; in France, on the other hand, 'official' textbooks no longer exist and none is recommended by the Ministry of Education. 'Even in the *collèges*, where textbooks are provided by the State free of charge, the authorities have no powers in this respect beyond merely setting a budget per pupil, which amounts to a technical guideline for publishers.'[12] In some countries, ministers, through their inspectors, recommend textbooks but leave the choice to teachers; others have a required list from which teachers must choose.

But the situation is not static. The trend is towards decentralization and the loosening of control. Some decentralization has taken place recently in Italy, France and Spain. In Austria, textbooks have to be approved by an education commission consisting entirely of teachers. Political changes in east and central Europe are prompting a radical re-examination of centralized syllabuses and approved textbooks. Although some measure of central control is very common, there was little enthusiasm at Braunschweig for any system of official approval and licensing of textbooks. 'It was,' as one speaker said, 'a political not an educational procedure.'

Throughout east and central Europe, the problem is rather different. Many schools have no textbooks at all. Lack of experience of writing non-ideological textbooks and of basic materials, outdated printing technology, a scarcity of maps and visual material and so on were reported to the Bruges Symposium by delegates from Albania, Estonia, Lithuania, Poland and Romania. Such textbooks as exist are often ideologically unacceptable, although in the Czech Republic a new textbook, based on previously unofficial underground publications, is being produced.

An uneasy coexistence between official, underground and popular folk history emerges. In Poland before the changes, as one delegate reminded the Bruges

Symposium, official history was obliged to coexist with unofficial underground history, different not only in content and its alternative sources but in sensitizing its pupils to reading between the lines, sometimes driving a wedge between the home, with its family and collective folk memories, and the public history in the school; on occasions doing little more than replacing the authority of the party with that of the Catholic church. 'Writing about truth is not easy.'[13]

The textbook's effectiveness as a means of control depends in part on its function. Is it to support a course? Or is it to be used as a resource? Does it aim to add to knowledge, or to identify tasks? And what kinds of task? Are they carefully defined and programmed by the book? Or do they demand some measure of autonomous learning by the student? These important distinctions were at the core of a debate, sometimes heated and frequently politically driven, on the pre-eminence of knowledge or skills that preceded the publication of the English and Welsh national history curriculum. An emphasis on the acquisition of knowledge was seen by some as encouraging passive and deferential learning, as a tool for transmitting rather than examining ideas. A skills- or process-led curriculum encouraged autonomous and critical learning but, so it was argued, lacked rigour and was at the expense of a firm foundation of knowledge of national and European history.

A textbook containing tasks which test memory and comprehension is quite different from one which enables pupils to select and evaluate source material. The former is more likely to be an effective intrument of control, the latter to offer pupils some prospect of making an informed estimate of interpretations.

Debates on the functions of textbooks frequently polarize and distort the distinction between knowledge and skills, which are not mutually exclusive but inescapably interdependent. Skills cannot be deployed unless we have knowledge. Knowledge-led and content-dense syllabuses can lead to breathless chronological gallops through the national and European pasts – 'Plato-to-NATO syllabuses' – limit professional choices by teachers, and leave little time for group work and rigorous discussion, the use of source material or individual research projects. Of course, the limitations placed upon professional choice and pupil autonomy are what attract some people, particularly those in authority, to such syllabuses.

But much depends on how we use the term 'knowledge'. In many history syllabuses, 'knowledge' can be used in three quite distinct ways. The distinctions are valid but, if confusion is to be avoided, have to be carefully defined and made explicit:

- *knowledge as information*: the basic facts of, for example, events, people, dates, places;
- *knowledge as content*: the subject matter of study – for example, periods such as 'the reign of Louis XIV' or 'the twentieth century' or themes such as 'the industrial revolution' or 'the Rise of Fascism';
- *knowledge as understanding*: the facts studied in relation to other facts and evidence about them, and placed in an explanatory framework which enables their significance to be perceived.

The first two definitions help define a syllabus; the third leads to learning. How these distinctions are applied and what weighting is given to them, particularly to 'knowledge as understanding', are of great importance in distinguishing between rote learning and developing critical faculties. They are also distinctions which authors of textbooks must keep clearly in mind.

No participant at the Braunschweig workshop believed that a textbook could be neutral. So it is also important to know who writes and publishes textbooks.[14] We need to know, for example, whether those who write the textbooks follow already prescribed syllabuses. This is a tidy but not entirely reassuring arrangement. Who commissions the authors? Are they people whose assumptions and criteria are understood by authors, or teachers and students? The 1992 *Histoire de l'Europe* was inevitably and skilfully selective, but its criteria for selection were not always clear. Should not attitudes, criteria and assumptions always be declared, or at least be easily excavated by their readers? Is it right that teachers and students should have to engage in a game of 'hunt the bias'?

So there was considerable support in Braunschweig for requiring all textbook authors and publishers to declare their assumptions. There are, of course, practical as well as some pedagogical objections to a required declaration of assumptions. If one objective for the learning of history is the ability to detect bias and distinguish between fact and opinion, then opinionated and biased materials must be studied. The force of complaints about biased books or partial materials depends in part on the use made of them by teachers. An initial response should surely be, 'Don't show me the resource, let us see the teaching!' Attitudes and biases compulsorily confessed and declared may misunderstand the rules of the game, and destroy the excitement and intellectual stimulus of the chase!

But, apart from official state publishing houses, what about the commercial publishers? A report from Sweden described a textbook market (1990) of which 80 per cent was controlled by three combines, 30 per cent of whose total lists consisted solely of textbooks aimed at primary schools, with 40 per cent for secondary schools. If knowledge is power, then those who control it are mighty indeed. And who writes the books? No comprehensive information exists. However, in the experience of one work group at Braunschweig with delegates from nine countries, almost all textbooks were written by men, living in capital cities, working in teams, and increasingly composed of practising teachers. The United Kingdom again appeared to be an exception, with textbooks mainly written by individuals or pairs, although much of the supporting material for the Schools History Project (described in the next chapter) was the result of team work. The Braunschweig workshop supported research programmes into the processes of writing and publishing textbooks; it should not only have something to tell us about the control of the curriculum but also help us better to understand its distribution and weight, and enable it, with greater authority, either to be accepted contentedly or to be challenged anxiously.

There are some final questions about the central control of textbooks, which link with the next topic. They were summarized in the report of the Braunschweig workshop.

Do textbooks deprofessionalise teachers? ... Does an externally defined curriculum supported by approved and licensed textbooks recognise, let alone enhance, the role of teachers as professionals? Can professionalism flourish if much of teaching is based on the centrality of textbooks related more to content than to pupil learning? 'If ..., the prime actors are not teachers and their students, teachers may be seen as passive spectators.'[15] Can passive teachers produce anything but passive learners? Are *they* the kinds of learners which open societies seeking to defend, and sometimes struggling to develop, participatory democracy really need?'[16]

All of these considerations help us towards establishing some criteria for maintaining the integrity and independence of teaching resources.

CONTROL BY TEACHERS: THE ISSUE OF PROFESSIONALISM

Are teachers professionals? How do we recognize a profession when we see it? Here is one suggested checklist:[17]

- Professionals perform crucial social functions which require considerable degrees of skill.
- Professionals work in situations which are not wholly routine or predictable and in which new situations have to be handled.
- They draw upon a systematic body of knowledge acquired during a lengthy period of higher education in which there is a process of socialization into professional values.
- These values are pre-eminently concerned with the clients' interests and made explicit in a code of values.
- Professionals have freedom to express their judgement and have some voice in the formation of public policy.
- Thus professionals have some autonomy in relation to the state, and control over their exercise of professional responsibilities. They enjoy a measure of public status and reasonable remuneration.

This an an ambitious but still valid agenda. All its criteria are unlikely to be met, whichever part of Europe we work in, but it is offered as a realistic and sobering measuring rod. It is an agenda that will only be attractive to those who believe that education benefits from professionalism, and that our task is not to diminish it, but to identify and enhance it.

If these criteria are to have any reality, professionals need some form of institutional voice. In some countries, this is divided between professional subject associations and the trade unions. The former are concerned principally with the teaching and status of particular subjects in primary and secondary school classrooms, and sometimes in maintaining links between schools and universities; the latter with the working conditions and pay of teachers. In England and Wales, the voice of the unions for secondary school teachers is split, sometimes uncomfortably so, between three unions. Only in Scotland is there a General Teaching Council which gives a *professional* voice and some status to teachers of all subjects, although vigorous attempts are being made in England and Wales to follow the Scottish example, with the establishment of a Forum for a General Teaching Council.[18] So far, proposals have been met with ministerial scepticism.

In most European countries, teachers are represented on the governing bodies of schools, although in England their influence is restricted by law: their numbers are now limited to two members out of 18 in most secondary and high schools; teachers who are also parents are not allowed to be parent members either in their own school or in any school in the same local (that is regional or city) educational authority.

CONTROL OF TEACHERS: ACCOUNTABILITY

The professional autonomy of teachers cannot ever be absolute. It operates within the structure of the state and the needs of society. Thus, it is limited by the principle of accountability: an obligation on teachers to those who pay their salaries and fund their schools and universities – the tax-payers – to explain what they are about and why, and to produce some evidence that compulsory education helps pupils and students. But sometimes it can be overlooked, even in democratic states, that accountability is not just a vehicle that travels in one direction. The tax-payer also pays the salaries of ministers of education, their inspectors and civil servants, and those who administer examination boards. They too are obliged to tell us what they are about and why. Tortuous strategies are sometimes adopted to avoid doing it. However, they must not inhibit the stubborn assertion of our right to pose the questions and expect some answers.

There are, of course, other limitations to the complete professional freedom of teachers. National needs cannot be ignored. Comments from the French-speaking group at the Braunschweig workshop, quoted at the head of this chapter, recognized this, as did the question asked by the German-speaking group at the same conference: 'Does the concept of the textbook correspond to the legitimate interests of contemporary society for the transmission of certain knowledge – with regard to both subject matter and the way of teaching it?' Both comments and questions are valid, but they also beg some important questions. Just *who* defines a nation's 'cultural and scientific needs' and 'the legitimate interests of contemporary society'? Who diagnoses our needs? And by what processes? Have they been identified as the result of sustained and public debate, not only at national level in parliaments and during election campaigns, but also within the education world and professional organizations? The voice of the legislature alone is often no more than the voice of a parliamentary majority. Professional teachers then have the right and public duty to decide whether they accept the result of legislation or, within the law, seek strenuously to change it.

But accountability does not just give new tasks to teachers and schools, it often places them in the dock. 'It is all a matter of education' is a convenient slogan for passing the blame, and the subsequent solutions, for social and moral problems onto the already burdened shoulders of the schools: problems arise because the schools have failed to meet the needs of industry, because young people no longer respect their elders, or are more promiscuous and take drugs, because their hair is too long or they are football hooligans, or they cannot spell or add up, or do not go to church. This does not argue that education has *no* effect on such issues. But the alleviation of such problems is more likely to result from effective partnerships between schools, their clients and central government than from any rhetorical buck-passing.

But how should 'accountability' manifest itself professionally? At one crucial level, it shows itself in the effectiveness of parental access to schools and to records kept on their children, the strength of parent teacher associations, clear and detailed school prospectuses, the availability of interpreters and translations for those parents with a mother tongue other than that of the school, the level of parent representation on school governing bodies, and so on. Some teachers may see parental rights as a potential threat to their professionalism; nevertheless, parents deserve a professional response. To ignore or marginalize the rights of parents in education would not protect professionalism, it would be a betrayal of it.

There is another, more uncomfortable aspect of accountability which cannot be ignored, and that is the appraisal of teachers. It is difficult to resist the principle of appraisal, and it is not the task of this book to analyse the arguments and possible strategies for it. But who does the appraising, and who defines the criteria for appraisals? Is the process one of partnership between professionals? And if shortcomings are identified, does it lead, in the first instance, to discipline and dismissal, or to diagnosis, in-service training and improvement? In other words, is it *primarily* a tool of discipline, or is it a means of career development? The way these questions are answered supplies important evidence on the balance between the public control and professional autonomy of teachers. And however we answer them, teachers of history must be able to say not only what they are doing, but how and *why*. These are answers due not only to parents, future employers and higher education but also to pupils and students.

CONTROL OF TEACHERS AND PEDAGOGY: THE ISSUE OF EXAMINATIONS AND ASSESSMENT

But there is a final aspect of accountability which can be as much a threat to professionalism as a manifestation of it. That is assessment and examinations. In England and Wales, for example, before the professional autonomy of teachers began to be restricted by the 1988 Education Reform Act, it was already severely limited by the external examination system. The examination boards – eight independent bodies funded by examination fees and only indirectly by the tax-payer – controlled the content and the pedagogy of pupils aged 14–16 and 16–18. In the past 10 years, there has been a steady increase of central control of these examination bodies by the Schools Examination and Assessment Council (SEAC) whose task on behalf of the government was to monitor and accredit the work of the examination boards.[19] Central control, some of it much more directly governmental, is common enough in many European countries, although in the main it is limited to external, end-of-course examinations for 18-year-olds; school-based and continuous assessment, administered by schools and controlled by their teachers, sometimes externally moderated by other teachers, is more usual at the age of 16.

Central control in itself need not necessarily threaten the professionalism of teachers, but much depends on what the intended *functions* and public perceptions of examinations are. Again, current English practice is used as a model, although it is not necessarily exemplary. Current policy is that children will be tested, in the main by externally devised and accredited, short, written tests, at the ages of 7, 11 and 14, and at 16, by existing external examinations. These tests will supply information about what pupils have done, and will be essentially *summative*. Ostensibly they aim to raise standards. But as the results are, by law, to be aggregated and published, they will in effect become an evaluating and monitoring tool for measuring teacher performance and comparing schools. Examination 'league tables' have entered the vocabulary of the English educational system and are affecting classroom teaching methods, the aspirations of pupils and their parents, and the morale and anxieties of some teachers. The function of these new procedures is to monitor and control.[20]

There is nothing wrong with parents and others knowing examination results, and competition is part of life and not, *per se*, wrong. Parents and children are irredeemably competitive: word of mouth, stars on charts, pupils' perceptions of each other's performance, can soon establish crude league tables. But it remains a question for us all to debate sensitively whether it is more in the interests of pupils' learning to complement and compensate for competitiveness, or to institutionalize and encourage it.

End-of-course written tests may be reliable, where reliability means that if the same tests, marked by somebody else, were given to the same pupils on another occasion, the scores would be the same. But how *valid* are the results of these tests? In other words, do they measure what they purport to? If they claim to measure, say, the sum total of pupils' learning and their progress, such tests clearly do not do so, and themselves fail. A simple score, for example, based on a single reading test is statistically convenient and is measurable. It will *not* tell anyone about *all* the pupil's reading skills. Test results will enable comparisons to be made between whole classes or even schools, but do they, indeed can they, take into account gender, class or culture bias? Are they tests of learning or of teaching? Do the results allow for the number of pupils with different mother tongues, or the social and economic character of the school's catchment area? These questions in themselves do not challenge the aim of institutional comparisons, but they remind us all that the exercise is very complex, and that crude scores may do more to deceive than to inform.[21]

Examinations and tests are also educational currency. Whether or not they are made of base metal, their grades and certificates can be exchanged for desirable goods – a job, a place in a university, parental approval and rewards; good grades and certificates also benefit teachers, enhance their careers and increase the public esteem of schools. Teachers will inevitably teach to the examinations and their particular demands; they cannot ignore the contribution of examinations to the ambitions and needs of their pupils. Most examinations, particularly if they are solely written, test a limited range of skills (see Chapter 5 on this issue). This also restricts the functions which examinations are able to fulfil and the range of information they can deliver.

Many external examinations tend to be summative. They summarize, often in a single grade or mark, what pupils have done. They make statements about *levels*. But levels compared with what? Often with the levels of other pupils in the same class, or in other schools, or in cohorts of pupils of the same age. But what kind of information does this convey? It tells pupils and parents that, for example, 'Between 2.30 and 4.00 p.m. yesterday afternoon, 12 pupils knew more than you did about Hitler, or Pombal, or the nineteenth-century iron industry, and 18 knew less'; or 'None knew less – or more – than you.' How useful to anyone is this information? It does not tell an individual pupil that '*You* now know much more about these things than you did three months ago', or 'although you *know* less, you seem to *understand* more.'

Summative results neither recognize effort nor measure progress. They do not tell teachers which pupils need special help, or identify particular learning problems and their causes in individual pupils; that is, many exams and tests neither screen nor diagnose. Nor are they *formative*; that is, they do not, in themselves, help improve future performance of either pupils or teachers. Unless, of course, teachers want them to. But then they may have to become quite a different kind of examination. They cease to be a competition. They lose the spur of success and the goad of possible failure. They lose their disciplinary function and, to some extent, a measure of their ability to control. Other formative purposes can of course be met on other occasions during the school year. They can contribute to student profiles or records of achievement, covering all aspects of a pupil's learning, interests and behaviour. But such documents, if they exist at all, do not necessarily have the currency of public status, the hushed rituals, anxieties and hopes, of external examinations.

Many employers and universities want grades. This is not only because they are what the education system in many countries gives them, but also because public perception has invested examinations with another function, which is not always deserved. That is *selection*. Thus, we assume that essentially summative procedures based on timed and written examinations can also be *predictive*. What they are believed to predict is how well a pupil will perform in a work place or in a university, in circumstances often quite different from those in the school. It is all very odd and unsatisfactory. Evidence of the predictability of single, terminal examinations is vulnerable and depends on the type of examination, the subject being tested and the equality of access by candidates of different genders and cultures.

External assessment and centrally organized examinations can, in the eyes of pupils, teachers and parents, diminish the status and seriously limit the range and diversity of pupil learning, undermine professionalism by influencing class organization and teaching strategies, and, in the end, convey to the clients misleading information. More than centrally prescribed content, externally imposed assessment procedures and tests are, potentially, the greatest threat to the professionalism of teachers and the needs of their pupils.

None of this is an argument against tests, examinations or assessment. But if we want to recognize the diversity of achievement as well as the shortcomings of school pupils, if the priority of the clients' needs is part of a teacher's professional code, if in an open society we need to identify the extent and motives of central control, we need, as a start, to be able to ask of examinations: just *what* information do they need to convey, *to whom* and for *what purposes*?

CONTROL BY CLIENTS

On whose behalf do governments make education compulsory? We 'know' education benefits society as a whole, although it is a 'knowledge' based on faith rather than on demonstrable evidence. But the concept of 'society' is too abstract to be of much use. In this instance, clients are *parents, employers* and *universities*.

Education takes place on behalf of, and at the same time with, parents, but not instead of them. '*In loco parentis*' is an inappropriate and misleading phrase when applied to schools. Parental rights of access to information are generally recognized, less often implemented. Sometimes they are protected by legislation. In England and Wales, the 1988 Education Reform Act guarantees parental representation on school governing boards and enshrines the principle of parental choice as central to government policy, although its benefits are unevenly enjoyed and are still dependent as much on economic and social circumstances as on decree.

What are employers entitled to expect? Certainly, at the very least, that their young employees should have basic skills of literacy and numeracy. It is reasonable for them to want reliability and honesty (although it is far from clear whether the lack of these qualities is a matter of inadequate schooling, family circumstances, or economic or social circumstances). For teachers, including those of history, to brush aside the needs of employment as being uncomfortably instrumental would be to condemn themselves to life in a self-indulgent cloud-cuckoo land. But the problem is that the needs of employers are diverse and always changing. Many pupils will need not only vocational skills, but the basic skills of survival in the unemployment market, and it is difficult in a rapidly changing world to anticipate for 12- and 13-year-olds just what their employment needs will be in five or six years' time. The words of Alan Cowie quoted on p. 125 are pertinent. He defends the flexibility of the humanities, including history, and argues that the needs of employers would best be met by widening rather than narrowing the options of young people. In fact, he is asking for a strategy which must give 'education for change' more substance than a mere slogan. Cowie also implicitly seeks some clear definition of the relationship between education and training. Moreover, there are plenty of signs among many European employers that his voice is neither lone nor aberrant.

Education is concerned with the development of a whole person: intellectually and physically, morally and aesthetically, socially and sexually, politically and domestically. Some of this education takes place in schools. Education also embraces training in vocational skills which qualify young people for the job market. Much of this training and its updating will occur in the work place. But if education becomes driven principally by the unpredictable needs of employment, there is a danger that the needs of employers will exercise too powerful an influence, the curriculum may become unbalanced, and the personal development of young people will be impoverished. To ignore or marginalize the needs and opinions of employers, however, would be an abandonment by education of one of its responsibilities, and would sell young people short.

History has an important part to play in a curriculum for change and, potentially, in empowering all young people as more informed and effective operators in a bewildering and unpredictable society, in which they seek work, vote, become parents and enjoy leisure. For only a few of them will the outcomes of learning history be vocational, a part of their training to become, say, teachers of history, museum curators, archivists, researchers, documentary producers in the media, journalists, authors; for many such students, the *intent* had been perhaps quite different and the vocational outcome recognized only retrospectively.

But the function of school history is not primarily to train teachers, curators and archivists or students in university history departments, although some university teachers think it is. Only a tiny minority of 16-year-old Europeans studying history as part of a compulsory core curriculum will continue with its study, and the percentage is not much greater for 18-year-olds. Nevertheless, university historians can still have a powerful voice in the setting of examination syllabuses, in the writing of history textbooks and on curriculum change. Proposals for decreasing the narrowness of much of the school curriculum for 16–18-year-olds in England has often been derailed by powerful voices in the universities. Some university voices complained that British students of the 'new history' (described in the next chapter) arrive with inadequate basic knowledge of British and European history, thus making their tasks as university teachers more difficult. But school history is not just to serve universities. The new history was not designed to help the minority of pupils who will be taught by anxious academics.

There may well be the broader educational and social reasons for equipping young people with the basic knowledge of their national and European history, but that is a different issue. Dissemination of ideas and academic demands have too often been from the top down and have affected the content and teaching styles throughout the whole of secondary education. But nowadays this problem may be diminishing. There are an increasing number of university historians and researchers who work with teachers and school pupils, and whose perceptions of history and the needs of young people are based on direct knowledge of the realities of under-resourced departments and unbiddable pupils; an increasing number of excellent books and resources for use in schools are the result of effective partnerships between teachers in schools and university historians; and, since 1953, many university historians have contributed to Council of Europe conferences and workshops.

PARTNERSHIP OR CONTROL?

Democracy is a partnership based on a contract, either defined in law or enshrined by tradition. At the centre is a partnership between legislature, executive and judicature, and it represents a balance that is one of the safeguards of many parliamentary democracies.

But does democracy necessarily safeguard education and the teaching of history? Is the status and development of history in schools a result of a partnership between schools and central government? Attention has already been drawn to the legal diminishing of teacher representation on governing bodies. In recent years in the United Kingdom, for example, not only ministers of education but prime ministers have made public statements on particular teaching styles for the learning of mathematics, on reading and writing, and, for history, on the pre-eminent status of knowledge and the chronological limits to syllabuses. At least their concern has been obvious and public.

We should not be resentful if politicians express clear opinions about the status and importance of education; in too many countries, it has often been ignored by them. We cannot expect, either, always to be in agreement with their opinions. However, concern can grow if the appointment of independent professionals to advise them on the definition and implementation of their opinions becomes politicized. There was, for example, some concern, in England at least, at inadequate representation of practising class teachers on the national curriculum subject working groups, and there remains some worry that the criteria for appointment to independent government advisory bodies may be more political than professional.

These comments are not attacks on the integrity of individuals or on the competence and hard work of the History Working Group, but they send out some warning messages. The politicizing of independent professional advice remains a matter of public concern, as does any diminution of the advisory role of teachers. They are symptoms of a growing imbalance between political and professional control. Some countries may be puzzled at some of the trends in the United Kingdom; in others they may strike a familar note. But for all teachers they pose further questions:

- First, who are the partners in curriculum development? If a government delegates its responsibilities to bodies representing the minister, do they include, for example, representatives of the inspectorate, history teachers, university historians and researchers, parents and employers? If they include members of pressure groups representing partial views or vested interests, are they balanced by professional associations and the lay opinions of parents and employers? We must be able to answer 'yes' to both these questions.
- Second, what is the status of the recommendations of these bodies? Are they merely advisory? Is the evidence on which their recommendations are based, or rejected, made public? Do these bodies control their own agendas, and the timing of their meetings and recommendations? We should also be able to answer 'yes' to both these questions.
- Finally, how are the members of these bodies appointed? Are they *all* ministerial appointees? Or all representatives of professional associations, trade unions and other interest groups? We should be anxious if the answer to either of these questions is 'yes'.

These questions, of course, do not suggest a recipe for speedy decision making, but they seek some guarantee that government policies are professionally influenced and implemented. In democratic societies, they are questions that need constantly to be asked.

The issue of control should be about not power but *partnership*. The constitutions of open democratic societies in a New Europe depend not just on a separation but also on a balance of powers. This chapter has not been arguing for the end of central government power or for the exclusion of parents, employers or universities, and certainly not for the dominance of educationists or the teaching profession. We do not want control by the power of one of the participants, but control by the joint and planned authority of them all. So the task before us is to find a way to establish an effective working partnership between all the clients, so that none of their needs is misunderstood or their experiences wasted, and all their differences of opinion are *publicly* resolved.

There is another book to be written surveying patterns of educational control throughout Europe. There is much to learn from each other's procedures, priorities and mistakes.

THE FORGOTTEN CLIENTS: THE AUTHORITY OF PUPILS

Public authorities may, though they should not, have their own reasons, perhaps political or economic, for ignoring the real interests of pupils ... What is wrong with this is both, to use the Kantian formula, that they treat the learner not as an end (which is the true purpose of education) but as a means, which is radically anti-democratic.[22]

One does not just go around instilling knowledge into pupils.[23]

Pupils are clients. But are they participants in the partnership? In the scheme of things, pupils do not have much power, but the argument so far has been less about power than about authority. Power is associated with strength, authority with credibility.

Pupils as authorities

At the Braunschweig workshop, criteria were defined for the evaluation of text-books. 'Do they meet the needs of society?', ask the curriculum controllers. 'Will they enable my pupils to learn?' ask the teachers. The publishers want to know 'Will they sell?' But what do the pupils ask, if given the opportunity? 'Can I understand them? Will they bore me? Can I use them?' Pupils *are* authorities on, for example, whether they are bored, whether they have understood a lesson or a school rule, their experiences of being the child of a one-parent family living on the twelfth floor of a vandalized block of flats, what it is like being a refugee, or being the object of racial or sexual abuse, or, more positively, having lived for the first 10 years of their lives in Jamaica or Vietnam, or experiencing the cultural and spiritual support of Sikhism or Islam. In a history class, pupils may well know things and have had experiences of human behaviour not shared by the teacher. Those experiences and reactions have authority and credibility. What the pupils may not have is the expertise which enables them to organize, critically reflect on and *use* those experiences. This is where the teacher can become an authoritative guide. But the teacher as a know-all monopolist in history classes is inappropriate.

The rights of pupils

We want to learn how it *was* in order to go forward.[24]

The legal rights of pupils vary considerably between the countries of Europe. However, much recent legislation on children's rights across Europe implement such declarations of intent as the UN Convention on the Rights of the Child (1989), the recommendations of the Council of Europe, deliberations of the European Court of Human Rights on physical punishment in schools (1985 and 1987), and on directives of the European Union.

In 1989, the European Parliament issued its Draft Convention on the Rights of the Child. It complements and extends the scope of the UN Convention. It concerns itself with such issues as the rights of the children of migrants and immigrants whose parents lawfully reside in a member state, as well as those of refugee and stateless children, to enjoy the same treatment as nationals of the state, although it stops short of defining a right to citizenship. It states the rights of children to be consulted in all matters that affect them, including their placement in particular educational institutions; the rights of disabled children; the rights of access of all children to knowledge about their identity, including 'biological origins'; the rights of access not only to paid employment but to protection against exploitation in the labour market. Other declarations of the Council of Europe and directives from the European Union define the specific cultural and linguisitic needs of the children of migrant workers, immigrants and national minorities.

During the 1980s many European countries introduced legislation banning the use of corporal punishment in schools, although in the United Kingdom it is still permitted in private schools. More controversial, in terms of both public opinion and implementation, has been legislation banning the use of physical punishment in the home (in Sweden and Norway, for example). Since 1991, children have been able to appear on their own behalf in courts of law in the United Kingdom, and cannot be replaced by lawyers or social workers or other adults. On the other hand, since 1988 senior-school students have been effectively excluded by an age limit from membership of school governing bodies, thus ending a trend which had hitherto been gaining some support. Practice and legislation vary across Europe on, for example, the right of parents to have access to all records kept by schools on their children. A recent European Union survey revealed that, across member states only approximately half of all school principals recognized this right.

But the rights of most pupils in classrooms are more often a matter of accepted practice, random and arbitrary, dependent on the priorities or whims of school principals or individual teachers. In any case, those matters which most directly affect children would be difficult to define by law – for example, the rights to understand, to have an opinion, to question, and to appeal. The acceptance of such rights depends on the sensitivity and patience of teachers, on their ability to listen as much as to talk. If a national curriculum defines what pupils are entitled to learn, they also have the right to know why. Syllabuses taught but never explained have no place in a genuinely open and democratic school.

In Denmark, for example, teachers cannot decide for themselves what to teach; they have to discuss the content of syllabuses and their assessment with students; until 1980, and a change of government, decisions on curricular change were made by an advisory commission consisting of teachers and pupils. Iceland appears to represent a European high-water mark of teacher autonomy and the definition of student rights:

> Formal end-of-term tests are written and graded by the teachers themselves, and there are no governmental checks upon what they are doing. As a security measure, the pupil has a right to see his paper and discuss the grading with his teacher after the examination, and the pupil can have his test re-evaluated by a teacher at another school if there is a disagreement on the grade ... At the beginning of the term, the teacher has to make up a plan for the course with information on content, course work, individual work, tests and assessment, and the pupils tend to remind the teacher sharply if he does not abide by the plan that he made and *they agreed* [author's italics] at the beginning. Changes in the plan during the term have to be approved by the pupils.[25]

But we still know very little about pupil and student attitudes, and not enough about their understanding of important historical concepts. Much of what we know is anecdotal, random and unsystematic. However, some current research projects (already described in Chapter 3) concerned with student and pupil learning are producing more systematic and usable data in this key area.

Autonomous pupils as partners

History is taught in the main by specialists, often by enthusiasts for whom history has always been stimulating; for some, what happened in their history classes was perhaps what motivated them most to become teachers. But enthusiasms can also impose blinkers. Historical empathy with people in the past should surely enable us to have some empathy with our pupils in the present. Our imaginations must help us appreciate what it feels like to sit, bewildered and bored, in a classroom accumulating inert information about famous, predominantly male, dead people. Why should pupils be obliged to engage in an activity of no apparent value or interest? Adults would not put up with it. Pupils are at least entitled to some explanation. School rules that may be self-evidently sensible to teachers may not appear so to young people. Just as rational explanations may, if we are lucky, increase the likelihood of rules being observed, so history taught with a clear rationale *may* be learned with a touch more enthusiasm (although our expectations must be modestly sanguine). Pupil response is also one tool of evaluating the effectiveness of our teaching and the rationality of our rules.

The task of teachers is to identify not simply pupils' learning difficulties and their special needs, but also their particular enthusiasms, interests and hobbies. This is an argument not for pupil power, or for the simplistic concept of a 'child-centred' curriculum, but for the recognition that the experiences and views of pupils have their own autonomous credibility and authority. To allow them to control curricular decisions would be foolish. To ignore them would not only be arrogant but also display an unprofessional indifference to the needs of the most important clients in the educational partnership.

A distinction was made by a delegate at the Bruges Symposium between what pupils *should* know, *need* to know and *want* to know. It seems a useful agenda item for all of us. There are plenty of people too eager to answer the first question; some of us are quite good at answering the second; too few of us pay enough attention to the last.

Delegates at the 1990 Braunschweig workshop and at the 1991 Bruges Symposium were much exercised over the issue of external control and its potential threat to the professionalism of teachers. The concern prompted the proposal, described in Chapter 3, for a charter for European teachers of history.

There is an obligation on history teachers to define and proclaim their professionalism. This chapter has been about control. Its argument has been concerned with partnership, and less with the power of the partners than with their authority. In open democratic societies, teachers have the right to speak, be listened to and participate. They have the obligation to explain, justify and be accountable. In a democratic society, ultimate responsibility lies with freely elected governments whose decisions remain open to influence and can be subject to change. We are all entitled to hope and expect that democratic governments will not exploit majority rule to assert power in order to control, but use it to establish the authority of a partnership. Without such a partnership, the complementary skills and experiences of the partners will be wasted. Society as a whole, and more particularly the clients in the classroom, will be the losers.

A FINAL QUESTION: HOW EFFECTIVE IS CONTROL?

We know very little about the relative impact on teaching of autonomous and centralized systems, and far less about its outcomes in both. Teachers do not always teach what official policies require of them. Pupils do not always learn what centrally defined syllabuses prescribe. Inadequate resources, the particular circumstances in schools and the unpredictable needs of particular pupils define professional and local priorities, which are not always readily deferential to central decree. There is a certain stubbornness about professional autonomy which must not always be pandered to, but must never be ignored.

NOTES

Quotations in this chapter are drawn, unless otherwise attributed, from the papers submitted to the Council of Europe 1991 Bruges History Symposium. In the main these papers were written by representatives of the national ministries of education.

1 M. Ferro (1981), *The Use and Abuse of History or How the Past is Taught*, Paris, Payot: p. vii (English edition: London: Routledge and Kegan Paul) 1984. Ferro's book pursues these ideas by examining the teaching of history in South and Black Africa, the Caribbean, India, the Islamic world, the then Soviet Union, Armenia, Poland, China, Japan and the United States, and the histories of the national state in Europe, Chicanos (Hispanic residents in the US) and the Aborigines.

2 From the recommendations of the French-speaking discussion group at the Braunschweig workshop published as H. Bourdillon, (ed.), Amsterdam, *History and Social Studies – Methodologies of Textbook Analysis*, Swets and Zeitlinger, p. 103.

3 J. Froude, 'Oxford Essays', 1885, quoted in P. Slee, (1986) *Learning and a Liberal Education*, Manchester: Manchester University Press, p.42.

4 The terms 'ideology' and 'ideological' refer here, and throughout this book, to value-systems with meta-explanations of human behaviour, from which subsequent explanations of individual and group behaviour can be deduced. They are contrasted with 'historical explanations', which are subsequent to, and dependent upon, evidence of the behaviour of identifiable human beings. The contrast may be further described by saying that the emphasis of ideological explanation is on the transmission of values, while the emphasis of historical explanation is on the examination and analysis of values.

5 (1994) *The National Curriculum and its Assessment* (The 'Dearing' Report), London: School Curriculum and Assessment Authority.

6 (1994) *History in the National Curriculum – Draft Proposals*, London: Schools Curriculum and Assessment Authority.

7 This paragraph draws on P. Szebenyi (1992) 'Decentralisation and centralisation – to be, or not to be bound', in *Perspectives on Change in History Education*, London: University of London Institute of Education. The book is based on the proceedings of the Second Anglo-Hungarian History Teaching Seminar.

8 R. Stradling (1993), *History in the Core Curriculum 12–16: A Feasibility Study for Comparative Research in Europe*, Scottish Consultative Council on the Curriculum.

9 (1990) *National Curriculum History Working Group: Final Report*, London: Department of Education and Science and the Welsh Office, pp. 10–11.

10 *Final Report* p. 11.

11 See Bourdillon, *History and Social Studies*.

12 E. Børre Johnson (1992), 'Textbook research in Norway', J. Dominguez (1992), 'History and social science textbooks in Spain', and H. Bergeron (1992), 'School textbooks: books like any other?', in Bourdillon, *History and Social Studies* pp. 149, 159, 126–7.

13 From the comments of Danuta Wisniewska at the Bruges Symposium.

14 Comments in the following three paragraphs are drawn from J. Slater (1992) 'Report on the 1990 Braunschweig workshop on textbook analysis', in Bourdillon, *History and Social Studies*.

15 K. Wain (1992), 'Different perspectives on evaluating textbooks', in Bourdillon, p. 38.

16 J. Slater, 'Report on the Braunschweig workshop', pp. 19–20.

17 This list was first proposed by Professor Eric Hoyle (1983), 'The professionalization of teachers: a paradox' in P. Gordon, (ed.), *Is Teaching a Profession?*, Papers 15, London: University of London Institute of Education.

18 More information from John Sayer, 27, Britannia Street, London WC1X 9JP.

19 This body and its functions have now been merged with the National Curriculum Council as the School Curriculum and Assessment Authority (SCAA).

20 At the time of writing (November 1994) there are signs that policy is changing in the face of much disquiet from teachers, as well as some determined resistance. It is possible that, as a result of the Dearing Report's recommendations, the system of external tests will be simplified and applied only to a few core subjects, such as English, mathematics, science and a foreign language. The use of test scores to create 'league tables' of comparison

between schools may also be modified. Scotland, with a more established system of prior consultation, has not been faced with this particular problem.

21 The possibility of a 'value-added analysis' of results, that is, of raw academic tests results enhanced, or diminished, by social, economic, linguistic and cultural factors is now being examined as a proposed change in policy.
22 K. Wain (1992), *Different Prospectives on Evaluating Textbooks*, in Bourdillon, *History and Social Studies*, pp. 37,39.
23 A Dutch delegate at the Bruges Symposium, 1991.
24 A Swedish student quoted by a Swedish participant at the Bruges symposium.
25 E. Brynjolfsson (1991), 'Teaching history in the Icelandic upper secondary school', paper submitted to the Bruges Symposium.

PART 2

THE FUTURE

CHAPTER 5

A New History for New
Europeans?

History is a way of organizing the past so that it does not weigh too heavily on
the shoulders of men ... History has no choice in the matter, it systematically
gathers in, classifies and assembles past facts in accordance with its present
needs. It consults death in accordance with the needs of life.[1]

The good historian is like the giant of the fairy tale. He knows that wherever
he catches the scent of human flesh, there his quarry lies.[2]

History is what historians say about the past. It is less than all the past, but it is more
than people remember. All the past cannot be encompassed, and our individual
memories are too personal, selective, incoherent and deceptive. Collective memory
is too myth-laden, imposed by tradition and clung to for motley reasons of personal
and cultural pride, national esteem and aggrandizement.

History is a unique subject. It is the only one on the school curriculum which is
predominantly concerned with evidence of the behaviour, as it has changed through
time, of human beings *who have actually lived*. But it is not merely an accumulative
subject, with historical facts stored like marbles in a row of jam jars, or categorized
like stamps in albums. It is much more than 'just one damn thing after another!'
History is not written as a chronicle but organized as an explanatory narrative.
Historical statements and narratives are inescapably bound to evidence; if they are
not consistent with existing evidence, they are not historical. But history also inter-
rogates the evidence, enabling us not only to understand *why* people behaved as they
did but also to make some estimate of human success and failure. Thus it depends
not only on knowing about the past, but on authenticating and critically evaluating
what we know.

History is also an *organized* and *public* activity: in school history departments and
university faculties, in agreed syllabuses and public examinations, in museums, by
the authors of textbooks, by producers of television programmes, by ministers of
education and inspectors, and in the proceedings and recommendations of history
symposia organized by the Council of Europe. Public history is above all *taught*

107

history. Because it is organized, the question is 'By whom?' (see in particular Chapter 4).

If one of the characteristics of the New Europe is that it is composed of states either with some ostensible claim to be, or struggling to become, liberal democracies, is publicly and externally organized history acceptable? If education seeks to prepare young people to be active participants in open liberal democracies, to think autonomously and sufficiently flexibly to survive in a bewilderingly changing world, what kind of history does the New Europe need? This chapter will examine these questions.

It will argue that agreed content is less important than agreed criteria for its selection. Criteria for the selection of content depend not just on knowing what history *is* but also on what history is *for*. Historical understanding is a matter less of the accumulation of knowledge than of reflecting critically on and authenticating that knowledge; in other words, less of knowing the past than of thinking historically about it. Moreover, the chapter will argue if history is going to be taught in open societies it must be taught in open classrooms – that we have to consider not just the *what* and the *why* but also the *how*.

The first part will look at new content and its selection and the problem of function.

NEW CONTENT

New places

Since 1945, history syllabuses[3] in many European countries have widened the scope of their content. Chapter 1 suggested a number of European and world themes which might supply the content of a history syllabus in the New Europe. The list dethrones the nation state from its central position in many history syllabuses. After 1945, the balance of content in many European countries had already begun to alter. War-time alliances and enmities, the end of European empires, economic and environmental interdependence, and a post-war spirit of internationalism had increased the attention paid to the history of the United States, the then Soviet Union, and Asia and Africa. Content increased, but not time for teaching it, so pupils were whisked through breathless and superficial *tours d'horizons*, while established content – usually national histories – was squeezed or drastically reduced. Textbooks did not become longer but their style was threatened with becoming either more dense and daunting, or more terse and abstract.

By contrast, and alongside the adding of new continents, there were new demands to include local history, long ruled by enthusiastic and sometimes distinguished amateurs, and now supported by histories of the landscape, urban histories, histories of municipal transport and housing, studies of lost medieval villages, and the demography of late medieval and early modern parishes.

The problem of accumulated content is considerable, but it must not be exaggerated. World, European, national and local history do not necessarily mean the accumulation of new and distinct blocks of knowledge. Recent Council of Europe courses for teachers have focused on the link between local and European dimensions. The Trondheim and Visby (1993) Conferences showed how effectively the locality or a region could initiate and summarize great national European and world events. Coins and grave-goods are evidence of the movements of people and commodities; shops, restaurants and places of worship in towns all over Europe are among the legacies of the imperial pasts of many European states, of post-war political turmoil or economic circumstances in Asia or the Middle East; war memorials and random patches of post-war buildings are reminders of the impacts on small communities of two world wars. A single building – a castle or a factory – can be the sole focus of a local study, and become the starting point and exemplary evidence for a wider study of national events or of industrialization.

The case for local history is strong. It gives status to and recognizes the interest of people with lives like those of its students; it identifies and explores roots; it draws on a wide range of accessible primary source material; it offers its students opportunities for individual and group research and a new range of learning activities outside the classroom; and it gives immediate and concrete examples of past human behaviour, which can motivate pupils and are within their understanding.

But where are the boundaries of local history? Are they social, defined by where pupils live and limited by what they can easily explore on foot and with their eyes? Or are the boundaries geographical – say, the Baltic Sea, the Grampians, the Île de France or the Douro Valley? And when does local become regional history? And what if the boundaries are linguistic and cultural? The local or regional histories of, say, Esztergom or Trastevere, Warwickshire or the High Tatra, are potentially quite different from and far less controversial than, say, studies of Anderstown or the Falls Road, Macedonia or Ilidze.

Local history has its own agenda of delicate and sometimes complex problems. It can be a way of deliberately avoiding national political and military history: it can be a safe sometimes a deferential past. It can also be a painful past when it defines, in a particularly personal and confrontational way, controversial issues in the recent past of a small community. In Norway, the law prevents the naming of individuals until 80 years after their deaths, and has presented obstacles to a local study of everyday life during World War II. Local history is often a private past when family history, a rich source of materials and a fascinating strategy for engaging pupils in genuine historical investigation, reveals painful incidents and hidden relationships, not best examined in the public arenas of classrooms. A truthful past may well undermine, or at least be at variance with, powerful myths, which give social cohesion and act as a focus for local pride, or conceal the unpalatable. Thus local history can be a mythical past. The Trondheim Seminar attended *The Play of St Olaf*, written in the 1950s. It concerns the life and particularly the death in battle in 1030 of King (later St) Olaf Haraldsson, the site of whose death is now the setting for this play, performed annually and attracting some 20,000 people. But as the programme admitted: 'We do not have historical evidence for everything that happened.'

How can we possibly sift fact from fiction when even the most substantial source we have for Olaf ... an old 13th century Icelandic epic, is so heavily biased by nearly two hundred years of colourful and powerful popular tradition.[5]

These issues, identified by teachers with experience of them, counsel discretion and caution. They are not arguments against local history. They remind us of the uncomfortable tension between our own lives and the recent past of shared memories and experiences.

Different groups

But new content was not only geographically more extensive. New groups of people began systematically to be studied, first in universities, often corralled in fringe or postgraduate courses: women's history, black history, gay history; the history of the dispossessed and illiterate, of childhood, of death and of private life. The arrival of these themes was in part a result of the influence on history of sociology, psychology and anthropology, epitomized most famously by the *Annales* school of French historians[6] and the concept of total history – the history of all human activities and their reciprocal relationships.[7] In the United Kingdom, the journal *Past and Present* was founded in 1960 with similar ambitions and aims. Serious study, influenced by the social sciences, gave not only a focus and a new arena to the study of groups hitherto largely ignored or under-represented by traditional history, but also an academic cutting edge to their political discontent. Many of these studies were given a distinguished platform in the journal *Historical Workshop*, founded in 1976, and enabling some of these groups, in the memorable phrase of E. P. Thompson, 'to be rescued from the enormous condescension of posterity'.[8]

Wider categories

The influence of the social sciences and the *Annales* school also widened the categories of historical content. Academic specialists in the histories of art, science and technology, in social, economic and constitutional history, were well established in universities before 1939 (the first professor of economic history was William James Ashley, appointed to Harvard in 1892). But much history in schools was still dominated by the political, military, diplomatic and, for the medieval and early modern periods, ecclesiastical histories of nations. The Council of Europe history conferences from 1953 up to the present have regularly urged widening the scope of school history syllabuses. In England and Wales, the so-called PESC formula (political–economic–social–cultural) sought to widen the content of the new national history curriculum.

The arrival of the present

Many history syllabuses, including, until well after World War II, degree courses at Oxford and Cambridge, ended at a comfortable distance from the present, keeping at arm's length sensitive or embarrassingly controversial issues. In 1990, an English Secretary of State for Education refused to sanction the learning of history after 1960. The last thirty years he felt were more properly the province of 'civics' or 'current affairs'. However, a regular message from delegates at Council of Europe conferences has been the need for young people to understand *present-day* societies by studying them in their historical context of change through time. This demand was particularly strong at the 1991 Bruges Symposium, most notably so from delegates from central and eastern Europe. They could not afford, and did not dare, to keep the events of the very recent past at arm's length. They were perhaps too jealous of their own newly won political freedom to marginalize its historical context. They had a sturdy confidence in history, and some would have shared the doubts of their predecessors at Elsinore in 1965, who saw 'civics' not only as a threat to history but as an insufficiently rigorous or defined tool for studying the present.

The reasons for all these changes were various: chance, the building of academic empires, an urge for European unity, a suspicion of nationalism, the urgency of global interdependence. Sometimes changes were carefully planned and considered attempts to correct long-established and discriminatory curricular imbalances; often they were unplanned and hugger-mugger. What is clear is that, in a multicultural Europe and an interdependent world, it is easier to add to the list of key topics and periods than to remove them. Resulting syllabuses soon bulge with importance and suffocate with priorities. They may well attempt to satisfy a range of national and cultural interests, but they will be unteachable.

THE ISSUE OF SELECTION

'Total' and 'world' history are both acceptable and comprehensible concepts. But neither the totality of human behaviour nor the history of the whole world can be learned. Content has to be selected.

When a historian writes a book or delivers a lecture, its content will be the result of choice, a consequence, perhaps, of the author's specialisms and interests, possibly the terms of his or her appointment, or gaps in public knowledge, or what publishers think will sell. Book titles declare their contents, potted biographies may tell us something of the author's career, previous publications and credibility. The reader is free to ignore, read, be impressed or be irritated. Free choice has been exercised by the author and the reader.

The situation is different when teachers, inspectors or examiners plan a history syllabus to be learned by young people between the ages of 11 and 16. History pupils are not free spirits like the members of the reading public. They are conscripts of compulsory education. They are also not, in the main, specialist readers of history, and only a minority are likely to become historians, or even continue with its study after the age of 16. The syllabuses they study will not simply reflect the specialist interests and enthusiasms of their teachers and examiners, they will also seek to put the past in a wider national, European and global context. Their content must inevitably be ruthlessly selective.

Centrally selected content runs the danger of riding roughshod over regional and cultural differences, not answering the diversity of needs of young people living in different social, cultural, economic circumstances, and ignoring the dramatic contrast between the recent pasts contained within Europe. A prescribed curricula, centrally defined and imposed by national governments, can not only marginalize the diversity within Europe, but sit uneasily with the values and realities of open societies to which virtually all the nations of the New Europe claim to aspire. Is a debate about common content fruitless? Is there nothing to share?

If, in open societies, we are going to engage in historical discourse, evaluate evidence and different interpretations, two fundamental questions have to be posed: who selects the past we study, and with what criteria? Chapter 4 considered the first question; here we consider the second.

No history syllabus exists without considerable gaps in content. Selection is not an occasional and irritating distraction, it is the core of the matter. Compromises and sacrifices always have to be made. However, declared criteria help ensure that these are planned and explicit rather than arbitrary and concealed. Common criteria may produce similar curricula but not necessarily uniform syllabuses. They can be the product of associations of European teachers, or embodied in Council of Europe recommendations. They can still acknowledge national policies, be aware of regional and local circumstances and cultural diversity, while at the same time recognizing the professional autonomy of teachers. More important, they can even, if they so choose, be sensitive to the needs of *pupils*, their enthusiasms, quirks and hobbies, and embody statements of entitlement for all pupils within our compulsory educational systems. Above all, they can make values, which too often lurk unrecognized below the surface but which in fact lie at the heart of historical choice, explicit public property. The task is to seek not agreed content, but some measure of agreement on the criteria for the selection of content.

Essentially these criteria must be historical – 'Historical accounts are ... *selective* in order to be *explanatory*'.[9] – and not the result of tradition, political whim or sheer, blind chance. But recent developments in the teaching of history have been not just a matter of absorbing new knowledge, but one of assessing how students of history acquire, learn and use that knowledge. We ask not just how much more these students know after three years of studying history, but what, after that time, they can now *do*. The progressive acquisition of historical skills now sits alongside the accumulation of historical knowledge.

A NEW HISTORY: ONE ENGLISH APPROACH

In the 1970s a history curriculum project in England began to tackle the issues of criteria for selection and the development of historical skills. There had been some shifts in the content of history syllabuses in England in the years after 1945, and new syllabuses on United States and world history were introduced as options into the public examinations system. But it was not until the 1970s that changes affecting pedagogy and a rationale for content selection began systematically to be considered and become influential. These changes have sometimes been termed 'the new history'.

Its main aims were, first, to establish a balance between content and the processes of learning; second, to emphasize that the basis for the selection of content is the educational objectives to be achieved and the historical skills to be acquired; third, that the overall strategy is what has often been termed 'the enquiry method'. 'Knowledge' is neither inert nor an end; the new history is concerned not only with the criteria for its selection, but with its use. Evidence is seen not merely as confirming what is already known, but as a means of authenticating and testing what is known. Thus the new history clearly distinguishes between knowing about the past and thinking historically about it.

In 1972, David Sylvester of the Department of Education at the University of Leeds initiated, and was the first director of, 'the Schools Council Project: History 13–16 (SCHP).[10] By giving 'the new history' an agenda and a rationale, it was to provide a seismic change in the teaching of history in schools in England, Wales and Northern Ireland.[11] The project was based on the following assumptions:

- Teachers have too much history to teach. Consequently, the difficulties of syllabus construction and selection of content remain, even if unacknowledged by some, as a central issue for history teachers.
- The raw material of history is evidence from the past, too often omitted from school history teaching.
- History teaching has seen the recent growth of a variety of approaches in the classroom, such as the use of documents, games and simulations, and local history.
- The relevance of history in terms of its use for adolescents needs not only analysis, but also discussion and transmission among both teachers and pupils if history is to remain in the school curriculum and – what is more important – make a significant contribution to the education of young students.

So the Project aimed to give teachers a rationale for selecting content, make evidence central to history teaching, review some of the new approaches to its teaching, and help teachers arrive at reasons for their belief in the value of history as a school subject:

> since it is only this conviction that history has such a value, which sustains the Project. Certainly the Project does not see the reason for its existence as a means of ensuring that history stays in the school curriculum because it has been there for the last hundred years, or because thousands of teachers would face redundancy if it disappeared.[12]

The Project produced, 'for its well-being', as Sylvester put it, some account of the educational uses of history for adolescents. They were that it:

- helps explain their present;
- helps them understand people of a different time and place, and this is a widening, and therefore a valuable social and educational experience;
- provides material for the understanding of human development and change in the perspective of time and also of the complexity of causation in human affairs;
- can stimulate leisure interests which may be pursued in adult life;
- gives experience of general analytical skills which may be useful in other fields.

In order to meet its objectives, the Project team had to do three things: provide a suitable framework for constructing a history syllabus for 13–16-year-olds; write and compile resources to support the teaching of the syllabus; and establish a group of pilot schools so that the teaching and learning could be evaluated.

To begin with, the team rejected a number of possible frameworks for syllabus construction. First, they could find no adequate conceptual structure. There was no shortage of concepts, but they were either too general, such as 'cause' or 'change', or too numerous and specific, such as 'war', 'tolerance', 'trade', 'the family' or 'feudalism'. It is not that these concepts lacked validity or importance – some were to play a key role in the development of the Project – but they were not a helpful starting point for syllabus construction. Similarly the Project failed to isolate an adequate methodological structure for history. Most would agree that historians look at evidence and then construct some kind of narrative based on it, but that in itself does not form a useful base for syllabus construction. Nor does a structure based on a taxonomy of educational objectives. Clearly these are relevant for teaching history, but not as a foundation on which to build a syllabus.[13] The most familiar and common structure in schools was chronological. This too was rejected by the Project as being too linear and limited and 'the cause of many of the past ills of history teaching.'[14]

In the end, the syllabus was based on the *uses* of the past for adolescents – in other words, on the *function* of history. Initially the syllabus for 14–16-year-olds consisted of:

- *a study in modern world history* (a choice of one of, 'the Arab-Israeli conflict', 'the rise of Communist China', 'the Irish Question' and 'the move to European unity');
- *a depth study of some past period* (a choice of one of, 'Elizabethan England', 'the Victorian age' and 'the American West');
- *a study in development through time* (to begin with, 'the history of medicine', with the later addition of 'the history of energy' as an alternative);
- *a study of history around us* (a local history study).

These four units were later to be followed by an introductory unit for 13–14-year-olds called 'What is history?'

Finally, a group of pilot schools was established, later to be expanded into a network of 'cluster' groups covering most of England, Wales and Northern Ireland. These schools ensured that from the outset teachers and pupils influenced this important development. No longer was the model of curriculum development only downwards from universities to the schools; it was now upwards and sideways too. These early schools also provided the basis for an independent evaluation of the Project by Dennis Shemilt, whose report is one of the most important and persuasive arguments for the 'new history' that has been published.[15]

The Project team finally took the realistic decision that, in order to give their ideas some status in the eyes of pupils and their parents, the SCHP would have to be embodied in one of the officially endorsed public examination syllabuses for 16-year-olds. This decision was also to have important effects on the future development of history examinations and their assessment.

'What is history?'

The 'What is history?' unit was designed to introduce young people to what historians actually did, in particular to the critical evaluation and use of evidence. The first part, not to everyone's liking, was based on the discovery by a roadside of the body of a fictitious young student, 'Mark Pullen'. The evidence was his wallet and its contents: a bus ticket, a student union membership card, a ticket for a student dance and so on. The pupils became historians as detectives. What conclusions could be drawn from this evidence about the death of Mark Pullen? Did the evidence permit different conclusions? Young people began to see that evidence does not supply one answer, that different answers can all be valid, and that the evidence may not enable the discovery of the 'right' answer, which may not exist.

The unit on the fictitious 'Mark' was succeeded by another with a real corpse, that of Tollund Man. A series of photographs of this unknown man buried some two thousand years ago in a Danish peat bog was supplied, together with virtually all the available information about him. On the back of the folder was a sheet headed 'Things to find out', followed by these questions:

1 Who found the body?
2 Where was the body found?
3 What clothing or possessions were found on or near the body?
4 What was the age of the man?
5 How long had he been dead?
6 Which of the following was the most likely cause of death: old age, disease, suicide, murder?

Each of these questions was followed by a 'yes/no' option and a space for the pupils' explanation for their choice. Finally, the pupils were asked to give a *reason* for the death, and their own theories. A third unit was concerned with the mysterious death in 1483 in the Tower of London of the nephews of Richard III.

Three years later, when 16-year-olds sat examination papers based on the Project, they were faced with one paper and a series of questions based on source material – photographs, cartoons, paintings, documents, statistics – dealing with a topic outside the periods or themes they had been studying.

Although the Project has been immensely popular, it has not met with everyone's approval. Evidence presented to pupils out of its historical context – as in 'What is history?' and the source-based examination paper – was *not*, so some argued, how historians worked. Others objected to the fragmentary and incoherent nature of the subject matter of the Project. Critics, some of them in university departments of history, were concerned because their students would no longer arrive with a basic knowledge of the key events and personalities of British and European history. Others were concerned that the new curriculum was unsuitable for the less able pupil.

The first complaint, that key elements of the Project were not how historians worked, confused the aim of helping young people understand how historians worked with their working like historians. Nor were the ideas of the Project just for the most able. Provided that the content of the source material was accessible, and that the language of the questions was comprehensible, the Project showed that it could support the learning of the whole ability range of examination pupils. It was true that the content did not offer a framework of knowledge of British and European history, and to many it certainly appeared incoherent; these doubts helped prompt moves towards a national history curriculum more than fifteen years later. Fragmentary the content may have been, but it *did* have a declared rationale; within its carefully argued terms, it had coherence. The evidence of Her Majesty's Inspectorate (HMI) was that, taught by teachers who understood and believed in the philosophy of the Project, it motivated pupils, gave them insights into the complexities of the key concepts of 'change', 'cause' and 'evidence', and stretched their minds. One university teacher of history, on being introduced to the work of 14- and 15-year-old Project pupils, commented: 'If this is what 15-year-olds can now do, what on earth am I doing with my second-year undergraduates?'

In Dennis Shemilt's evaluation of the Project, he included a summary of comparisons between pupils in control and in Project schools,[16] reproduced in Table 4. It explains in part the popularity of the project with some pupils, but also why others, as well as some teachers, found it daunting.

The Schools History Project was attempting to provide criteria for selection which were explicit and argued. The criteria could, of course, have produced quite different content, and have been subsequently used to do so. The Cambridge History Project (CHP), for example, has built on the thinking and experience of SHP, and developed a two-year advanced course for students aged 16–18. Here again, the criteria for the selection of its content are carefully argued. The syllabus is built round the themes of 'People, power and politics'. Students study the themes in two distinct ways: through an in-depth study of mid-seventeenth-century England titled 'Was there a mid-seventeenth-century English revolution?', and through a development study, 'Political change through time'. The in-depth study includes a comparative study, of the French Fronde, while the development study includes an analysis of different accounts and interpretations of Russian history.

SHP is concerned with two to three years of learning history, and CHP will be studied by only a small minority of young people aged 16–18. These two syllabuses were designed to be taught in the United Kingdom and developed at a time when teachers still enjoyed considerable autonomy and a free choice between syllabuses. Aspects of these projects can contribute to our search for some frameworks within which to build a history syllabus for all pupils right across Europe during their years of compulsory education, from the age of 5 to that of 16.

Table 4 Summary of comparisons between pupils in control and in Project (SCHP) schools

Pupils on established courses	Pupils on SCHP courses
1 History is a compendium of pre-existent and inalienable Facts.	1 History constructs knowledge from evidence; constructions are negotiable.
2 History is a descriptive subject not concerned with explanation.	2 History involves both description and explanation.
3 History is a rote-learning discipline.	3 History is a problem-solving discipline.
4 History is a chronicle of the rich, powerful and famous.	4 History is about ordinary people like you and me.
5 History is a useless and pointless record of the past	5 History records the biography of the pupils' species, culture and society, and can be considered an extension of their own biographies.
6 History is personally irrelevant.	6 History is personally relevant.
7 History is easier than mathematics.	7 History is harder than mathematics.

COMMON CRITERIA

What might common criteria for constructing history syllabuses in Europe look like?

A future Council of Europe symposium might propose, for example, that history syllabuses should:

- contain a balance of local, national, European and world history;
- include the study of some cultures that are markedly different from those of today;
- provide the opportunity to study short periods of the past in some depth;
- provide the opportunity to study the development of a major theme over a long stretch of time.
- include substantial elements of contemporary issues studied in their historical context.

But within this framework there are still many empty spaces. It says nothing about how pupils should learn history or with what resources. As it is thus baldly stated, it would be little more than one of the initial tools of planning a syllabus and one of several criteria for its subsequent evaluation. We need to add a network of related criteria to help us decide priorities and emphases and to give substance to our selection.

Contemporary society and the new Europe as criteria

Delegates at the Council of Europe conferences have regularly defined 'the contemporary world' and 'the new Europe' as criteria for selection. A number of possible themes were proposed in Chapter 1. The section on 'The recommendations' in Chapter 2 adds the criteria of economic, social, cultural and technological developments. Together they offer us important headings but not as yet a detailed and teachable syllabus.

Criteria of resources and location

Choices of particular content will be conditioned by what is on the shelves of school libraries, by what is in departmental stock cupboards, and by the knowledge and enthusiasms of the teachers. ('Teachers' are resources; their personal interests and enthusiasms should not be wasted, although they can sometimes dominate and distort the choice of content.)

Access to radio and television programmes, including the availability of satellite transmissions, electronic links and computer link-ups, will increase the variety of resources and the school's control of them, and can widen the choice of themes and topics which can be studied. But such technology, even in many schools in the relatively affluent west, is often not available. Even when it is, the complexity, cost and quality of the technology do not always guarantee historical source material of comparable quality or of matching intellectual demands. Computer games may well provide ingenious pastimes but contribute little to developing critical thinking. Programs may be more effective in developing keyboard skills and computer literacy than in developing historical understanding. These comments are not intended to be Luddite, but there is a strong case for as rigorous tools of critical analysis to be applied to history computer software and television programmes as have been used in the past at Council of Europe workshops on textbook analysis.

But the immediate environment of the school and its region is also a key resource and criterion in making detailed decisions about content. Often it is free. What can pupils see from their classroom windows? What can they walk to and from in the course of a school morning or afternoon? Is there a museum nearby, or an archive collection? Is either supported by education officers anxious to work with school pupils? When was the local church built? Is the prominent building near the school a medieval castle, or an eighteenth-century manor house, or a great nineteenth-century railway terminus, department store or prison? When were the school, the post office and the bank built? Is there the site of a seventeenth-century battle or a World War II airbase? Is there visible evidence that the Romans or the Greeks or the Ottomans once ruled in the region? Or that a town was bombed by the Royal Air Force or the *Luftwaffe*? Is there evidence in the ownership of shops and in the cuisine of restaurants and cafés of a colonial past and the movement of peoples?

A history syllabus in a school in the middle of an industrial city or in the middle of the countryside, in the Scottish highlands or on the banks of the Elbe or Danube, in

Catalonia or Northern Ireland or even in different parts of one city will not be the same, and *ought not* to be the same, although all these schools could share a common curriculum.

Pupils as a resource

The selection of content should also be done with a sensitive awareness of the cultural mix of the pupils in a classroom. History should enable pupils to have some estimate of their worth and understanding of their roots. Furthermore, pupils whose families are from Vietnam, the Indian subcontinent, the Caribbean, will know things and have had experiences which their teachers have not (unless the teachers share the pupils' background). Wise and perceptive teachers will realize that they are not the monopolists of knowledge or experience and recognize their pupils not just as learners, but as a resource. We need knowledgeable teachers, not 'know-alls'!

Concepts and ideas as criteria

We cannot have love without lovers, nor deference without squires and labourers.[17]

Historical understanding and expression depend on using historical concepts. Some concepts often appear to describe concrete and particular situations, for example, 'Communism', 'revolution', 'frontier', 'warfare', 'feudalism'. Sometimes these are described as 'substantive' or 'first-order' concepts. 'Second-order' or 'structural' concepts are not specifically historical; they are aids to categorizing, analysing and applying historical knowledge. Some, as in the Schools History Project, are described as 'key' concepts, for example, 'cause', 'change' and 'evidence'. First-order concepts are more than glossaries of technical terms; dictionary definitions are not enough. 'Part of what communism is must be found in what communists have done ... The past gives our concepts concrete content. Concepts carry temporal luggage.'[18] Peter Lee's beautifully compressed observations remind us that the *historical* dimension of concepts depends on knowing how particular people have behaved in the past. Understanding concepts also depends on their being used to illustrate a variety of historical circumstances. 'Revolution' is a common enough historical term. But a simple definition does not help us or our pupils appreciate why the word is applied equally to events in, say, France after 1789, Russia after 1917, developments in eighteenth-century science and agriculture, or changes in the lengths of women's skirts and men's hair in the late 1960s. Such concepts are more than simple historical terms.

If, for example, we want pupils to understand and *use* the terms 'emperor', 'colonialism' or 'right wing', then the deeds of real emperors must be learned about, as must particular colonies and colonialists and right-wingers. A group of concepts might well suggest the structure and help select the detailed content of a particular theme. For example, the concepts of 'progress', 'improvement', 'change', 'science' and 'technology' could help select the content, as well as its interpretation, for the study of industrial change in the nineteenth century.

Concepts will only be valuable if pupils begin to appreciate their limitations and the over-simplifications they seem to suggest. But which concepts? In 1985, HMI in England published a list of concepts with which, it was suggested, pupils might become familiar by the age of 16.[19] Not all pupils, even by the age of 16, will be able to use all the terms on the HMI list. Some may only appreciate them indirectly by being introduced to events which illustrate them. Many pupils, for example, will never be able, or indeed need, to use terms such as 'oligarchy'. Nevertheless, there is no reason why they cannot understand how a few men ruled the Venetian Republic, or a small group administer their school. Young children may say of a teacher, 'Who the hell does she think she is!', or of another, 'She knows what she is talking about!' Some of these pupils may, at a later stage, recognize the distinction between 'power' and 'authority', but all of them have already experienced the distinction.

But there are three key concepts which must be omnipresent in learning about the past and developing historical thinking. They are *cause, change* and *evidence*. Their understanding and use does not demand particular content. Rather, they suggest particular ways of learning, authenticating statements, and looking for explanations. These concepts do not in themselves select substantive content, but they can help us prioritize and emphasize particular aspects and treatment of it.

The HMI list was not meant to be either exclusive or prescriptive; it was offered as part of the criteria for selection. Different teachers, schools and districts would doubtless amend it. As part of shared European criteria, such a list of concepts and historical terms would be unthreatening and possibly provide a second framework for the selecting of content.

Criteria of skills

General skills of study and specific historical skills (which are the essence of the subject) offer a further group of criteria for the selection of content. For example, one general study objective in history teaching is to develop in pupils the skills of working independently, including the confident use of a library. So it is not much good selecting content that is not supported by an adequate supply of appropriate textbooks or library books. If the object is to give pupils an opportunity to develop the skills of evaluating a wide range of source material – newspapers, statistics, old photographs, street names, parish records and the memories of old people – then the history of an area and of a time when these sources are available has to be chosen. In 1969, the Braunschweig Conference argued that accessibility to historical methodology should be one criterion for selecting local history. (But local history is too important, not only for its intrinsic interest, or as one source of illuminating national and world events, or for putting the lives of ordinary people in their historical context, for it to be justified solely as a kind of classroom sports-hall for exercising skills to be deployed elsewhere.)

If history is going to encourage the critical evaluation and comparison of different kinds of source material – for example, written, pictorial, statistical – it must be in a language and form that is accessible to the pupils. Such work takes time. Inevitably, less content will be covered. A judgement will have to be made whether the coverage of content is more important than developing skills of critical analysis, synthesis and communication. That judgement will depend on clearly understood and declared criteria for selection.

The development of a historical methodology obliges us to define progress in historical learning in terms not just of the accumulation of knowledge, but of the acquisition of increasingly demanding skills. In England, there has been a somewhat barren debate on whether history is a skills- or a content-led subject. Clearly, historical skills and understanding cannot be developed independently of knowledge. The new history is not a victory of skills over knowledge. Rather, it challenges a long-established imbalance in favour of factual recall and reasserts the mutually supportive partnership between knowledge, understanding and skills.

Pupils' interests as criteria

A subject such as history has no clear vocational value, and its intrinsic, social and intellectual functions may appear neither very obvious nor particularly persuasive to the majority of young people. Part of the attraction for them, if it exists at all, will lie in the interest and enjoyment of history. Indeed, without these, history's status in the eyes of pupils faces a bleak future. But pupils' interests in that sense often tend to be individual rather than collective. Should planned school syllabuses offer opportunities for particular hobbies, quirky enthusiasms, even personal obsessions? Our answer depends, in part, on whether we think our societies are the better for their presence or absence.

There has been a growth in many European countries in the encouragement of pupils' own choice of project work and personal studies. This has not been confined to older students but extended to the whole age range of compulsory education. It has become a planned and timetabled part of the history syllabus and frequently contributes to externally assessed examinations. Sometimes, examination regulations restrict the subject matter to issues related to the main courses of study, although in many countries the choice of individual topics, particularly for 18-year-old students, is often much freer.

Doubts have been expressed over some of these developments. They have been seen by some as undermining the uniformity, coherence and thus comparability of the outcomes of learning, of national curricula and public examinations. In curriculum development, the importance of 'coherence' is often stressed. The trouble is that the antitheses of coherence are all pejorative: 'incoherence', 'disorder', 'uncertainty', 'unpredictability' and so on. But pupil choice *is* often unpredictable. Should we plan and control it? If we allow pupil choice, is not control slipping from the teachers' hands? What if they choose war games? The social history of fashion or association football, or their own families? Collecting old bottles? Whatever next! Who could possibly want 'incoherence'? But perhaps there *is* something to be said for it. Can we not rescue some lost positives in the defence of, say, some *disciplined serendipity* in the learning of the past? In any case, it is surely odd and paradoxical if a subject which attempts, quite properly, to help young people think autonomously, and to live in an open society, excludes choice from their learning. We should surely welcome some organized space in the syllabus in which the content is selected by the criterion of pupil choice. As adults, much of our work is coherent and structured because of the demands of writing or teaching commitments. When we can escape from these, we become random adventurers in our choice of reading, the galleries and museums we visit, the buildings we look at. There is no reason why the delights and excitement of the unexpected or the pursuit of freely chosen enthusiasms should be denied to young people in schools.

There has recently been some backlash against such approaches by the educational right wing; government policies may seek to reduce the amount of work done outside the examination rooms that can be officially recognized and credited. Sceptics base their disquiet on the three issues of 'control', 'standards' and 'coherence'.

Such developments may be seen by some as undermining the power of the syllabus makers and teachers to control content and its learning – and of course they do. But in fact these developments are not challenges to their *authority*. Guidance from teachers will still be needed to give free choice some structure and direction, help locate resources, and deepen and extend pupils' interests with some suggestions based on experience. For centralists, such learning may deliver too much autonomy back to teachers and limit control over what may be seen as vested teacher interests or, more unpredictably, the learning of pupils. But it would be a touch paranoid to interpret anxieties just as a matter of losing control. Centralizers are concerned with raising and monitoring standards. Who is not? Unconsciously, some may still be gripped by a Puritan tradition that sees the absence of pleasure as a virtue; they confuse increasing perspiration with raising standards. Teachers, of course, know better. They know the importance of motivation and that excitement and enthusiasms support rather than threaten standards. They must remain on our agenda of criteria.

SOME FURTHER DIFFERENCES

History's central preoccupation with the evidence of the changing behaviour of human beings who have actually lived, sets it apart from, although neither above nor below, literature, sociology, law or ethics. At this point some further differences are described, or at least differences of emphasis, which distinguish the learning of history from some other subjects.

First, historical skills are not tidily sequential and hierarchic. A taxonomy of historical skills is not like, for example, learning to play the piano or high jumping or, for that matter, mathematics. Algebraic skills are not just subsequent to, but are dependent on, mastering multiplication and division; the two-times table necessarily precedes the twelve-times. While historical skills are sequential in that they contain steps of increasing difficulty, teachers know that children often leap-frog, sometimes quite unpredictably, intermediate processes to demonstrate skills at an unexpectedly advanced level. Progress zigzags; an understanding mastered on one day has disappeared on the next. Historical skills are not like riding a bicycle: once learned they are quite often forgotten, or temporarily mislaid. Thus lesson plans and hierarchies of objectives interpreted too rigidly can inhibit the enthusiasms and interests of pupils and teachers, stifle inventiveness and the expression of opinion, and fail to exploit the experience that all pupils can bring to a history lesson.

The differences between arithmetical tables or grades in piano playing are readily observable and generally understood. Not only the height of the hurdles but also the distance between them are easily regulated. But it is not so in history. Levels of attainment are imprecise and problematic. Is it obvious that pupils who can 'put together information from historical sources' are doing something more difficult than those who can 'make deductions from historical sources'; that it is more difficult to 'show an understanding that change and progress are not the same' than to 'distinguish between different kinds of historical change'; or that it is easier 'to identify differences between times in the past' than 'to recognise that over time some things changed and other remained the same'? These examples are from the English and Welsh national history curriculum. Arguably, some of these level descriptions are not different but synonymous and, like much source material, open to more than one interpretation. There is a danger that defined levels of attainment impose a rigid programme, without any strong evidential base for the vastly problematic and uncharted area of what actually happens, and why, when pupils acquire historical skills or think historically. Such levels can also inhibit excitement and surprise at the unexpected achievements and insights of our pupils.

Does all this mean taxonomies of educational skills are useless? Not at all. They can offer us a menu for planning teaching strategies; they can be one of the tools in subsequent evaluation; they can contribute to the criteria for content selection; they can help us identify and articulate levels of achievement. What they cannot do is to state in advance *how* pupils learn.

Nor do they present a developmental learning pattern in terms of content. The history of the twentieth century is not more intrinsically difficult than that of the fourteenth century or the Roman Empire. Yet many chronologically organized syllabuses assume that pre-history and the histories of Greece and Rome are more appropriate for young children than, say, the building of European railways or World War I. While one of the intrinsic aims of learning history is to acquire a sense of chronology and anachronism – more useful terms than a 'sense of time' (how do we recognize it when we see it, and what do we do with it when we have it?) – it does not follow that the past has to be learnt chronologically. Arguably, a 'sense of chronology' might be more effectively and *usably* instilled if we were able to move backwards and forwards in the past, leap-frogging some periods, backtracking to others, than relentlessly trudging from the distant past to wherever the clock or the timetable allows us to reach.

Further, as levels of attainments are not tidily hierarchic or predictably sequential, it follows that the pedagogical objectives of history cannot easily be defined in terms of precise destinations, completed tasks, or problems to be solved. History does not permit us to say, 'Ah, *now* I know all about the Reformation!', 'At *last* I understand why there was war in Vietnam, or fellow Europeans imposed their culture and beliefs on those of Africa and Asia.' Our understanding is never complete, our knowledge never total. Rather, it is a matter of lessening misunderstanding and diminishing our ignorance. Meanwhile, there remains the exciting possibility that there is always more to discover. The outcomes of studying history are unpredictable, often unexpected, usually modest. 'The quest for precision is analogous to the quest for certainty, and both should be abandoned.'[20]

Finally, history often presents its students with simple and accessible images and ideas: tidy explanations; comfortably sharp distinctions between right and wrong, good and evil; generalizations about class or gender; conveniently enumerated causes and consequences – 'the free world' and 'the Evil Empire', 'freedom fighters' and 'terrorists', six causes of the Great War, 'Prussian militarism', 'French culture', 'English democracy', 'European civilization'. All these are distinctions and concepts sometimes perpetuated by the authors of textbooks and examination papers; often they are part of our inherited culture and traditions, in the attitudes of our families and our peer groups, from comics and the media, or sometimes partially understood and uncritically borrowed from the social sciences. Such broad categorizations often fail to distinguish between what evidence permits us to believe about the past, on the one hand, and our current anxieties and political and personal aspirations for the future on the other.

Historical thinking obliges us to recognize the subtleties, complexities and contradictions which lurk behind myths, and to challenge simple moral categories. It maintains the centrality of *speculative* thinking. Collingwood reminds us that our criterion 'is not a criterion of what did happen, but what could happen'.[21] Thus historical statements tend to be tentative and are always provisional. The enemies of historical thinking are stereotypes and dogma. So when we listen to pupils talking and read their writing and attempt to find evidence of historical thinking, it is not just the language of time and chronology we must look for – 'before', 'after', 'since', 'during' – or that of cause and consequence – 'because', 'therefore', 'as a result' – but that of qualification, speculation and hesitation – 'perhaps', 'on the other hand', 'although', 'probably', 'uncertain', 'unclear'. History establishes the status and moral stature of doubt.

THE ISSUE OF FUNCTION

So far, my comments have largely been on what history *is*, and less on what it is *for*.[22] But has history *functions*, or should it be studied only 'for its own sake?' If not, is the alternative a crude instrumentalism in which historical study is used, some would say exploited, for social, political, even economic ends outside itself?

'History for its own sake' is a metaphor, and we should be the better for abandoning it. Who is this 'it' on whose behalf history is learnt? Someone other than the learner and the historian? Clio perhaps? Alas, she does not exist, any more than does her virginity, or the need to protect it from the harsh threats of instrumentalism. 'History for its own sake' has become a slogan sometimes invoked by the educational right wing, striving to divert students of history away from uncomfortable critical skills which question and challenge assumptions rather than transmit values. On the other hand, history which internalizes its aims is seen by some on the educational romantic left as a protection against the instrumentalism of a nasty market economy and unworthy, wealth-acquiring activities. Suspicion of 'instrumentalism' has always been just a little defensive and prim.

History is a human activity performed in a social context. A retired, financially independent person studies history, not for 'its' sake but happily and indulgently as a hobby, for his or her own sake. A university scholar immersing herself in aspects of, say, medieval land tenure is perhaps not unaware of the esteem, or envy, of her fellow medievalists or of her stipend and fellowship, justified by her scholarship. More obviously and publicly instrumental is the young postgraduate education student, with his history degree, continuing with the study of the subject in order to find employment as a history teacher. Or there is the 18-year-old school leaver with a good grade in her A-level history examination, being interviewed for a post in industry or business, and encouraged by the words of an employer:

> The study of English or History teaches not only the object of the discipline but also the method. The object may subsequently be discarded, dates and kings forgotten, but the methods by which they were learnt remain and provide the means to acquire new information and expertise ... A general arts and humanities education provides the young school leaver with the ability to adapt to a range of work demands. It makes them more employable than technologists with a single perishable skill. The need to equip young school leavers in the job market should be reflected in widening their options, not narrowing them.[23]

All four people love history. None has undermined its integrity. All have used it, in some part, for ends outside history. All are instrumentalists.

But what about those who see history as a means of training young people to take part in a liberal democratic society? Or the delegates at Calw in 1953, who stated that history should 'avoid any interpretations of historical developments which might be used in the particular interest of one state, or might disturb the friendly relations between two people', and that it was 'desirable not to introduce into the past contemporary national antagonisms'? Or those at Braunschweig in 1979 who referred to 'tolerance, both with regard to European neighbours or to contacts with the world at large', and to those at Tuusula in 1991 who saw history as fostering 'a pan-European approach'? They too were instrumentalists. But are these aims *historical*?

Here we must make another distinction: that between 'intrinsic' and 'extrinsic' aims. (I find this a more useful distinction than that between the metaphor of a personalized history for whose sake it is studied, and instrumentalism.) Intrinsic historical aims might be, for example, 'to understand the economic circumstance in

Germany in the early 1930s and their effect on the rise of Nazism', 'to study the role of women in early medieval rural societies', or 'to study the evidence in early Renaissance painting of family and civic loyalties in fifteenth-century Florence and Siena'. Intrinsic learning objectives, say, for school students might include 'knowing the difference between AD and BC', understanding the concepts of 'cause' and 'change', 'understanding that historical statements must be consistent with available evidence,' and so on.

On the other hand, learning 'to participate actively in a liberal democratic society', 'to counter racism or gender discrimination', 'to develop tolerance' or to become 'European citizens' is *extrinsic* to history. All these aims are concerned with changing society. But history is concerned with changing what we know about past societies and how we think about them. Peter Lee talks about 'the transformative aims' of history: 'The reason for teaching history is not that it changes society, but that it changes pupils.[24] There are irresistible social and ethical reasons for helping young people to live in liberal democratic societies, or be opposed to sexism or racism, but these are broader *educational* aims; they are not historical. However, historical perspectives and thinking can make a crucial contribution to our understanding of race, discrimination and liberal democracy. Such aims are not just concerned with studying the contemporary world. When we decide to study the pasts of our cultures and nations, the significance of revolutions, the role of women or black people, or urbanization, or the importance of our village or suburb, our decision will inevitably be affected by, for example, patriotism, kinship, outrage, nostalgia, politics – and they will often powerfully influence our criteria for selection. Historical, personal and social aims are enmeshed and not always easily unravelled, but their emphasis is different and the distinctions remain. They are none the worse for that, provided, that is, we recognize and publicly declare these distinctions. Broader and extrinsic educational aims may well help us select issues which will then be studied with intrinsic historical procedures.

It might be helpful to make a further distinction between intrinsic aims which history seeks to *guarantee*, and extrinsic aims which it may *enable*. History may enable, for example, students to pursue a lifelong enthusiasm for local history, or visit battlefields, or become absorbed in genealogy or the history of IBM; it may enable others to pursue careers in museums, archives or classrooms and lecture-rooms; perhaps it may enable others again to become more informed politicians, trade unionists, priests or, for that matter, farmers, actors or restaurateurs; or to become more informed and reflective Marxists or advocates of European federalism, or their more informed and reflective opponents; or to become decorous, or troublemaking, members of liberal democratic societies. But history does not seek to guarantee any of these. It does, however, remind us of the distinction between intention and consequence.

Do these distinctions matter? I believe they do. Extrinsic aims often seek to transmit values; intrinsic aims seek to examine them. The fact that the values may be good – 'tolerance', 'world peace', 'liberal democracy', 'European unity' – is neither here nor there. Self-evidently worthy values, as much as those that are suspect, must be ruthlessly examined and supported with evidence. Unless we do that, our ability to defend the former and challenge the latter will be enfeebled.

Subjects do not justify themselves merely by saying what they are about or by defining their procedures, but by declaring what they are *for* and by saying what they are trying to *do*. Would it matter if history were not learned in the schools of Europe? Lucien Febvre tells us that history must be 'in accordance with the needs of life'.[25] But what are these needs? What *is* it all for? More important, perhaps, *whom* is it all for?

Identity and roots

The great R. G. Collingwood had his answer:

> history is 'for' human self-knowledge ... Knowing yourself means knowing, first, what it is to be a man; secondly, knowing what it is to be the kind of man you are; and thirdly, knowing what it is to be the kind of man *you* are and nobody else is. Knowing yourself means knowing what you can do; and since nobody knows what he can do until he tries, the only clue to what man can do is what man has done. The value of history then, is that it teaches us what man has done and thus what man is.[26]

One can add that history might possibly help us make some estimate of what men and women might conceivably become.

Arthur Marwick too had his reply:

> To those who pose the question – What is the use of history? – the crispest and most enlightening reply is to suggest that they try to imagine what everyday life would be like in a society in which none knew any history. Imagination boggles, because it is only through knowledge of its history that a society has knowledge of itself. As a man without memory and self-knowledge is a man adrift, so a society without memory (or more correctly without recollection) would be a society adrift.[27]

The only evidence we have about human behaviour is the past. The future does not exist, and 'to live in the present', as G. K. Chesterton reminds us, 'is like proposing to sit on a pin. It is too minute, it is too slight a support, it is too uncomfortable a posture.[28] So we are landed with the past whether we like it or not. History gives us our individual, cultural and national identities. Without a historical context we could not define or understand ourselves either as individuals or as members of a community, culture, faith or nation.

Cause and explanation

Second, history is the never-ending pursuit of cause and explanation. It is more than just recollections and our knowledge of what happened in the past; facts alone neither explain nor justify. History also gives us the tools to *reflect* on what we know and understand, evaluate and apply it, in the cause not simply of knowing but of explanation.

The contemporary world

Third, history is for reducing our misunderstanding and ignorance of the world in which we live by putting it in its historical context of change through time. Our ability to assess our present predicaments and circumstances depends in part on seeing the mix of continuity and change in all human societies. Things as they are have not always been so, and will not necessarily continue to be so.

Statements about people: evidence and empathy

Fourth, history supplies us with procedures for authenticating statements made about other human beings. It gives our judgements a measure of authority and compassion. History demands evidence. It constantly asks, 'How do I know this is true?', 'What is the evidence?' History relentlessly insists that statements about other human beings be supported by and consistent with existing evidence. Interrogating evidence means understanding how language is used, by whom and for what purposes; spotting emotional and metaphorical language; detecting bias; distinguishing fact from opinion. It provides us with a necessary kind of 'drill' to precede, and subsequently test, our judgements. So it is an awkward and uncomfortable subject, refusing to accept easy judgements, sweeping generalizations and comforting assumptions.

'We can add to our knowledge, but we cannot subtract from it. When I try to see the Universe as a Babylonian saw it around 300 BC, I must grope my way back to my own childhood.'[29] Historical understanding also depends on developing 'historical empathy'.[30] It poses the question, 'What was it like to be someone different from me?' In everyday talk, empathy is taken as 'the ability to put oneself in someone else's shoes'. It was expressed more formally by Collingwood:

> Historical knowledge is the knowledge of what man has done in the past, and at the same time it is the redoing of this, the perpetuation of past acts in the present ... To the historian, the activities whose history he is studying are not spectacles to be watched, but experiences to be lived through in his own mind.[31]

Shemilt analyses this view critically and describes the empathizing historian who 'literally relives the thoughts and feelings of his subjects' as a 'psyche-snatcher' or a 'stealer of souls'; or as 'a time-traveller' who projects his or her own psyche into the past; even as 'a necromancer' conjuring up 'apparitions of, but not from, the past to appear and address the present in the language of the present'.[32] Over-ambitious claims for empathy can undermine its credibility.

But there are also some common-sense, everyday reservations about its unqualified use. We are all guilty of the well-meaning arrogance of: 'I know just how you feel' and 'If I were you ...' But the objects of our sympathy cry out: 'But you *don't*, and you're *not!*' Our sympathy may be genuine, but our claims are exaggerated. At best we are seeking some measure of identification with our friend's problems, with whom we at least share a language, perhaps some experiences, and a culture. So let us dispose of two common objections to empathy. It is *not* identifying with other people, which is impossible. Nor is it necessarily a matter of sympathizing with other people. That would be morally dubious. *Tout comprendre* is not always *tout pardonner*.

But there are always gaps in the evidence. The pursuit of our quarry, our irrepressible historical nosiness, require us to speculate, to imagine, to seek explanations that are not just based on evidence but are *plausible* in the light of our own experience. Historical empathy is much more than mere fantasy or caprice; it is a disciplined, evidence-based supposition which seeks *a measure* of informed but *speculative* understanding of the predicaments and attitudes of people different from us.

Historical empathy depends on being able to detect anachronism, sometimes or an awareness of the inappropriate and the ridiculous. A colleague once observed a class being asked to write 'an imaginary telephone conversation between St Peter and St Augustine'. A pupil wrote: 'Hello! Is that you, Pete? Gus here.' That pupil had a sense of the ridiculous. The author watched a class asked by their teacher 'to imagine a conversation between Columbus and the first natives he met when he landed on the Caribbean island'. A pupil asked: 'Please sir, what language were they using?' That pupil had an awareness of the inappropriate. Neither teacher had a sense of anachronism. Bad empathy assumes similarities between the present and the past. Good empathy is one means of exploring the differences. But in our exploration of the past we must not confuse making the past 'more intelligible' with making it 'wholly recognizable'. The past remains a foreign country.

Historical empathy also warns pupils against hindsight. In her book *The March of Folly*,[33] Barbara Tuchman tells us that for past actions to be judged as 'folly', they must have been perceived to have been so at the time, and that reasonable alternative actions must have been available. To let in the Trojan Horse was folly because Cassandra, who was about at the time, told the Trojans they were fools; they did not need hindsight to have rejected that very odd Greek gift.

Hindsight allows us to forget that once upon a time the great events of the past were still in the future. But this involves us in intellectual play-acting. We have to assume an ignorance we do not possess. We have to use our imaginations and pretend not to know the end of the story. Why did Duke William of Normandy decide to cross the Channel in October 1066? Just because he believed he had a claim to the English throne, or was ambitious? But *he* did not know what we know: that his ships would not be scattered by equinoctial gales, that he was to meet a Saxon army which had just completed a remarkable and exhausting forced march from the north of England, that a chance blow would kill the Saxon king, and that his victory was to be relatively swift and complete. So perhaps discontent among his fellow barons was more important in prodding him than were the dubious prospects of victory across the sea. Similarly, our subsequent knowledge of the devastation of

Europe between 1939 and 1945, and of Auschwitz, must not distort our assessment of why many Germans voted for Hitler in 1932.

Empathetic thinking is quite within the understanding of young pupils, but to develop that understanding depends on our teaching strategies and on how we present the subject matter we have selected. There is a difference between starting a lesson with 'Today we are going to talk about the Norman Conquest' and 'Today we are going to look at a duke who has to make up his mind whether to cross the sea and seize a throne', or alternatively 'Let's pretend we do not know what happened when William landed near Hastings.'

In sum, historical empathy is one tool for seeking out explanation and understanding. It uses evidence, refined by imagination and tempered by experience, to enter into some informed appreciation of the predicaments and points of view of other people in the past. It asks the question: 'What was it like to be someone different from me – because he or she was of the other sex, was poor, a millionaire, an empress, or German, Jewish, Irish or Muslim?' These are not just historical questions, but social questions of crucial importance.

It is our ability to empathize that sometimes seizes us by the arm and captures our emotions, lifts curtains on the strange worlds of other people's lives. In the years after World War II, Sybil Marshall, who was teaching in a tiny Fenland village school near to Cambridge, met an 87-year-old woman who showed her the shawl her great-grandmother was married in. She told Sybil Marshall about the wedding day: 'They were married in church here in the morning, but after that they didn't know how to spend the rest of the day. So they walked into Cambridge to see a man hanged.'[34] We think we are in a familiar world. Then suddenly, after the first full stop, we are jolted into strangeness.

Or a chance remark, a memory or a picture can hint at an adventure or a tragedy which we have to know more about. We see a nineteenth-century photograph. An unsmiling, lined, white-haired woman looks directly at us. She seems resigned and is probably very tired. She is wrapped in a plaid shawl; her hands are crossed over her knees. It is difficult to say how old she is. We know her name:

> She is Mary Nye, once happily married in England to a farm labourer. Her husband, walking home after work, found a hen's egg by the roadside and took it home. A neighbour reported the incident to the magistrates. Nye was sentenced to seven years transportation for 'having an egg in his possession for which he was unable to satisfactorily account'. Determined to follow her husband, Mary Nye committed a trifling offence, and was also shipped to Van Diemen's Land (Tasmania). But her husband had disappeared into the interior. She never saw him again.[35]

Compensation and opposition

Fifth, history has a compensatory oppositional function. It compensates and counters the influence of the myth makers and the inventors of tradition. Tradition and myths have their function, but both limit debate and resist analysis and explanation. Myths offer a coherent but essentially a metaphorical explanation of the incomprehensible or unacceptable: the 'creation of the world', 'the cultural integrity of a region or locality', 'the economic decline of once-great nations', 'the virtues – or iniquity – of imperial power', 'the sturdy American virtues of the frontier', the lost virtues of golden ages – Hellenic Greece, the Victorian age, *Blut und Boden*. In Britain, Victorian values of self-help and competitive individualism, of sturdy moral family values and economic rectitude, were used to justify the competitive free market economy of the 1980s.

Myths are also highly selective views of the past, often emphasizing triumphalism, the benevolence of the victors or the fecklessness, treachery or backwardness of the vanquished. Many imperial myths were born this way. New nations create their own pasts to justify the characteristics their new leaders have chosen for them. Past outrages are selectively remembered in order to justify continuing sacrifice and violence. The left wing can emphasize working-class struggles against capitalism and overlook working-class Conservatives and strike-breaking socialist ministers. Myths demand simple and exclusive moral categories: 'patriots' and 'traitors'; 'resistors' and 'collaborators'; those who fight for their class and those who betray it; women who seek power and equality as opposed to those who work at home for their children and husbands. Some myths are official, enshrined in national ceremonies, monuments and public invocations. The 'Dunkirk spirit' or Lord Tennyson's 'Charge of the Light Brigade' were invoked, and turned a retreat and a Crimean shambles into kinds of victory. Myths also find scapegoats and become weapons of persecution: medieval plagues were explained by Jewish intervention; current levels of unemployment by immigration from southeast Asia and the Caribbean.

If some myths are officially sanctioned, and tradition can be deliberately created,[36] other are popular. They are folk history, inherited perceptions maintained by collective recollections and nostalgia.

'Like the poor, the past is always with us; not because we choose to tolerate it (as we do poverty) but because we cannot escape it.'[37] Peter Rogers, who wrote those words, lives and teaches in Northern Ireland; he knows and despairingly loves the province. The past is known only too well and thoroughly there. Little is forgotten. But what is remembered is used to punish, not forgive. Propaganda, not understanding, is its function. Despite the quality of much of the history learning in some of its schools and where the Schools History Project took firm root, popular and politically exploited myths have so far seemed the stronger.

> ... and we are at Mohacs. The ancient battlefield, on which in 1526 the Kingdom of Hungary was overwhelmed by the Turks and obliterated for centuries ... Mohacs, in its way, is a museum – a painful museum, not the display of something, but life itself, its transience and its eternity. Beside the date someone has laid some fresh flowers: that old defeat still smarts and those dead are recent.[38]

The function of myths is political, ethical, confessional, to transmit values and bind together or reassure societies. But history does not set out to dethrone King Olaf, to mock May Day or demean the pride of *le quatorze juillet*. The function of history is to identify myths, analyse their metaphorical and often emotive language, explain their function and limitations, and sometimes, implicitly, offer rational alternatives or warn of potential excesses. It is neither improper nor necessarily ignoble to see past events as metaphors for present achievements, to maintain pride and morale in the face of adversity. No society or cultural group exists without the cement of shared perceptions of its past; they can give us identity, confidence and pride. But they are not easily compatible with historical thinking.

'Today, in nearly every country ... collective memory and official history thus confront each other in a real test of force.'[39] The intrinsic aims of history do not choose sides, and we cannot expect either of the contestants to disappear. With even-handed scepticism, historical thinking can act as a kind of arbitrator between collective memory and official history.

Curiosity, leisure, enthusiasm and enjoyment

Sixth, history is for satisfying curiosity, for developing leisure interests and enthusiasms, and for offering pure enjoyment. There is evidence of a vast public interest in the past from the numbers visiting museums, country houses, castles and cathedrals, from the buying and borrowing of books, from the attendance at part-time classes and courses for adults, in the membership of local history and archaeological societies, in the content of television programmes, in the support for conservation groups, and in holiday destinations. Learning history in schools is part of the professional underpinning of all these activities. But young children do not come to schools ignorant of the past; they bring with them spontaneous enthusiasms for the distant and the exotic, a bubbling curiosity about their own early years and about what adults can remember of their childhood. History in schools should be for nurturing and developing these enthusiasms. But what a responsibility! Too often the association with enjoyment is snapped by a relentless didacticism and the demands of examinations focused on the competitive acquisition of knowledge. Standards must be raised, certificates acquired, but enthusiasms and excitement wither away. This function of history bears the heaviest of responsibilities and faces the greatest of challenges.

Diversity and achievement

Finally, history is for recording the diversity and complexity of human achievement. History places these achievements, and their changing reputations and stature, in the social and political context of their own time. It reminds us that greatness gives us transcendental insights, but that it is also human and sometimes flawed (this is not a cynical but an immensely optimistic view), and that achievement can be not only variously interpreted, but fragile. The characters of great artists may not always have been admirable. The motives of martyrs and heroes may have been mixed. Brave sacrifices can be made on behalf of ignoble causes, executioners may have passionate convictions about better futures; sincerity may not always have been enough. History shows us the peaks, the depths, the banality and the contradictions of human behaviour. In that case, is not the final function of history to be both exemplar and warning?

HISTORY AND VALUES

Here another distinction must be made: between the value of history and the values within history. The 'value' of history is a metaphor for what history can be exchanged for, 'history as currency'. A suitable grade in an examination can be swapped by an 18-year-old for a place in a university history department; the manuscript of a study of medieval rural life can be exchanged for the possibility of a tiny royalty, while one on the peccadilloes of minor royalty can be traded for one substantially larger. 'Values' implies some moral worth, distinguishing what is acceptable from what is not. For some, 'values' may be transcendental, absolute and unnegotiable; for others they may relate to a particular culture, society or group.

To see the past as an exemplar, or as a warning and thus as a guide to Utopian futures, has been one of history's most persistent characteristics. Europeans have long since used the past as a measuring rod of current achievements, or sometimes of decay. In the fourteenth century, Jean Froissart told stories of chivalrous behaviour to be emulated, or of villainy to be avoided. But the favoured model for the good life was classical antiquity. Its rediscovery was that not only of an artistic style but of an ethic. Petrarch wrote letters to long-dead classical authors. This one to Livy, for example: 'I should wish (if it were permitted from on high) either that I had been born in thine age or thou in ours; in the latter case in our age itself, and in the former I personally should have been the better for it.'[40] And four hundred years later Johann Winckelmann wrote: 'To take the ancients for models is our only way to become great, yes, unsurpassable if we can.'[41] Sir Joshua Reynolds, his London contemporary, exhorted his Royal Academy students to emulate the ancients as much for ethical as for artistic reasons. (But for some antiquity meant paganism and licentiousness. Rousseau, for example, reminded us that antiquity presented us with:

> images of every perversion of heart and mind, drawn ingeniously from ancient mythology and presented to the early curiosity of our children, doubtless that they may have before their eyes models of vicious actions, even before they have learnt to read.[42])

Nevertheless, for better or worse, Europe was firmly married to the classical past, and by the end of the eighteenth century that had become translated into the Greek ideal of universal and unchanging nature, embodying not only aesthetic qualities but the supposed Greek virtues of truth, purity, honesty and courage. A century later in England, the Pre-Raphaelite Brotherhood looked to the simplicity of early Renaissance art, not because it was Italian, but because it too embodied Greek virtues.

But antiquity had its competitors. Gilbert Scott, William Burgess and above all Augustus Welby Pugin revivified Gothic architecture, not just in nostalgia for the medieval past, but because it provided, so the ecclesiologists claimed, the only valid setting for the rituals and sacraments of the true Catholic faith. Marxism, although not all Marxist historians, gave historians not only new tools of analysis but an explanatory meta-theory and a prophetic determinism for the ethics of a classless society. And in our own days, 'Victorian values' as a metaphor had some force. As history they had less to commend.

But to see the past as an ethical source-book has been challenged, often implicitly, first, by a much more objective, systematic and scientific analysis of evidence. Herbert Butterfield, commenting on English Whig historians, wrote: 'And if we have clung to the past, it has been a nicely chosen past – one which was conveniently and tidily disposed of for our purpose.'[43] This was the tidy, or tidily comprehensible, past of Petrarch, Winckelman, Reynolds or Marx. It was *not* the past of Ranke (not intentionally anyway) or of Bloch and Braudel.

To see the past as a form of parable or metaphor sustaining a contemporary ethic or political stance is not improper, but it depends on emphasizing continuities and similarities, and argument by analogy, whereas thinking historically depends equally on differences, discontinuities and change. This does not invalidate metaphors, parables and analogies, but we must recognize them, and their limitations, and see them for what they are. They *use* the past, but they do not think historically about it.

We must also recognize that if we are entitled to raid the past for our own moral and political purposes, we have allowed a genie to escape from the bottle. The past, which can sustain the ideals of nature, free markets and free trade, or family life, can also be conjured up by fearsome necromancers to give credence and powerful emotional justification to Fascism, Nazism and the ugly faces of nationalism. At its best, Marxist history provided a conceptual framework for analysing the past, and also offered a challenge to the comfortable traditions of narrative and narrowly focused national history from which they have never entirely recovered. But as we have seen, and many have experienced, Marxist history ceased to be an analytical tool and became an ideology, looting the past in order to justify its own conclusions. It became party history, manipulating the past for its own ends at the expense of the intellectual freedom of generations in east and central Europe. 'Things fall apart; the centre cannot hold.'[44] The past as morality has been part of a clutch of philosophical, political, economic, scientific and aesthetic ideas which emerged during the eighteenth century as the Enlightenment and, ever since, have deeply influenced much of European social behaviour and artistic expression. They characterize what many would term 'the modern age'.

We now live in what others call a post-modern age. There is a new and often very healthy disillusionment with the global interpreters of the past – the antiquarians, the *philosophes*, Newton, Marx, Spengler, Toynbee – who persuaded us to dream either that the world could be brought under rational human control, or that it could be explained by what the post-modernists call 'meta-narratives'. If post-modernism may too precipitately have freed us from the Enlightenment, it also helped liberate us from the thought police of east Europe. 'The post-modern condition is modernity emancipated from false consciousness, from unrealistic aspirations and unrealisable objectives.'[45]

If we need to make a sober reassessment in the light of recent European history of the moral authority of the past, if we must redefine our objectives in more modest and humble terms, is there no firm centre left? If history cannot claim a moral high ground, or explicitly seek to prepare its students to be active participants in liberal democratic societies, what *is* there left to us? Are we obliged to remain helpless spectators, wringing our hands on the touchline?

In fact, to trim our aims, to depose some of our pretensions, does not mean that history is either amoral, value-free or impotent. Historians of art, for example, develop our powers of observation and deepen our understanding of pictures, but they do not decide for us just which artists move or influence us; and so it is with historians of human societies. History offers us the means of understanding and critically evaluating a range of human activities and lives, but history itself does not place them in a class order, or offer a consumers' guide, with a recommended 'best buy'. There is a commitment to *choice*, but not to what is chosen, just as a judge's commitment is not to 'guilt' or 'innocence', but to impartiality.

Our value-laden subjectivity, born from our circumstances and our aspirations, is not an irritant, distracting us from the real business of history; it lies at history's very heart. We cannot divorce our feelings and understanding of the past either from our social environment or from our own culture, emotions and experiences. Emotions precede cool reflection. When we, or our pupils, are faced for the first time with the bare facts of a marriage or a victory, a betrayal, an execution or an act of heroism, we all instinctively admire or condemn, applaud or sit on our hands. We do not first acquire knowledge and understanding about genocide before deciding to be appalled. Our urge to know more about Balkan history does not justify our horror over the fate of Sarajevo, it is a consequence of it.

Further, the very language we use to describe the past is replete with concealed judgements and prejudices masquerading as objectivity. 'Massacre', 'crusade', 'Reformation', 'conquest', 'terrorist', 'freedom fighter', 'resistor', 'traitor', 'rebel', 'peasant', 'civilization', 'discovery', 'bourgeoisie', and 'imperialism' all describe situations, but they also reveal attitudes to them.

Finally, our selection of content is, inescapably, a value judgement. 'In all the endless debates generated by Ranke's *Wie es eigentlich gewesen* ('How things really were'), a first question is often neglected: *what* things merit or require consideration in order to establish how things really were?'[46] For *professional* historians, the selection of a particular theme or period in the past may say little more than: 'It is important to me, the author, because I am an acknowledged specialist and authority on the subject matter, and it merits time spent by myself and my readers.' But to pupils in schools, selection has been made less by an authority than by someone *in* authority – a teacher, the author of a textbook, a chief examiner, a minister of education. Their selection confers status on what has been selected in the eyes of pupils and, by implication if not by intention, denies it to what has been left out. A decision to study Leonardo rather than Kepler, Martin Luther rather than Martin Luther King, creates priorities and pantheons for pupils. To select or reject a nation or a cultural group conveys estimates of worth not only to a history class, but to cit-izens of that nation and members of that group. Such priorities for study are certainly not value-free. Those which suggest, for example, that the Turks were principally concerned with invading or massacring, that the Irish were starving, emigrating or rebelling, that women, apart from a few empresses, were only interest-ing when they were militant suffragettes or workers in war-time munitions factories, or that Jews are victims, are not only selective but judgemental. A black pupil asked by the author about black history raised his eyes to the ceiling and said: 'But it's always slavery, sir!'

Selection is often a matter of inherited and rarely questioned assumptions and traditions. Male- and Euro-dominated history is less a deliberate conspiracy than a mixture of laziness, insensitivity and a deferential acceptance of tradition. The argu-ment for declared and publicly discussed criteria at least obliges those who select to explain and justify omissions. But it does not dispose of selection. Content remains value-laden, even when the knowledge it contains may strive to reach a degree of objectivity.

So history cannot purge us of our subjective reactions to the past. What it can do is to oblige us to face and scrutinize them, and so enable us to hold them with a greater degree of informed responsibility and evidence.

OBJECTIVITY AND NEUTRALITY

If we cannot talk about objective *content*, we can talk about objective *procedures*. Procedures are objective if they cannot be modified either by the idea being exam-ined or the conclusions we hope to reach. Objective *historical* procedures demand that statements about people be consistent with available evidence and linked to it by what we recognize as logical and rational thought.

Why is this distinction between objective content and procedures important? Because it reminds us that if the same evidence can produce different interpretations, it does not justify *any* interpretation. The distinction reminds us that while historical statements are provisional and tentative, they nevertheless do provide a valid and acceptable basis for a shared understanding of the past. They are neither purely subjective nor arbitrary. Historical statements do not sustain accusations of either historical or moral relativism. They remind us that although insights into human behaviour are strengthened by the exercise of imagination and backed by our own experience, they must nevertheless be grounded on evidence and not mere whim.

So are we as historians, proceeding objectively to study what we have subjectively selected, participants or spectators? Should we strive perhaps for *neutrality*? If this implies some form of even-handed non-involvement, it is not a helpful term. Historians can point to examples in the past where the non-involvement of, say, Spain, Ireland or Sweden in World War II was a committed act of policy which demonstrably strengthened or weakened one or other of the combatants. Nor is 'impartiality' a preferred word, even though Herbert Butterfield was suspicious of historians making judgements: 'I don't think passing judgements is in the province of technical historians ... I think that is God's job, that is God's history.[47] Only God can judge? Surely only the gods can be spectators?'[48]

History is not in itself a value-system, and it does not have an explicit or particular moral intent. Nevertheless, history as it has been described in this book is inconsistent with certain value-systems and attitudes. History insists constantly on the question: 'How do I know this is true?' (that is, on a question about evidence). Evidence does not simply remind us of and illustrate the past, it has to be interrogated in order to disinter and explain the past. History also requires us to ask: 'What was it like to be someone different?' It tries to discern our shared humanity with someone whose views and behaviour we may find puzzling, even abhorrent.

As historical evidence is incomplete, always diverse, sometimes contradictory and subject to various interpretations, its procedures depend on discussion and debate and the examination of assumptions. Historical statements are provisional and tentative, tend to be more like informed judgements than the assertion of confident conclusions, and can in no way be predictive. Thus the procedures of history, and its values, are neither determinist nor Utopian.

From all this it follows that the values of history *cannot be those of closed and authoritarian systems.* History does not aim to prepare its students for active participation in liberal democratic societies, but, as it has been described in this chapter, it is unlikely to flourish outside them. A liberal democratic society which does not encourage historical thinking about the past compromises itself and disables its citizens.

JOINT COURSES: INTERDISCIPLINARITY OR INTEGRATION?

In many European countries history is taught, or is planned to be taught, as part of integrated or interdisciplinary syllabuses, as papers submitted to the Bruges Symposium revealed. Structures and alliances vary.

In Austria, history is taught as a separate subject within a course called 'history and social studies', while Norway emphasizes local history within a course of social studies. Flemish-speaking Belgium stresses the important complementary relationship between history and other subjects and areas like social education and civics; in Swedish secondary schools, history is taught as a distinct subject associated with geography, religion and civics under the heading of 'society-related subjects'; and one course in Ireland for the first years of secondary schooling also links history with geography and civics, but under the organizing theme of 'environmental and social studies'. In England, an increasing number of secondary schools place history within joint 'humanities courses', in alliance usually with geography and social studies and sometimes with religious education; in France, in both the *collèges* and the *lycées*, history is taught as a joint interdisciplinary subject with geography and 'civic instruction'; while in Portugal, history is linked with geography, Portuguese and a foreign language within a multidisciplinary course. The new Spanish curriculum seeks to combine history, geography and other disciplines such as sociology, anthropology, economics and the history of art. A Swiss paper, presented to the Bruges

Symposium, quotes one of its prestigious schools: 'The human sciences are by definition interdisciplinary'; Bulgaria regrets the purely symbolic link between history and other subjects and the difficulties of establishing history and geography as a joint subject; and Romania states that 'interdisciplinarity' represents one of the aspirations of its current educational changes.

The case exists for a future Council of Europe initiative to share the considerable European experiences of joint and shared courses. However, comparison and evaluation of joint courses are difficult, as there is no shared terminology to describe them, and their constituent elements often ally areas of study quite different in kind – for example, single subjects, such as history or sociology, are linked to integrated themes, such as 'civics' or 'environmental studies'. A task for the Council of Europe might well be to seek some agreement on terminology. As a starting point, the following definitions are offered:

- *Interdisciplinary courses* contain distinct and identifiable subjects, such as history and geography, working together, using their complementary and contrasted procedures and skills, to study a topic of common interest – say, the changing nature of a village or region.
- *Cross-disciplinary courses* contain alliances between subjects normally taught separately, to study themes which cross subject boundaries, such as 'economic understanding', 'civics', 'citizenship', 'European understanding', 'environmental education' and so on.
- *Multidisciplinary courses* are looser arrangements where subjects happily coexist – in joint degree courses of, say, history and literature, or engineering and economics – but do not necessarily explore the links between themselves.
- *Modular courses* contain quite distinct units or 'modules' of, say, history and geography. Such courses may prescribe a common core for all students, but the core is accompanied by a menu of modules selected by the students, which can be, for example, divided equally between the two subjects or produce a course that is predominantly either historical or geographical.
- *Integrated courses* submerge distinct subjects, sometimes even deny their validity, to synthesize them into a new discipline or area of study. It is a model defended by those who see knowledge as a 'seamless web'. 'Integration' perhaps better describes an organizing theme, such as 'civics' or 'the environment', or to developments within subjects rather than relationships between them.

So far this book has argued the unique qualities of history, not only in its content preoccupations but in its intrinsic aims and procedures. To that extent it opposes a positivist view of history, that is, one that asserts that human beings should be studied in the same way as other natural phenomena, or that, as the famous statement of Bury says, history 'is a science; no less and no more.'[49]

Integration tends to be implicitly *positivist*, whereas interdisciplinary courses are implicitly *idealist*, that is, they sharply distinguish between human and natural events. To quote Collingwood again:

When a scientist asks, 'Why did that piece of litmus paper turn pink?' he means 'On what kinds of occasions do pieces of litmus paper turn pink?'. When an historian asks, 'Why did Brutus stab Caesar?', he means 'What did Brutus think, which made him stab Caesar?'[50]

If history is more idealistic than positivist, then it is a *humanity* rather more than a science.[51] But we are still left with more questions than answers.

What are the elements that make interdisciplinary partnerships?

These elements are what we call 'subjects' or 'disciplines'. The evidence of HMI in England and Wales is that a crucial precondition for effective interdisciplinary courses is that they are taught by those who have a more than usually confident understanding of the particular procedures and preoccupations of their own subject. Without that understanding, it is unlikely that the complementary contributions of the partners in a joint course can be defined, let alone effectively taught.

Joint courses: servants or task-masters?

Interdisciplinarity has been, and is likely to remain, an important strand in the curricular development of history.[52] However, if the aim of such developments is to help the understanding and learning of pupils, we have to recognize that inter-disciplinarity and integration can, on occasions, be inhibiting rather than enabling. It is still true, judged by a number of European statements, that interdisciplinarity is seen as a self-evidently desirable aim. Alliances are seen as more important than the cause which unites them. Themes are studied *predominantly* as tools of integration, not for their intrinsic importance. Examples observed by the author are reminders of the dangers which can distort the coherence of learning, as well as the potential strengths of the strategy.

In one school, much of the curriculum in successive terms was organized round the concepts of 'earth', 'air', 'fire' and 'water'. These concepts could well have provided a coherent and progressive strategy for studying the natural environment. But successive projects on 'Anglo-Saxon farming and settlement', 'the Montgolfier Brothers and Blériot', 'the Great Fire of London and the Blitz', and 'the voyages of Magellan and Captain Cook' produced a history syllabus which was random and incoherent. Interdisciplinarity had ceased to be the servant of learning and become its arbitrary task-master.

However, another school had decided to develop a course on 'the history of the English landscape'; clearly an alliance between history and geography was necessary. A curricular aim was an understanding of aspects of the local environment and its past. Interdisciplinarity was its supportive tool. A third school wanted to study and record ecclesiastical architecture in the nineteenth and early twentieth centuries as evidence of religious and social attitudes in a Welsh mining valley. An alliance between the departments of history, religious studies and art logically followed.

Distortion can also result from misplaced egalitarianism, which makes obligatory an equal contribution from all subjects throughout a course. A survey was made of a group of schools which were studying the environment and which linked history, geography and science. Those courses in which the three areas of study contributed equally throughout were weaker. The stronger were those where, in successive terms, the learning was subject- or single-discipline-led, emphasizing, for example, the changing human past, or the natural and physical environment, or the effect of it on human settlement. Strategies were flexible and pragmatic, and the particular insights and procedures of separate disciplines were effectively developed within interdisciplinary teams.

These observations suggest that interdisciplinarity is strongest when seen as a strategy, as a helpful tool, and not as a crusade or a doctrine. It is unlikely to provide the basis for a whole curriculum, or necessarily for a single course or examination syllabus, although there are persuasive examples of both; it can provide the basis for short-term, *ad hoc* alliances to study an important theme for one term or even less.

Choosing allies

Evidence submitted by delegates at the Bruges Conference was that history's natural ally is seen mainly to be geography. This seems also to be an assumption of the Council of Europe. Its 1990 workshop on textbook analysis linked history, geography and social studies, although in the event history dominated the discussions and the final recommendations. But is geography a humanity or a natural science? When the English Secretary of State for Education set up an advisory working group on the teaching of geography, its specialist geographers declared the subject's natural allies to be the physical sciences and mathematics, although geographers generally seem divided on this issue. Certainly an alliance between history and geography makes sense when the focus of study is, for example 'human beings in their environment', 'urban change' or 'frontiers'. But there is a danger that familiar and, on occasions, appropriate links are little more than inherited habits without a declared rationale and based on unexamined assumptions. If history is a humanity, where are its curricular links with literature and language and the creative arts? And should not history also explore links with mathematics and science?

Curricular development between or within subjects?

Opinion at the Council of Europe seminars has constantly supported widening the range of historical content and defining and refining its learning objectives. To these ends, the Schools History Project and the equally important Geography for the Young School Leaver were both key developments *within* subjects, as are moves to widen the focus of historical study to include scientific, technological and cultural change. We might add that historians who seek to understand the impact of the physical environment on human behaviour and use maps do not cease to be historians and become temporary geographers; they become better historians. Geographers who understand the interaction between the environment and human behaviour are not becoming part-time historians; they are more effective geographers. (See also the section below on the relationship between history and sociology.) These are examples of *internal* integration.

Some arguments for interdisciplinarity have posited a suspicion of separate subjects and distinct disciplines. This book argues for the distinct characteristics of learning history. Teaching skills can be diluted and wasted if interdisciplinary courses oblige teachers to work outside their specialism, particularly in the teaching of secondary-school students.

The reservations expressed in this section do not challenge the principal of interdisciplinarity or its appropriateness for learning about some aspects of key issues. To assert the integrity of history, geography and sociology must not divert historians from thinking much more ecumenically about their subject, teaching in federal teams with other specialists, sharing their resources, and widening the focus of their own historical understanding. Working in such teams can be important in the building of confidence and the career development of teachers. All this makes not only good curricular sense but also, in these sober days of limited resources and diminishing funding, sound economic sense.

Summary

A suggested agenda of criteria for the teaching of joint courses follows:

- Subject-based and interdisciplinary courses are distinct, complementary, and not contradictory strategies.
- Both strategies can be, on appropriate occasions, delivered by interdisciplinary teams.
- The choice of strategy should depend on the theme to be learned, not the other way round.
- The quality of the subject alliances and the effectiveness of learning depend on an interdisciplinarity which maintains and contributes the distinct characteristics of separate subjects.
- An interdisciplinary team need not feel obliged either to deliver a wholly interdisciplinary syllabus or to resist separate subject teaching.
- Themes may be integrated, although the organization of their teaching will be interdisciplinary.
- Integration does not helpfully define relations between subjects but better defines developments *within* subjects.
- Curricular developments within subjects impose new and increasing demands on subject teachers; pupils may be less effectively taught if specialists are required to teach outside their own specialisms.

- Interdisciplinary teams can share resources and provide an important context for curricular and career development.
- The existence of such teams, composed of, say, historians, geographers and social scientists, should not limit the exploration by historians of links with, on the one hand, languages, literature and the creative arts, and, on the other, science and mathematics.
- With pressures to add content to syllabuses and develop increasingly demanding skills, the problem of time is urgent, so the need to share not only criteria for selecting content but also experience of joint and, in particular, *modular* courses may enable us to maintain, with an acceptable degree of compromise, the study of history, geography and the social sciences in schools.

A particular issue: history and sociology

The relationship between history and sociology is complex, interwoven and interdependent. What are the essential differences between them? Can one replace the other? After all, sociology, like history, studies human behaviour, and both require and analyse evidence. Nevertheless, the differences are significant.

First, the emphasis of sociology tends to generalizations about the structures of human society. History emphasizes the differences between societies:

> Sociologists learn to turn to tables on figures, while many historians skip them and look for conclusions in words. Sociologists look for rules and often screen out the exceptions, while historians are trained to attend to detail and often fail to see general patterns.[53]

Second, historians have an investment in time; their attitude to it is different from that of the sociologist. They are concerned not only with the differences between societies but with how those societies have changed over time:

> the historian can never get away from historical time: time adheres to his thought like earth to the gardener's spade ... Sociologists are not opponents of history as history, but of historical time ... they flee either to the perpetually fixed moment, which is, as it were, suspended above time, or to recurrent phenomena which belong to no particular age ... History, by its very nature, is called upon to give its special, privileged attention to duration.[54]

Third, sociology much more specifically seeks to give us particular guidance, to help solve problems; its very nature is to be an applied science.

This does not mean that sociologists are the enemies of historians, apart from those occasions when two distinct disciplines are obliged to compete for limited money to buy books, or for time for teaching. In fact, they have both developed an interdependent and mutually enriching relationship. History has been rescued from its imprecise and cavalier use of such concepts as 'feudalism', 'capitalism', 'middle-class', 'society' and 'power' by the sociologists' much more rigorous and defined use of concepts and models. However, historians use models and concepts as useful initial tools of analysis, as frameworks for the preliminary organizing of evidence, or as hypotheses, but not as generalizations masquerading as conclusions or laws. Weber's model of the relationship between capitalism and protestantism, or Frederick Jackson Turner's frontier thesis, provided powerful focuses for historical investigation. After Weber and Turner, or indeed Marx, capitalism and expansion never looked quite the same again. But ultimately, these great overarching theses had to be *tested*, not uncritically accepted.

Second, the sociologists taught historians how to count or, as they have taught us to say, 'to quantify'. Statistical methods enable historians to categorize their evidence in quite different ways, and give them the tools to evaluate statistical source material critically. Historians now have a powerful additional weapon in 'the testing of common sense assumptions and literary statements', which 'brings out in to the open assumptions that must, if the words mean anything at all, be behind the traditional historians' use of such adjectives as "more", "less", "greater", "smaller", "increasing", "decreasing" etc.'[55]

Quantification has helped us not only to understand the limits as well as the extent of the achievement of the first industrial revolution, but to disinter from parish records changing patterns of family life, of births, including illegitimacy, of deaths and of levels of literacy, and so to penetrate and recreate the lives of ordinary people.[56] But if historians have learned from the sociologists, the latter in their turn have increasingly embodied a historical perspective in their work. Ultimately, the validity of the sociologists' models and concepts depends on their being tested by historical procedures and evidence.[57]

HISTORY, POLITICAL EDUCATION AND CITIZENSHIP

Council of Europe conferences and workshops continue to reiterate the importance of political education and citizenship. This section explores the relationship and contribution of history to those concepts.

Political education

Political education seeks to give students the knowledge, understanding and skills to understand political behaviour so that their own individual attitudes and values will be more informed and confident and, if they so choose, their active participation in society more responsible and effective.

Political education is different from *political behaviour*. Such a distinction makes political education different from other school studies. For example, science, history or art education seek to train in the classroom young scientists, historians or artists. Political education *enables* its students to define and develop political convictions and, if they choose, to behave politically. Political education is essentially concerned with the examination of a series of alternative points of view. Political behaviour depends on commitment to one point of view. Thus it is a different activity; it may take place as a result of political education, but it is outside and separate from it.

Politics studies the issues in society over which we disagree, in particular those issues related to power and authority, the creation and distribution of wealth, and individual freedom and human rights; all are related to public and personal attitudes and values. Politics also studies the behaviour and machinery which individuals use to disseminate and discuss their beliefs, either by converting others to them, or by reconciling their differences. Finally, politics studies the actions we take when there is public disagreement, so that decisions can be taken. *Democratic politics* seeks in particular to involve in this process all points of view in such a way that all parties survive the resolution of differences while maintaining the possibility of changing the decision. (There are of course other well-tried and familiar ways of resolving differences of opinion: imprisoning the opposition, censorship, beating people with batons, excluding opponents from public and professional life; but as the term is used here, these methods are not *political*.) Thus political education is not value-free. It can only flourish in open societies.

Civics and citizenship

'Civics' studies societies where authority and power are organized on behalf of their citizens. Those societies may be open and democratic or closed and wholly authoritarian. Citizenship has an instrumental function in that it educates and trains young people to participate in civic societies. A society may depend on its citizens being autonomous, enfranchised and disputatious, or on their being deferential and loyal. Citizenship in itself, which may or may not have a legal status, is no guarantee of liberal democracy and has no one set of declared values. The mere existence of 'civics' and 'citizenship' on a school's curriculum tells us little about the underlying assumptions and values of the civic society which are being taught.

'Political education', like 'civics' and 'social studies', is a federal term, embracing contributory disciplines. In English schools, the political awareness of young people can be enhanced across the curriculum. Here are some examples observed by the author:

- A theatre-in-education group working with English and drama teachers explored some of the political and moral issues raised by the Falklands War; another, using as a starting point Nat Turner's slave rebellion in Virginia in 1831, examined values and attitudes in a multicultural school.
- A geography class examined urban development in relation to poverty, unemployment and ethnic communities.
- A religious education class examined the moral debates and the range of attitudes on issues such as abortion, contraception and homosexuality.
- An English literature class examined the concepts of 'power', 'authority', 'social order' and 'resistance' as illustrated in some of Shakespeare's plays.
- A chemistry lesson studied the problem of masking the effects of radiation from

nuclear waste, which the government was proposing to bury in disused coal-mines beneath the school.

- A mathematics class taught its pupil to interpret and evaluate statistical information on issues such as unemployment, the state of the economy and patterns of immigration.

Political education is concerned primarily with publicly controversial issues, and only incidentally with the machinery established to resolve them. It is not concerned solely with the issues of central government or of international relations; it is concerned equally with those in the community, the village, the street and the school.

Political attitudes and experiences are not formed only in civics or politics classrooms. Indeed, teachers may only be an incidental influence; they are in competition with the media, family attitudes, peer groups and what the 1985 Recommendation of the Committee of Ministers called 'the climate of the school'. But the first experience young people have of the ability of adults to organize a community is when they go to school.

Everything that is formally intended in the school is its curriculum. It is far more than the sum total of taught syllabuses or what is taught in history, geography, economics or politics classes. Who makes the rules? Are they clear? Or fair? What happens when someone breaks a rule? How are differences of opinion resolved? Who has power? The principal and the teachers? The senior pupils? Boys more than girls? The school bullies? What is it like to be a member of a minority? Black? Or bad at games? Or clever? Or to be confined to a wheelchair? Is it easier to be a boy in the school? Does a school attach more importance to correct dress or to respectful attitudes to adults than it does to racist or sexist remarks? School policies, or their lack, are evidence of the seriousness with which the school addresses these questions. The pedagogy employed throughout the school also has political implications. For example, do we train young people to live in a democracy by talking at them excessively rather than inviting their views? Does learning from textbooks or copying from worksheets produce autonomous citizens? Are teachers as good at listening as they are at talking?

Placing political skills, knowledge and understanding in the context of the school and the local community[58] not only is a realistic aim, but may help make politics more persuasive to the increasing number of young people who are bored and disillusioned with national partisan politics, and find it difficult to accept the customary forms of organizing political life.

There is support for, and much experience of, using elected student councils and joint staff-student management committees as a means of developing political education. This is not the place to discuss their impact and influence, although the evidence is not entirely encouraging. Too many of these strategies are seen, in Patrick Rayou's words, as a Trojan horse, which: 'merely serves to confirm the weak position of young people in relation to adults and threatens to cut them off from their only legitimate base, their peer group.'[59]

Unless, at the very least, the school and its classrooms are open and tolerant, neither of which is inconsistent with control and effective learning, political education for open democratic societies is likely to go for naught.

The contribution of history

Implicitly, history creates a necessary if not sufficient basis for political education, because it:

- places controversial issues in their historical context of origins, cause and change through time;
- demands and critically evaluates a range of source material not only in order to know about past human behaviour but also as a means of authenticating the statements we make about it;
- helps us understand that there can be several valid interpretations of past events.

In other words, history establishes a cast of thought, and provides some of the necessary procedures for making informed and critical choices between alternative points of view.

But for history to claim a more direct contribution to the political education of young people, its agenda will have to be rather more focused. It is true that knowing about the Roman Empire or Periclean Athens may help the understanding of concepts such as 'empire', 'power', 'citizenship' or 'democracy'; that Russian and Ottoman rivalries in the Balkans, or the South Slav question and the Bosnian Crisis of 1908, may help us a little to understand the current strife in what was once Yugoslavia; but there is no evidence that school pupils translate their knowledge of the past into an understanding of the present unless the past is explicitly related to current circumstances.

An agenda to guide history teachers in selecting particular themes and topics could look like the one that follows. By the age of 16 all young people should:

- *know about some problems which are currently controversial* – for younger pupils these may be issues in the school or in the local community; for older pupils they may also include national and international issues;
- *know about some of the current and past debates and disagreements over those same problems*, and understand that those debates may be over aims, outcomes and priorities (such as preserving individual freedom or protecting individuals by, say, censorship or regulations against smoking, or whether to spend money on a new swimming pool or an extension of homes for the elderly), or over the means of achieving an agreed aim (for example, by working within the law, or by breaking it, by negotiation, by decree, or as a result of open debate);
- *know that debates, priorities and means are affected by the availability of resources* and the means of their creation and distribution;
- *know and understand that differences of opinions about issues are often associated with different groups and organizations* – within schools, by parents, teachers, senior pupils, gangs; by men or women, cultural and political groups, political parties

and trade unions, pressure groups, governments and opposition parties, Protestants, Catholics, Muslims, etc.;

- *know and understand that political procedures and machinery exist in order to establish agreed ways for debating issues, resolving disagreements and taking decisions*, or to seek support in order to gain power;
- *know and understand the limitations of democratic politics and power*, which result from democratic procedures and majority rule, from limited resources, and from the ability to change decisions by appeals through courts and elections;
- *know and understand that there are alternative procedures to those of open democratic societies*, through examples not only of authoritarian regimes in the more distant and recent past, but of alternative patterns of democracy from, say, the United States, France, the United Kingdom, the Third World and Periclean Athens.

This proposed agenda emphasizes knowledge and understanding, and a historical context is only part of it. But democratic societies depend on people *doing* things. The acquisition of progressively difficult historical skills is not specifically political, but the ability to locate, order, evaluate and use information is part of being politically confident and competent. Here again, the difference between the intrinsic aims of history, which it strives to guarantee, and extrinsic outcomes, which it may enable, is important. And in these tough days, with rising levels of youth unemployment, political education may also need to give young people, particularly from minorities, the means of 'using' the system, and weapons to help them survive with some vestiges of dignity in contemporary urban jungles.

Political education and indoctrination

Indoctrination is a process by which people attempt to persuade others to accept ideas and attitudes by suppressing evidence or teaching it so selectively that it deliberately emphasizes or conceals certain aspects.

There is sometimes a fear that political education is a form of indoctrination, and in the recent past the term has had some unhappy and ugly associations. There is also anxiety that teachers, when discussing issues that are currently controversial, cannot separate their own personal commitments from their professional responsibilities. But the situation is more reassuring than these anxieties suggest.

First, the distinction between the problems of objective content and the absolute necessity of objective procedures offers possible routes through sensitive and controversial areas, so that professional and academic integrity may be preserved.

Second, historical skills and historical thinking seek to instil a measure of informed and responsible scepticism, which offers particularly stony and hostile ground to the indoctrinator or the irresponsibility partisan.

Third, the evidence of HMI in England and Wales did not support fears that teachers were unable to distinguish between personal commitment and professional responsibility.

Fourth, teachers should not necessarily conceal their attitudes to public issues.

147

Indeed, they are unlikely to be successful if they try, particularly if they are successful in stimulating interested debate. There are considerable benefits if teachers are known to be active members of a community, with commitments to particular points of view, a church or a football team. In any case, for teachers to conceal their own attitudes when they are encouraging pupils to display and justify theirs is surely an unsatisfactory base for good teacher-pupil relations. Keith Joseph, a Conservative Secretary of State for Education, said:

> If asked by pupils for their own views teachers should, when appropriate, declare where they as individuals stand, but explain at the same time that others, in particular the pupils' parents and other teachers, may disagree with them. The teacher should explain that such disagreements are legitimate given the complexity and value-laden nature of the issues and that pupils too need to weigh the evidence and considerations for themselves and try to reach their own opinions, respecting as they do the possible contrary opinions of others.[60]

Finally, does indoctrination work? There is evidence to suggest that deliberate and persistent attempts to alter attitudes are more likely to be counter-productive, as demonstrated by some curricular policies against racism. There is a significantly higher level of church membership and attendance in the United States, where the constitution forbids the teaching of religious doctrine in schools, than in England, where religion and Christian education are a compulsory part of the curriculum in all state schools. Did years of ideologically led teaching in east and central Europe produce generations of young Marxists? Indoctrination in schools in the United Kingdom is very rare. When it occurs, it is professionally unacceptable, not because it subverts the minds of pupils but because it wastes their time and bores them. Political indoctrination is a denial of political education and inconsistent with the proper learning of history.

FOUR FINAL QUESTIONS WITH FOUR SPECULATIVE ANSWERS

The four questions are concerned with the level of children's understanding, the openness of the historian's agenda, the effects of historical thinking, and history less as a humanity than as a humanizing subject.

First, as history is concerned with provisional and tentative statements, with problems that often have no solutions, with questions that have more than one answer, with establishing doubt, are we not seriously underestimating the need for clarity and predictability, particularly in the learning of young children and those with some academic difficulties? It is an important question and it is difficult to give a confident answer. We still lack research findings on just how children understand human behaviour, and what alters that understanding. Perhaps we are still too influenced by vestigial Piagetian theories of children's understanding, which often encourage teachers to think in terms of what aspects of the adult world children will *not* understand. There is enough evidence which encourages us to have a much more open-minded attitude to the possibility of children's ability to understand 'more complex aspects of society than those apparently allowed for by Piaget'.[61]

Evidence from schools tends to confirm this view, and suggests that the nature of historical thinking does not present a real problem, provided, that is, teachers are aware of the issue, and ask historical questions in accessible language. Nowadays most teachers are much more aware of the need to monitor language in worksheets, textbooks and their own questioning. Sometimes it needs to be simplified; the wording of source material has to be explained in advance, perhaps accompanied by a glossary or, if necessary, suitably 'translated'. But the need to simplify language for younger pupils and the less academically confident does *not* mean that, correspondingly, the level of intellectual demand has to be lowered. Indeed, the very contrary is often true; accessible language can offer opportunities for the demands to be raised.

It may well be that the issues of speculative and tentative historical thinking are less an issue of age or intelligence than one of temperament. There are adults as well as children who are drawn more to predictability, precision and problem solving; others to ambiguity, puzzles and mysteries. The task is not to exempt either group from ways of thinking they do not find easy, but to encourage their access to them.

Second, how open is the historian's agenda in an open society? After all, the aim is to enable pupils to make future choices from *their* agenda. But is there perhaps a concealed agenda limiting choice? As history teachers, we would be gratified if an ex-pupil told us that what he or she had learned in our history classes had enabled him or her to continue with his study at the university, or develop an enthusiasm for local history or Renaissance Venice, or given him insight into his or her local and cultural roots, or become a more confident business person, trade unionist or politician. But a more informed Fascist? A more confident racist? What if an excitement with the past, born in our classroom, had strengthened his or her nationalist convictions and enabled him or her to become a more convinced sniper or grenade thrower? Would it then be reasonable for us, as defenders of an open society, to feel disconcerted and anxious? Is history after all in the business of limiting choice? If so, by what criteria? I believe there are two.

One is historical. Prejudice, racial and cultural stereotyping are inconsistent with historians' insistence that statements about individuals, groups, whole cultures and nations must be consistent with available evidence. There is no evidential basis for racism. This is no more negotiable than is '$12 \times 12 = 144$'. History attempts to understand humanity's inhumanity and examines a range of explanations for it. But history is inescapably value-laden. The need for 'balance' must not drive us into moral neutrality. A 'balanced' view of genocide is unacceptable. 'Next week, boys and girls, we shall look at the case for Auschwitz' – surely not! We cannot prevent our pupils becoming Fascists, scrawling xenophobic graffiti on walls, beating up Pakistanis or Vietnamese, or lobbing grenades into food markets. The past may be invoked in their defence. But we cannot allow history to be used as their justification.

There are also sound general educational criteria for limiting the agenda. History is taught in *schools*. Their function is to enable learning. They must strive to be havens. They will fail if any of their learners feels under-valued or threatened. A school fails, contradicts its very nature, if it seems to endorse, even indirectly, prejudice and discrimination. The liberal agenda is not limitless.

The third question concerns the aims and consequences of historical thinking. 'The politician has to simplify in order to do business with his public; but the historian can be so obsessed with the falsity of simplification as to qualify his subject out of recognizability.'[62] It is proper to ask how societies can survive without decisions being taken and problems solved, if confident beliefs are eroded by doubt, if the need to judge is blunted by the compassionate awareness of circumstances and alternatives, if the absence of evidence can delay decisions – all encouraged by history. Enoch Powell's warning is pertinent. But historical thinking is only one strand of thinking. History is rational, demands evidence, and accepts a range of alternative interpretations based on it. On the other hand, for example, political thinking (as opposed to political education) is concerned with the assertion of one partial point of view. Government and its civil servants *have* to take decisions, as we do in our professional and personal lives, often with inadequate evidence and without having solved the problem. Religious belief is not authenticated by evidence in an historical sense, nor is the love between two people or the emotional impact of landscape or *The Marriage of Figaro*; mathematics and science depend on a far greater degree of predictability than does history. Constitutionally, a liberal democratic society is characterized by a separation and a balance of powers. None dominates, all contribute. So it is with strands of thinking. Historical thinking does not claim a priority, but without it our societies will be grievously disabled. But only if history humanizes.

But *does* history humanize?[63] The history of Europe in this century does not offer an encouraging answer to this question. George Steiner, in *In Bluebeard's Castle*, argues relentlessly and pessimistically: 'the axiom which we can no longer put forward without extreme qualification is that which correlates humanism – as an educational programme, as an ideal referent – to humane social conduct.'[64] Has a study of the past, a history degree, ever disturbed the consciences of camp commandants, of napalm throwers, of ethnic cleansers? Nations and communities celebrate their own pasts but can remain imprisoned by them – in Germany after 1933, and today in parts of Northern Ireland, in what was Yugoslavia and in many of the new nations of Africa and Asia – and use them to explain, justify, even dignify, oppression and brutality.

But does not history even *tend* to humanize? And what is humane behaviour? Where might it be found? Perhaps in groups – national, cultural, political – which can take pride in their identities, while at the same time recognizing and welcoming the diversity and eccentricity which lie within them. Humanity is found within groups which do not just celebrate success and give status to majorities, but also understand their failures and losers, and respect their minorities. A humane society is one where estimates of human worth, or inadequacy, depend on evidence moderated by imagination, and are not imposed by tradition, law or blind loyalty.

History might, just, if we are determined enough, tend to humanize, if it is not primarily concerned with the passive accumulation of knowledge about the past whose criteria for selection have not been defined, and which is seen principally as a prop to attitudes that have to be accepted rather than interpreted and understood.

History will tend to humanize if it is not solely concerned with the doings of great people and thus implicitly suggests the supreme unimportance of most people's lives. When Dennis Shemilt was evaluating the Schools History Project, he asked young people whether their lives could ever be of interest to historians. One pupil replied: 'We don't stand out enough, we don't do anything.' Another, who lived in a small coal-mining town in the north of England, said: 'No, not in Castleford. Maybe if I lived down south.'[65] What an indictment of history, that it gives, in Shemilt's phrase, 'this sense of personal powerlessness'.[66] *That* is a humanity dehumanized!

Stereotypical thinking, which places human beings into generalized cultural, gender or moral groups, will overlook and diminish the complex, contradictory, many-faceted behaviour of human individuals. It dehumanizes not only people generally but specifically, the historian. For that reason we must never decry the importance of evaluating evidence and using historical imagination. Their enemy is stereotypical thinking, which lies at the heart of much prejudice and hatred, and of humanity dehumanized.

But the issue is not just a matter of how we select historical knowledge and develop historical skills. In a subject which deals with human behaviour, no pupil enters the classroom entirely ignorant; many already know a great deal about the past. It has been estimated that most of the historical knowledge of primary school children comes from outside the classroom, from grandparents, television and comics, from family holidays and visits. Many pupils of all ages have experiences of human behaviour not shared by their teachers, of, for example, racial abuse, drugs, violence, as well as the support of historic cultures and faiths or having lived some of their lives in distant countries.

The 'new history' supports those teachers who recognize what their pupils already know, and who *listen* to them, encourage their independent learning and welcome their unexpected questions and explanations. They are redefining the traditional relationship between teacher, learning and pupil. This is not a negotiated curriculum, nor is it an equal partnership. The teacher remains an authority who helps pupils to tease out reality from myth, and to understand, reflect on and use their knowledge and experiences. But good teachers know that they are no longer monopolists of knowledge and experience (as are perhaps, for a short time, teachers of a foreign language, the calculus or the piano), and see their pupils as a resource, which recognizes the worth and validity of their lives.

Such consideration affects the pedagogy and organizing of classrooms. But teachers are not entirely free to choose how they do this. External obligations have to be met, in particular to public examinations whose currency may buy jobs or more education. What examinations demand, teachers will, understandably, teach. But what many exams want is evidence of what young people can do working in silence, writing on paper against the clock, often as isolated individuals in competition with each other. Now there is nothing wrong with any of these activities, although it is worth asking ourselves how often in our professional and social lives we have to use them in that combination. But if they produce marketable certificates and grades, those activities are endowed with status. What does not have status is the equally demanding activities of young people working in groups, talking and listening to each other, and working collaboratively. A humane society may need all these activities, but it is under threat if the latter group is seen as second best.

We live in a Europe which, for the most part, struggles to reject closed and authoritarian societies. But an open and democratic Europe still remains an aspiration. Even in established democracies, freedoms have to be jealously guarded. As historians, we must not get ideas above our station. History alone cannot guarantee or even enable democratic societies, but it can offer some intellectual weapons to be used in their defence. With them, young people may be marginally less vulnerable to Burkhardt's *terribles simplificateurs*,[67] concealed within politics, the media, churches and popular mythology. History is, to pillage a phrase of Hemingway's, 'a crap-detecting subject'. Without it, our claims to live in open and democratic societies will be grievously compromised.

NOTES

1 L. Febvre (1949), 'A new kind of history', *Revue de Métaphysique et de Morale,* **lviii,** reprinted in P. Burke(ed.), *A new Kind of History and Other Essays'* New York: Harper Torchbooks, p. 41.

2 M. Bloch (1954), *The Historian's Craft,* trans. P. Putman, Manchester: Manchester University Press, p. 26.

3 The terms 'syllabus', 'curriculum' and 'scheme of work' are used in the following way. A *school curriculum* is anything that a school formally intends should happen: it is more than the sum total of taught syllabuses; for example, it includes rules and sanctions, relations with parents, school magazines, voluntary clubs and activities, and its attitude to minorities. A *history curriculum* is more than its substantive content; it contains a statement of aims and a rationale; defines skills to be acquired; identifies necessary resources and means of assessment, and the role of visits and fieldwork outside the school. A history curriculum should also be seen as a *scheme of work*: a practical guide to what teachers and pupils should know and do, and how and with what they should set about doing it. A *history syllabus* is a briefer document outlining the substantive content within a curriculum.

4 An example quoted at the Trondheim course, 1993.

5 Grete Raeder Ostby, in a talk to the Trondheim course, 1993.

6 *Annales: Economies, Societies, Civilisations* started publication in 1946 and became associated with such historians as Fernand Braudel, Emanuel Le Roy Ladurie and Carlo Cipolla.

7 'Total' in this sense is sometimes called 'global' history. In this book, 'global' and 'world' are used only as geographical terms.

8 E. P. Thompson (1968), *The Making of the English Working Class*, revised edn., Harmondsworth: Pelican, p. 13.

9 P. Y. Rogers (1987), 'History – the past as a frame of reference', in C. Portal, (ed.) *The History Curriculum for Teachers*, London: Falmer Press, p.5.

10 The Schools Council was established by the Secretary of State (the Minister) for Education, to initiate and monitor curricular developments. SCHP is now known as the Schools History Project.

11 Scotland enjoys a separate education system. Wales and Northern Ireland have their own administrations and ministers, although their educational policies follow, and sometimes improve on, those in England.

12 D. Sylvester (1973), 'First views from the bridge', *Teaching History*, III, 10. pp. 143–6.

13 History teaching in England had at that time begun to be influenced by the work of Jerome Bruner, and by the work of Jeanette Coltham and John Fines. See, for example, J. Coltham and J. Fines (1971), *Educational Objectives for the Study of History*, Teaching History Series 35, London: The Historical Association.

14 Sylvester, 'First views from the bridge', p. 145.

15 D. Shemilt (1980), *History 13–16 Evaluation Study*, Edinburgh: Holmes McDougall.

16 Shemilt, *History 13–16 Evaluation Study*, p. 25.

17 E. P. Thompson, *The Making of the English Working Class*, p. 9.

18 P. Y. Lee (1984), 'Why learn history', in A. Dickinson, P. J. Lee, and P. Rogers, (eds), *Learning History*, Heinemann, p. 1.

19 The list was published in HMI (1985), *History in the Primary and Secondary Years: An HMI View'*, London: Her

Majesty's Stationery Office, London, p. 15. The list, which has now some historic interest, was:

administration	diplomatic	peasant
agrarian	economic	policy
anachronism	emperor/empress	political
anarchism	empire	power
ancient	**evidence**	pre-history
archaeology	fascism	primary source
aristocratic	feudalism	progress
authority/authoritarian	frontier	propaganda
bias	government	proletariat
bishop	hero/heroine	Protestant
bourgeois	humanist	radical
capital	hypothesis	reaction
capitalism	imperialism	rebellion
Catholic	industrial	reform
civilization	inference	religion
class	international	Renaissance
classical	king/queen	republic
Commonwealth	labour	revolution
colony/colonialism	law	right-wing
Communist	left-wing	ruler
conclusion	legal	secondary source
conservative	liberal	secular
constitution	Marxist	science
continuity	medieval	social
conversion	modern	socialist
crusade	monarchy	society
culture	motive	state
cause	myth	technology
change	nation	treaty
democratic	noble	war
development	oligarchy	welfare (state)
dictator	parliament	

Those readers familiar with this publication may recognize sentences and phrases from it in the main text. As the author, with the essential help of his colleagues, was largely responsible for the writing of this publication, he pleads 'not guilty' to the charge of plagiarism. Nor is it, quite, laziness, as some of his views and beliefs have not altered during the last 10 years.

20 K. Popper (1976), *Unended Quest: An Intellectual Autobiography*, London: Fontana Collins, p. 24.

21 R. G. Collingwood (1946), *The Idea of History*, Oxford: Oxford University Press, p. 239.

22 Much of this section draws on J. Slater 'Where there is dogma, let us sow doubt', in J. White, (ed.), in *The Aims of School History: The National Curriculum and Beyond*, Bedford Way Papers, London: The University of London, Institute of Education.

23 Andrew Cowie (1988), an employer, *Observer* 24 January, p. 27.

24 P. Y. Lee (1991), 'Historical knowledge and the National Curriculum', in R. Aldridge, (ed.), *History in the National Curriculum*, London: Kogan Page, p. 43.

25 L. Febvre, 'A new kind of history', p. 41.

26 Collingwood, *The Idea of History*, p. 10.

27 A. Marwick (1970), *The Nature of History*, London: Macmillan, p. 13.

28 Quoted, but without a source, in W. H. Auden and L. Kronenberger (eds) (1964), *The Faber Book of Aphorisms*, London: Faber.

29 A. Koestler (1959), *The Sleepwalkers*, London: Hutchinson, p. 19.

30 One of the most perceptive and practical analyses of this complex concept is by D. Shemilt (1994), in 'Beauty and the philosopher', in Dickinson, Lee and Rogers, *Learning History*.

31 Collingwood, *The Idea of History*, p. 218.

32 Shemilt, *History 13–16 Evaluation Study*,.pp. 41–3.

33 B. Tuchman (1984), *The March of Folly: From Troy to Vietnam*, London: Michael Joseph.

34 S. Marshall (1963), *An Experiment in Education*, Cambridge: Cambridge University Press.

35 M. Cannon (1988), *Australia – A History in Photographs'*, Ringwood: Viking O'Neil and Penguin Books Australia, p. 10. The photograph is in the collection of the Queen Victoria Museum and Art Gallery, Launceston, Tasmania.

36 See E. Hobsbawm and T. Ranger (1983), *The Invention of Tradition*, Cambridge: Cambridge University Press.

37 P. Y., Rogers, 'History – the past as a frame of reference', p. 20.

38 C. Magris (1990), *Danube*, trans. P. Creagh, London: Collins Harvill, pp. 285–6.

39 M. Ferro (1984), *The Use and Abuse of History*, London: Routledge & Kegan Paul, p. viii.

40 Quoted in P. Burke (1969), *The Renaissance Sense of the Past*, London: Arnold, p. 21.

41 J. Winckelmann (1755), *Thoughts on the Imitation of Greek Art in Painting and Sculpture*, Dresden, reprinted in E. Holt, *A Documentary History of Art*, New York: Doubleday Anchor Books, vol. 2, p. 337.

42 Quoted in H. Honour (1968), *Neo-Classicism*, Harmondsworth: Penguin, p. 44.

43 H. Butterfield (1944), *The Englishman and his History*, Cambridge: Cambridge University Press, p. 6.

44 W. B. Yeats (1952), 'The Second Coming', in *Collected Poems*, London: Macmillan, p. 211.

45 A. Giddens (1992), 'Uprooted signposts at the century's end', *Times Higher Educational Supplement*, 17 January.

46 M. Finley (1975), 'Myth, memory and history', in *The Uses and Abuses of History*, London: Chatto and Windus, p. 13.

47 Quoted in V. Mehta (1963), *Fly and the Fly Bottle*, Harmondsworth: Pelican, p. 208.

48 This passage draws on the author's (1989) lecture 'The politics of history teaching: a humanity dehumanized?', London: University of London, Institute of Education.

49 J. Bury in *The Scheme of History*, lecture reprinted in *The Varieties of History*, F. Stern, ed. (1956), London: Macmillan, p. 223.

50 Collingwood, *The Idea of History*, p. 214.

51 There is danger of misunderstandings arising from the use of the word 'scientific'. In English, this would mean that history was like the physical sciences. But this is not necessarily the connotation of the French *scientifique* or the German *wissenschaftlich*. A more wordy but less misleading English equivalent would be 'systematic, organized and rational study which insists on objective procedures'.

52 The issue of interdisciplinarity across the curriculum *et al.* was analysed perceptively by Roy Wake (1979), *Innovation in Secondary Education*, Strasbourg, Council of Europe.

53 P. Burke (1980), *Sociology and History*, London: Allen and Unwin, p. 14.

54 F. Braudel (1958), 'History and the social sciences', *Annales*, p. 723ff, reprinted in P. Burke (ed.), (1972), *Economy and Society in Early Modern Europe: Essays from Annales*, London: Routledge and Kegan Paul, pp. 11, 38.

55 Both quotations from L. Stone (1987), History and the social sciences, in *The Past and Present Revisited*, London: Routledge and Kegan Paul, p. 18.

56 For example, in P. Deane and W. Cole (1962), *British Economic Growth 1688–1959*, Cambridge, and the work of the Cambridge Group for the History of Population and Social Structure.

57 Sociology and geography are not the only social sciences that have widened and deepened our study of the past. As well as economics, anthropology has influenced the work of historians like Keith Thomas, and psychology, particularly Freudian analysis, that of Peter Gay.

58 Some would also include the 'politics of the family', but there are sensitive issues of school-family relationships involved, and in any case, such a topic may more properly be the realm of the anthropologist.

59 On the attitudes and direct involvement of young people and associated research, see P. Rayou (1994), 'Of citizens and men: Political education and the socialization of pupils in upper secondary schools', in the Proceedings of the Seventh European Conference of the Educational Research Institutions on Education for Democratic Citizenship in Europe. Amsterdam: Swets and Zeitlinger.

60 K. Joseph (1984), 'Educating people for Peace', speech to the National Council of Women of Great Britain, 3 March 1984.

61 D. Lawton and B. Dufour (1973), *The New Social Studies*, London: Heinemann, p. 41, in particular their references to the research of Vincent Rogers and David Russell.

62 E. Powell (1992), quoted in P. Hennessey, *Never Again: Britain 1945–51*, London: Cape, p. 1.

63 See also J. Slater, (1989), *The Politics of History Teaching: A Humanity Dehumanized*, London: University of London, Institute of Education. This section draws on this publication.

64 G. Steiner (1970), *In Bluebeard's Castle*, London: Faber, p. 60.

65 D. Shemilt, *History 13–16 Evaluation Study*, p. 21.

66 *Ibid.*, p. 7.

67 Quoted in F. Meinecke, trans. S. Fay, (1950), *The German Catastrophe*, Boston: Beacon Press, p. 1.

Bibliography of Council of Europe Documents, 1953–1994

compiled by
Ruth Goodwin
Directorate of Education,
Culture and Sport

TEXTBOOK STUDIES

The European Idea in History Teaching: Report of the First Conference on the Revision of History Textbooks, Calw, Germany, August 1953 (EXP/CULT (53)33).

The Middle Ages: Report of the Second Conference on the Revision of History Textbooks, Oslo, Norway, August 1954 (EXP/CULT (54)44).

The Sixteenth Century: Report of the Third Conference on the Revision of History Textbooks, Rome, Italy, September 1955 (EXP/CULT (55)31).

The Seventeenth and Eighteenth Centuries: Report of the Fourth Conference on the Revision of History Textbooks, Royaumont, France, September 1956 (EXP/CULT (56)43).

The Period from c.1789 to c.1871: Report of the Fifth Conference on the Revision of History Textbooks, Scheveningen, Netherlands, September 1957 (EXP/CULT(58) 1).

The Period from c.1870 to c.1950: Report of the Sixth Conference on the Revision of History Textbooks, Istanbul and Ankara, Turkey, August 1958 (EXP/CULT (59) 1).

A History of Europe? by E. Bruley and E. H. Dance. A. W. Sythoff (1960).

Grundbegriffe der Geschichte: 50 Beiträge zum Geschichtsbild, Council of Europe/International Schoolbook Institute. eds., C. Bertelsmann Verlag (1964).

History Teaching and History Textbook Revision, by Otto-Ernst Schuddekopf. Council of Europe Publications (1967).

Europa Geschichte und Akualität des Begriffes, by Rolf Salter. Albert Limbach Verlag (1971)

Religion in History Textbooks: Louvain, Belgium, September 1972, by L. Genicot. Council of Europe Publications (1974).

Co-operation in Europe since 1945, as Presented in Resources for the Teaching of History, Geography and Civics in Secondary Schools: Braunschweig, Germany, December 1979. Council of Europe (1979).

The Place and Significance of Contemporary History in Textbooks and Secondary Education: Report of the International Historical Didactical Conference, Kerkrade, Netherlands, November 1981, by Marianne Strootmann, (DECS/EGT(82) 47).

Against Bias and Prejudice: The Council of Europe's Work on History Teaching and History Textbooks: Recommendations on History Teaching and History Textbooks Adopted at Council of Europe Conferences and Symposia 1953–83 (CC–ED HIST (95)3).

History and Social Studies – Methodologies of Textbook Analysis: Proceedings of the Educational Research Workshop, Braunschweig, Germany, September 1990, ed. Hilary Bourdillon. Swets and Zeitlinger (1992).

HISTORY TEACHING IN SCHOOLS

Teaching History in Secondary Schools: Report of the Working Group on History Teaching in Secondary Schools, Braunschweig, Germany and Copenhagen, Denmark, September 1963, by E. E. Y. Hales (CCC/EGT(63) 31).

History Teaching in Secondary Education: Report of the Course on History Teaching in Secondary Education, Elsinor, Denmark, September 1965, by Kjeld Winding (EGT/Stage (66) XVII 2).

History Teaching in Lower Secondary Education: Final Report of the Course on History Teaching in Lower Secondary Education, Braunschweig, Germany, September 1969, by E. E. Y. Hayles (CCC/EGT(69) 37).

The Place of History in Secondary Teaching: A Comparative Study, by E. H. Dance. Harrap/Council of Europe, (1970).

History Teaching in Upper Secondary Education: Meeting of Experts, Strasbourg, France, December 1971 (DECS/EGT (71) 150).

Education and Culture, No. 17: History Teaching in School: Review of the CDCC and the European Cultural Foundation. Council of Europe (Autumn–Winter 1971).

European Curriculum Studies No. 8: History, by E .E. Y. Hales. Council of Europe Publications (1973).

New Trends in History Teaching in Upper Secondary Education: Fourth Donaueschingen Seminar, Germany, May 1979, by Erik Rudeng (DECS/EGT(79) 63).

The Teaching of History in Primary Schools: Aims, Methods and Problems: 19th Donaueschingen Seminar, Germany, May 1983, by Otto Stephan (DECS/EGT (84) 1).

New Approaches to History Teaching in Upper Secondary Education: 54th Donaueschingen Seminar, Germany, November 1991, by Traute Petersen (DECS/SE/BS/Donau (91) 4).

History Teaching in the New Europe: Symposium, Bruges, Belgium, December 1991, by Michel Charriere (CC-ED/HIST(93)1).

Problems of History Teaching in Post-Communist Societies: 62nd Donaueschingen Seminar, Germany, November 1993, by Christine Sauerbaum-Thieme (DECS/SE/BS/Donau (93) 4).

History, Democratic Values and Tolerance: Conference, Sofia, Bulgaria, October 1994, by David Harkness (CC-ED/Hist (94)28).

History Teaching in Schools in Democratic Transition: Conference, Graz, Austria, December 1994, by Ann Low-Beer. (CC-ED/Hist (95)2).

TOPICS IN HISTORY TEACHING

Teaching about the 'Portuguese Discoveries in Renaissance Europe' in Secondary Schools in Western Europe: European Teachers' Seminar, Lisbon, Portugal, July 1983, by Patricia Bahree (DECS/EGT(83)61).

Portuguese Expansion in the Fifteenth and Sixteenth Centuries and the World Encounter of Cultures: Workshop for History Teachers, Evora, Portugal, July 1984, by Patricia Bahree (DECS/EGT (85)61).

Teaching about Africa South of the Sahara: European Teachers' Seminar, Lahti, Finland, August 1984, by Elizabeth Gunner (DECS/EGT(85)15).

Teaching and Learning about Each Other: The USA and Western Europe: Conference, Washington DC, USA, November 1984 (DECS/EGT (85)57).

The Birth of Brazil: Roots of a Multicultural Society: European Teachers' Seminar, Lisbon, Portugal, December 1985, by Arlindo Manuel Caldeira (DECS/EGT (86)31).

The Viking Age in Europe: European Teachers' Seminar, Larkollen, Norway, August 1986.

Europe and the United States Constitution: 37th Donaueschingen Seminar, Germany, October 1987, by Godfrey Hodgson (DECS/EGT(87)38).

Teaching about the French Revolution in Secondary Schools in Europe: 39th Donaueschingen Seminar, Germany, May 1988, by Stephane Audoin-Rouzeau (DECS/EGT(88)30).

The French Revolution and its Consequences in Europe: European Teachers' Seminar, Esneux, Belgium, November 1988, by Jacqueline Delrot (DECS/EGT(88)63).

The Independence Movements in African Countries: 44th Donaueschingen Seminar, Germany, June 1989, by Jean Rossiaud (DECS/EGT(89)36).

The Conquest of Human Rights through History: European Teachers' Seminar, Esneux, Belgium, November 1989, by R. Cavenaile (DECS/EGT(89)45).

The Nationalities Question – From Versailles to the Present Day: European Teachers' Seminar, Esneux, Belgium, April 1991, by Jacqueline Delrot (DECS/SE/BS/Sem(91)2).

The Nationalities Question – from Versailles to the Present Day: European Teachers' Seminar, Esneux, Belgium, April 1991, by Jacqueline Delrot (DECS/SE/BS/Sem(91)2).

The Symbols of Freedom: Switzerland in the Thirteenth and Fourteenth Centuries: European Teachers' Seminar, Geneva, Switzerland, September 1991, by Guy Le Comte (DECS/SE/BS/Sem(91)5).

The Hanse in Norway and Europe: European Teachers' Seminar, Bergen, Norway, August 1992, by Sean Lang (DECS/SE/BS/Sem(92)1).

The Teaching of History since 1815 with Special Reference to Changing Borders: Symposium, Leeuwarden, Netherlands, April 1993, by Robert Stradling, (CC-ED/HIST(94)2).

The History of the Baltic Sea – A History of Conflicts: European Teachers' Seminar, Visby, Sweden, August 1993, by Sean Lang (DECS/SE/BS/Sem (94)15).

Vikings going Eastward – Explorers of the River Routes from the Baltic to the Caspian Sea: European Teachers' Seminar, Visby, Sweden, August 1994, by Richard Dargie (not yet available).

The Industrial Revolution: Birth of a European Technological Area: Teaching Pack, Provisional Version, by Marcella Colle-Michel, René Leboute and Danielle Leclerq (Secondary Education for Europe/provisional).

INTERDISCIPLINARITY IN THE SCHOOL CURRICULUM

Aims, Objectives and Methodology of an Interdisciplinary Approach to the Teaching of the Human Sciences in Secondary Education, by T. W. F. Allan, (DECS/EGT(75)46).

An Interdisciplinary Approach to the Teaching of the Human Sciences in Secondary Education: Report of the Meeting of Experts, Strasbourg, France, March 1976 (DECS/EGT(76)15).

Innovation in Secondary Education in Europe, by R. Wake, V. Marbeau and A. Peterson. Council of Europe (1979).

Project Based Teaching: The Multidisciplinary Approach to the European Dimension in Secondary Education: 55th Donaueschingen Seminar, Germany, May 1994, by Simone Barthel (DECS/SE/BS/Donau(92)1).

THE EUROPEAN DIMENSION

Introducing Europe to Senior Pupils, by Rene Jotterand. Council of Europe Publications (1966).

Europe in the Secondary School Curriculum: First Donaueschingen Seminar, Germany, September 1978, by Margaret Shennan (DECS/EGT(78)37).

Europe in Secondary School Curricula: Symposium Report, Neudiedl-am-See, Austria, April 1981, by David Peacock. Council of Europe (1982).

Teaching about European Co-operation and Integration in Upper Secondary Schools: Teacher Bursaries Scheme, Ebeltoft, Denmark, March 1987, by Margaret Shennan (DECS/EGT(87)31).

Europe: Knowing the Past, Understanding the Present. What to Know about European History by the end of Compulsory Schooling: European Teachers' Seminar, Oporto, Portugal, December 1988, by Marcella Colle-Michel (DECS/EGT (88)62).

Teaching about Europe, by Margaret Shennan. Cassell/Council of Europe (1991).

Teaching about European History and Society in the 1990s: European Teachers' Seminar, Tuusula, Finland, August 1991, by Sean Lang (DECS/SE/BS/Sem(91)4).

Teaching Local History in a European Perspective: European Teachers' Seminar, Trondheim, Norway, July 1993, by Ann Low-Beer (DECS/SE/BS/Sem(93)2).

The European Dimension in the Curriculum: European Teachers' Seminar, Cardiff, United Kingdom, October 1993, by Gianna Fruhauf (DECS/SE/BS/Sem(93)5).

The European Dimension in Education and Teacher Training: European Teachers' Seminar, Hildesheim, Germany, November 1993, by Sabine Pasler (DECS/SE/BS/Sem(93)6).

History Teaching and European Awareness: Symposium, Delphi, Greece, May 1993, by David Harkness (CC-ED/Hist(94)).

HUMAN RIGHTS EDUCATION AND EDUCATION FOR DEMOCRATIC CITIZENSHIP

Human Rights Education in Schools: Concepts, Attitudes and Skills, by Derek Heater (DECS/EGT(84)26).

Teaching and Learning about Human Rights, by Ian Lister (DECS/EGT(84)27).

Action to Combat Intolerance and Xenophobia, by Antonio Perotti (DECS/EGT (89)34).

Socialisation of School Children and their Education for Democratic Values and Human Rights: Proceedings of the Colloquy of Directors of European Educational Research Institutions, Ericeira, Portugal, October 1989, ed. Hugh Starkey. Swets and Zeitlinger (1991).

Education for Democratic Citizenship in Europe – New Challenges for Secondary Education: Proceedings of Seventh European Conference of Directors of European Educational Research Institutions, Nitra, Slovakia, October 1992, by Ken Fogelman and Pamela Munn. Swets and Zeitlinger (1994).

The Challenge of Human Rights Education, by Hugh Starkey. Cassell/Council of Europe (1991).

Human Rights Education, by Francine Best (DECS/provisional edition).

Teaching about Society: Passing on Values – Elementary Law in Civic Education, by François Audigier. Council of Europe Press (1993).

Europe versus Intolerance: Summary of the Proceedings of the Seminar, Strasbourg, France, March 1994 (SEM/INTOL).

Europe versus Intolerance: Contributions to the Seminar, Strasbourg, France, March 1994 (SEM/INTOL).

INTERCULTURAL EDUCATION

Compendium of Information on Intercultural Education Schemes in Europe, by Micheline Rey (DECS/EGT(83)62).

Training Teachers in Intercultural Education?: The Work of the Council for Cultural Co-operation: 1977–83, by Micheline Rey. Council of Europe (1986).

Roma, Gypsies, Travellers: Socio-cultural Data, socio-political Data, by Jean-Pierre Liegois, Council of Europe (1994).

Final Educational Evaluation of the Programme of Experiments in Intercultural Education from 1986–1991, by Antonio Perotti (DECS/EGT (90)37).

Intercultural Learning for Human Rights: Report of the Seminar, Klagenfurt, Austria, October, 1991, by B. Geremek. Council of Europe Press (1992).

The Case for Intercultural Education, by Antonio Perotti. Council of Europe

Press (1994).

WORLD STUDIES

World Studies in the European Classroom, by Edmund O'Conner. Council of Europe (1980).

Education for International Understanding – Teaching about a Non-European Culture: The Case of Japan: 11th Donaueschingen Seminar, Germany, May 1981, by Richard Tames (DECS/EGT(81)2).

Teaching about China in Secondary Schools in Western Europe: 22nd Donaueschingen Seminar, Germany, November 1983, Graham Thomas (DECS/EGT(84)2).

Teaching about the USA in Secondary Schools in Western Europe: 17th Donaueschingen Seminar, Germany, October 1982, by Roy Williams (DECS/EGT(84)39).

Teaching about Canada in Secondary Schools in Western Europe: 25th Donaueschingen Seminar, Germany, October 1984, by Maria Emilia Galvao, (DECS/EGT(84)43).

Asia in the European Classroom: European Teachers' Seminar, London, United Kingdom, September 1985, by Patricia Bahree (DECS/EGT(85)79).

Teaching about Canada in Secondary Schools in Western Europe: 31st Donaueschingen Seminar, Germany, May 1986, by Jean-Michel Leclercq (DECS/EGT(86)71).

The World in the European Classroom:

Conclusions and Recommendations of the Symposium, Haikko, Finland, September 1986 (DECS/EGT(87)58).

North-South Interdependence and Solidarity: Approaches to South America: European Teachers' Seminar, Lahti, Finland, August 1988, by John Hopkin (DECS/EGT(88)54).

Euro-Arab Understanding and Cultural Exchange: Conference, Strasbourg, France, November 1991. Council of Europe Press (1991).

DEVELOPMENT EDUCATION

Development Education: 7th Donaueschingen Seminar, Germany, March 1980, by Oliver Dunlop (DECS/EGT(80)47).

Development Education in Primary Schools: 21st Donaueschingen Seminar, Germany, October 1983, Sneh Shah (DECS/EGT(84)40).

Development Education in Secondary Schools: European Teachers' Seminar, Sintra, Portugal, January 1988, by Audrey Osler (DECS/EGT(88)34).

Development Education in the French Education System: European Teachers' Seminar, Royaumont, France, December 1987, by André Zweyacker (DECS/EGT(88)35).

Making One World: An Education Pack on Development and Environment, by John Widdowson. North-South Centre of the Council of Europe (1992).

Education and Training in the Fields of Environment and Development. Council of Europe (1993).

Development Education: Global Perspectives in the Curriculum, ed. Audrey Osler. Cassell/Council of Europe (1994).

SCHOOL LINKS AND EXCHANGES

Using the New Technologies to Create Links between Schools throughout the World: Report of the Colloquy on Computerised School Links, Exeter, United Kingdom, October 1988, by J. P. Carpenter (CDCC(89)10).

School Links and Exchanges in Europe: Report of the Seminar, Brighton, United Kingdom, November 1991, by David Rowles (DECS/SE/Sec(92)19).

An Intercultural Training Approach to School Links and Exchanges: Report of the Seminar, Colle Val d'Elsa, Italy, July 1992, by David Rowles (DECS/SE/Sec(92)51).

School Twinning and Local History: Implementation of the Pilot Programme during the School Year 1991–92, Information and Reflection Document, October 1992 (CPL1.Cult(27)6 rev).

The Educational Theory and Practice of School Links and Exchanges: 56th Donaueschingen Seminar, Germany, June 1992, by Roger Savage (DECS/SE/BS/Donau(92)2).

School Exchanges as a Factor in Curriculum Organisation: Report of the Seminar, Stavanger, Norway, September 1992, by Elspeth Cardy (DECS/SE/Sec (93)10).

School Twinning and Local History: Report on the Project of the Standing Conference of Local and Regional Authorities of Europe, Strasbourg, France, July 1993, by Olivier Jehin (CPL/Cult (28)5).

School Links and Exchanges in Europe: A Practical Guide, by Roger Savage. Council of Europe Press (1993).

School Links and Exchanges: The Role of the Local and Regional Authorities, by Roger Savage (Study No. 23).

European Clubs, by Margarita Belard. Council of Europe Press (1993).

Teaching for Exchanges – Aims and Ways of Teacher Training, by European Association for Teachers (EAT) and European Research Group on Training for School Exchanges (ERGTSE). Council of Europe Press (1993).

Electronic School Links: Final Report of the Seminar, Stockholm, Sweden, October 1993, by Gianna Fruhauf (DECS/SE/Sec (93)35).

Links: Newsletter of the European Network on Schools Links and Exchanges.

THE COUNCIL OF EUROPE ART EXHIBITIONS

Humanist Europe: Brussels, Belgium, 1955.

The Triumph of Mannerism from Michelangelo to El Greco: Amsterdam, Netherlands, 1955.

The Seventeenth Century in Europe: Realism, Classicism and Baroque: Rome, Italy, 1956–57.

The Age of Rococo: Munich, Germany, 1958.

The Romantic Movement: London, United Kingdom, 1959.

The Sources of the 20th Century: The Arts in Europe from 1884–1914: Paris, France, 1960.

Romanesque Art: Barcelona, Santiago de Compostela, Spain, 1961.

European Art round 1400: Vienna, Austria, 1962.

Byzantine Art as a European Art: Athens, Greece, 1964.

Charlemagne – His Life and Work: Aachen, Germany 1965.

Queen Christina of Sweden and her Epoch: Stockholm, Sweden, 1966.

Gothic Art in Europe: Paris, France, 1968.

The Order of St John in Malta: Valletta, Malta, 1970.

The Age of Neo-Classicism: London, United Kingdom, 1972.

Trends in the Twenties: Berlin, Germany, 1977.

Florence and the Tuscany of the Medici in Sixteenth Century Europe: Florence, Italy, 1980.

The Portuguese Discoveries and Renaissance Europe: Lisbon, Portugal, 1983.

Anatolian Civilisations: Istanbul, Turkey, 1983.

Christian IV and Europe: Denmark, 1988.

The French Revolution and Europe: Paris, France, 1989.

Emblems of Liberty. The Image of the Republic in the Art of the Sixteenth to the Twentieth Century: Berne, Switzerland, 1991.

From Viking to Crusader: Scandinavia and Europe 800–1200: Paris, Berlin, Copenhagen, 1992–3.

ART EXHIBITIONS HELD OUTSIDE THE SERIES

Exhibition-Dialogue on Contemporary Art in Europe: Lisbon, Portugal, 1985.

Space in European Art: Tokyo, Japan, 1987.

European Painters of the Eighties: Itinerant Exhibition, 1987–88.

THE CULTURAL HERITAGE AND THE EUROPEAN CULTURAL ROUTES

Museums: Treasures or Tools?: Symposium, Salzburg, Austria, September 1990, by Kenneth Hudson (DECS/SE(92)6).

Handbook on European Heritage

Classes: Group of Specialists on European Heritage Classes. Council of Europe (1993).

Architectural Heritage: Inventory and Documentation Methods in Europe: Proceedings of the Colloquy, Nantes, France, October 1992. Council of Europe (1993).

Pushing back the Horizon – European Cultural Itineraries and Explorations for the Third Millennium, by various authors. Editions du Rouergue (1994).

The Council of Europe's Cultural Routes, (Leaflet).

Routes – Newsletter of the Council of Europe Cultural Routes (Newsletter).

DECLARATIONS, RECOMMENDATIONS AND RESOLUTIONS

Council of Europe Summit of Heads of State and Government

The Vienna Declaration (Vienna October 1993).

Committee of Ministers of the Council of Europe

Resolution (52)17 on **History and geography textbooks** (adopted 19 March 1952)
Resolution (64)11 on **Civics and European education** (adopted 6 October 1964)
Resolution (65)17 on **The creation of national information and documenta-**

tion centres for the improvement of history and geography textbooks (adopted 25 September 1965)

Declaration regarding intolerance – a threat to democracy. (adopted 14 May 1981)

Recommendation No. R(83)4 concerning **The promotion of an awareness of Europe in secondary schools** (adopted 18 April 1983).

Recommendation No. (84) 18 on **The training of teachers in education for intercultural understanding, notably in a context of migration** (adopted 25 September 1994)

Resolution No .(85)6 on **European cultural identity** (adopted 25 April 1985)

Recommendation No.(85)7 on **Teaching and learning about human rights in schools** (adopted 14 May 1985)

Recommendation No R(88)17 on **Co-operation with the Georg Eckert Institute for International Textbook Research (history, geography and social studies).** (adopted 29 September 1988)

Parliamentary Assembly of the Council of Europe

Resolution 743 (1980) on **The need to combat resurgent fascist propaganda and its racist aspects**

Recommendation 897 (1980) on **Educational visits and pupil exchanges between European countries**

Recommendation 963 (1983) on **Cultural**

and educational means of reducing violence

Resolution 885 (1987) on **The Jewish contribution to European culture**

Recommendation 1111 (1989) on **The European dimension of education**

Recommendation 1162 (1991) on **The contribution of the Islamic civilisation to European culture**

Recommendation 1202 (1993) on **Religious tolerance in a democratic society**

Standing Conference of European Ministers of Education

17th Session (Vienna, Austria, 16–17 October 1991). Resolution No. 1 on **The European dimension of education: teaching and curriculum content** (doc MED-17-6)

18th Session (Madrid, Spain, 23–24 March 1994). Resolution No. 1 on **Education for democracy, human rights and tolerance** (doc MED-18-6)

18th Session (Madrid, Spain, 23–24 March 1994). Resolution No.3 on **The promotion of school links and exchanges in Europe** (doc MED-18-6)

Congress of Local and Regional Authorities of Europe

26th Session (19–21 March 1991).

APPENDIX
List of Addresses Relevant to History Education

INTERGOVERNMENTAL AND SUPRANATIONAL INSTITUTIONS

The Council of Europe

The Council for Cultural Cooperation,
Directorate of Education, Culture and Sport,
Council of Europe,
F-67075 Strasbourg Cedex, France
tel: (33) 88 41 20 00
fax: (33) 88 41 27 50

Congress of Local and Regional Authorities of Europe,
Directorate of Environment and Local Authorities,
Council of Europe,
F-67075 Strasbourg Cedex, France
tel: (33) 88 41 20 00
fax: (33) 88 41 27 51

European Centre for Global Interdependence (North-South Centre),
Avenida da Libertade 229–4e,
P-1200 Lisbon,
Portugal
tel: (351) 1 52 29 03
fax: (351) 1 353 13 29

The European Union

SOCRATES/Jeunesse Bureau
Rue Montoyer 70,
B-1040 Brussels,
Belgium
tel: (32) 22 33 01 11
fax: (32) 22 33 01 50

EURYDICE,
European Unit,
15, rue d'Arlon,
B-1040 Brussels,
Belgium
tel: (32) 2 238 30 11
fax: (32) 2 230 65 62

The European Schools,
Mr Jorgen Olsen,
Representative of the Board of Governors,
The European Schools,
200 rue de la Loi,
B-1049 Brussels
tel: (32) 235 37 46
fax: (32) 230 19 30

The Jean Monnet Action,
T-120 04–3,
DG 10,
200, rue de la Loi,
B-1400 Brussels
tel: (32) 2 299 92 67
fax: (32) 2 296 31 06

TEMPUS,
Fondazione Europea per la formazione,
Villa Gualino,
Viale Settimio Severo 65,
I–10133 Torino,
Italy
tel: (39) 11 630 22 22
fax: (39) 11 630 22 00

UNESCO
Associated Schools Project in
Education for International
Cooperation and Peace (ASP),
UNESCO,
7, Place de Fontenoy,
F-75732 Paris Cedex 15,
France
tel: (33) 1 45 68 10 89
fax: (33) 1 40 65 94 05

The Baltic Sea Project,
Siv Sellin, BSP General Coordinator,
National Agency for Education,
106, 20 Stockholm,
Sweden
tel: (46) 8 723 32 74
fax: (46) 8 24 44 20

Blue Danube River Project (BDR),
Yordanka Nenova,
ELS School 'Geo Milev',
Rousse,
Bulgaria
tel: (359) 82 623 820
fax: (359) 82 226 379

Mediterranean Project,
Miguel Marti,
Centre UNESCO de Catalogne,
Mallorca 285,
08037 Barcelona,
Spain
tel: (34) 3 207 17 16
fax: (34) 3 457 58 51

The Nordic Council of Ministers

The Nordic Council of Ministers,
18, Store Strandstraede,
DK–1255 Copenhagen,
Denmark
tel: (45) 33 96 02 00
fax: (45) 33 96 02 02

INTERNATIONAL NON-GOVERNMENTAL ORGANIZATIONS AND INTERNATIONAL PROJECTS DEVOTED TO HISTORY

Concepts of History and Teaching
Approaches at Key Stages 2 and 3
(CHATA),
Alaric Dickinson and Peter Lee,
Department of History, Humanities and
Philosophy,
Institute of Education,
University of London,
20 Bedford Way,
London WC1H 0AL
United Kingdom
tel: (44) 71 612 6543
fax: (44) 71 612 6555

European Standing Conference of History Teachers Associations (EUROCLIO),
Louise Henriette Street 16
2595 TH The Hague
tel: (31) 70 385 3669
fax: (31) 70 385 3669

The International Students of History Association (ISHA),
Justus Lipsiusstraat 44,
B-3000 Leuven,
Belgium
tel: (32) 16 23 29 26
fax: (32) 16 28 50 20

European Association of Young Historians,
David Parry,
Gonville and Caius College,
GB-Cambridge CB2 1TA
United Kingdom

International Society for History Didactics,
Kirchplatz 2,
D-88250 Weingarten,
Germany
tel: (49) 75 29 841
fax: (49) 751 501 200

The International Yearbook for History Teacher Education,
Frank Cass (Publishers) Ltd,
Gainsborough House,
14, Gainsborough Rd,
GB-London E11 1RS,
United Kingdom
tel: (44) 181 530 4226

The Georg Eckert Institute for International Textbook Research,
Celler Strasse 3,
D-38114 Braunschweig,
Germany
tel: (49) 531 590 990
fax: (49) 531 590 99 99

International Committee of Historical Sciences (CISH),
Ian Hill,
Regional Director for Europe,
44 rue de l'Amiral Mouchez,
F-75014 Paris,
France
tel: (33) (1) 45 80 90 46
fax: (33) (1) 45 65 43 50

The Young Historian Scheme,
c/o The Historical Association,
59a Kennington Park Road,
GB-London SE11 4JH,
United Kingdom
tel: (44) 171 735 3901
fax: (44) 171 582 4989

The European Studies Project,
Ulster Folk and Transport Museum,
153, Bangor Rd,
Holywood,
Co Down,
BT18 0EU,
Northern Ireland
tel: (44) 1232 425285
fax: (44) 1232 427992

The Historical Association,
59a Kennington Park Rd,
GB-London SE11 4JH,
United Kingdom
tel: (44) 171 735 3901
fax: (44) 171 582 4989

The Youth and History Project,
Bergen College of Education,
Mr Magne Angvik,
Landassvingen 15,
N-5030 Landas,
Norway
tel: (47) 55 205 864
fax: (47) 55 205 809

The Schools History Project,
Trinity and All Saints' College,
Brownberrie Lane,
Horsforth,
Leeds LS18 5HD
United Kingdom

**The Cambridge History Project
(CHP),**
The University of Cambridge Local
Examinations Syndicate,
Syndicate Buildings,
1 Hills Road,
Cambridge CB1 2EU.
United Kingdom
tel: (44) 1223 55 33 11
fax: (44) 1223 46 02 78

INTERNATIONAL NON-GOVERNMENTAL ORGANIZATIONS WHICH HAVE AN INTEREST (NOT EXCLUSIVE) IN HISTORY

**European Association of Teachers
(EAT),**
Guus Wijngaards,
Secretary General,
Koningsholster 64,
NL-6573 VV Beek-Ubbergen,
The Netherlands
tel: (31) 8895 42854
fax: (31) 8895 42902

**The European Association for Schools
for Cooperative Projects (EURELEM
2000),**
c/o OCCE,
101 bis, rue du Ranelagh,
F-75016 Paris,
France
tel: (33) (1) 45 25 46 07

International Schools Association,
Cyril Ritchie,
Director,
CIC Case 20,
CH-1211 Geneva 20,
Switzerland
tel: (41) 22 33 67 17

**International Baccalaureate
Organization,**
15, route des Morillons,
CH-1218 Grand Saconnex,
Geneva,
Switzerland
tel: (41) 22 791 02 74
fax: (41) 22 791 02 77

**International Association for the
Evaluation of Educational
Achievement (IEA),**
c/o SVO,
14, Sweelinckplein,
NL-2517 GK The Hague,
The Netherlands
tel: (31) 70 346 96 79
fax: (31) 70 360 99 51

**The Consortium of Institutions for
Development and Research in
Education in Europe (CIDREE),**
Cameron Harrison,
Secretary General,
The Scottish Consultative Council on the
Curriculum,
Northern College of Education,
Gardyne Rd,
Broughty Ferry,
GB-Dundee DDS 1NY,
United Kingdom
tel: (44) 1382 45 50 53
fax: (44) 1382 45 50 46

European Federation for Intercultural Learning (EFIL),
36, rue de la Montagne,
B-1000 Brussels
tel: (32) 2 514 52 50
fax: (32) 2 514 29 29

The International Association for Intercultural Education (IAIE),
Pieter Batelaan,
Sumatralaan 37,
NL-1217 GP Hilversum,
The Netherlands
tel: (31) 35 24 73 75
fax: (31) 35 23 92 44

International Society for Intercultural Education, Training and Research (SIETAR),
5, rue Adèle,
F-93250 Villemonble,
France
tel: (33) (1) 45 28 58 27
fax: (33) (1) 45 28 58 27

The European Educational Publishers' Group (EEPG),
Barbro Larsson,
Box 3095 750 03,
Uppsala,
Sweden
tel: (46) 18 123 114
fax: (46) 18 125 533

NATIONAL HISTORY TEACHERS' ASSOCIATIONS MEMBERS OF EUROCLIO

Austria
Konferenz für Geschichtsdidaktik Österreich,
Postfach 154,
A-1015 Vienna

Pädagogische Akademie des Bundes,
Elisabeth Buxbaum,
Ettenreichgasse 45a,
A-1100 Vienna
tel: (43) 1 505 73 72
fax: (43) 1 603 41 39

Belgium
Vereniging van Leraren Geschiedenis,
Robert Lenaerts,
Binnenveld 27,
B-2490 Balen
tel: (32) 14 81 14 55
fax: (32) 14 81 14 55

Vereniging van Leraren Geschiedenis en Maatschappijleer,
Paul Vandepitte,
Driesstraat 9,
B-8700 Tielt
tel: (32) 51 40 17 00
fax: (32) 51 40 17 00

Croatia
Ivo Rendi-Miocevic,
J Krasa,
51000 Rijeka
(*Association in foundation*)

Czech Republic
History Club, History Teachers Association,
Marie Homerova,
UD Auk,
Ovocny trh 15,
CZ-Praha 1 11000
tel: (42) 2 53 68 52
    (42) 2 53 55 84
fax: (42) 2 35 25 49
    (42) 2 78 15 05 4

Denmark
Dansk historielaerer forening for Gymnasiet
og HF,
Jens Dalsgaard,
Schleppegrellsgade 18 B 1 TV,
DK-8000 Arhus C
tel: (45) 86 19 99 47
fax: (45) 86 18 11 82

Estonia
Estonian Education Centre,
Sulev Valdmaa,
23 Sakala St,
EE-200105 Tallinn
tel: (372) 2 142 444 343/444 591
fax: (372) 6 142 440 235

Finland
Historian ja yhteiskuntaopin opettajien
hitto HYOL,
Fredrikinkatu 61 A 9,
SF-00100 Helsinki
tel: (358) 0 68 52 230
fax: (358) 0 68 52 235

France
Association de Professeurs d'Histoire et de
Géographie (APHG),
98-100 rue Montmartre,
BP 49,
F-75060 Paris Cedex 02
tel: (33) (1) 42 33 62 37
fax: (33) (1) 42 33 12 08

Germany
Verband der Geschichtslehrer Deutschlands
e.V,
Rolf Ballof,
Buchenweg 19,
D-37191 Katlenburg/Lindau
tel: (49) 55 52 71 66
fax: (49) 53 81 10 32

Hungary
Törtenelemtana'rok egylete,
Muzeum utca 7,
H-1088 Budapest

Eszter Glavinics Jahner,
Mirtusz U 17,
H-1141 Budapest
tel: (36) 1 11 86 00 2
     (36) 1 22 00 76 9
fax: (36) 1 11 86 00 2
     (36) 1 17 63 17 7

Ireland
History Teachers' Association of Ireland,
Mary O'Dubhain,
23 Butterfield Orchard,
Rathfarnham,
IRL-Dublin 14

Latvia
Latvijas Vestures Skolotaju Asociacija,
Andris Tomasüns,
Valnuzela 2,
LV-1050 Riga

Gumârs Kurlovics,
E Darzina Jelalu,
Talrunis,
LV-3008 Jelgava
(*Association in foundation*)

Lithuania
Lietuvos Istorijos Mokytojk Asociacija,
Eugenijus Manelis,
Architektu 77–59,
2049 Vilnius
tel: (370) 2 62 27 52
     (370) 2 61 01 65
fax: (370) 2 61 20 77

Luxembourg
Association Luxembourgeoise des
Enseignants d'Histoire (ALEH),
Michel Polfer,
10 rue du Pont,
L-9268 Diekirch
tel: (352) 80 97 40
fax: (352) 80 41 76

Netherlands
Vereniging van docenten in Geschiedenis
en staatsinrichting in Nederland (VGN),
Hélène Budé-Janssens,
Patrijislaan 12 A,
NL-2261 ED Leidschendam
tel: (31) 70 32 77 92 3
fax: (31) 70 32 01 29 8

Northern Ireland
Michael D. Millerick,
St Mary's College of Education,
191 Falls Road,
Belfast BT 12 6FE
tel: (44) 1232 327 678
fax: (44) 1232 333 719
(*Association in Foundation*)

Norway
Laererforbundet,
Harald Froehaug,
Hunnsv 22,
N-2800 Gjoevik
tel: (47) 22 03 00 00
fax: (47) 22 11 05 42

HIFO,
Elisabeth Edding,
Stormyrveien 9d,
N-0672 Oslo
tel: (47) 22 26 77 25

Portugal
Associaçao de Professores de Historia
(APH),
Rua da Arrabida N 10,
R/chao Esq,
P-1200 Lisbon
tel: (351) 1 38 80 98 1
fax: (351) 1 38 80 98 1

Romania
Romanian Society of Historical Studies,
Mihai Manea,
Bulevardul Republicii nr 13 Parter,
RO-70031 Bucuresti, Sectorul 3
tel: (40) 13 21 05 35
fax: (40) 13 21 05 35

Russian Federation
Tamara Eidelman,
Pl Pobedy,
RF-121293 Moscow,
Moscow 12 12 93
tel: (7) 095 14 85 87 7
fax: (7) 095 14 81 55 6
(7) 095 14 81 53 2
(*Association in foundation*)

Scotland
Scottish History Teachers Association,
Ian McKellar,
Strathclyde University,
Jordanhill College of Education,
76 Southbrae Drive,
Glasgow, GB-G 13 1 PP
tel: (44) 141 950 3397
fax: (44) 141 950 3268

Slovak Republic
Jana Huttova,
Gymnazium Jura Hronca,
Novohradska 1,
821 09 Bratislava,
Slovak Republic
tel: (42) 7 625 81
fax: (42) 7 625 81
(*Association in foundation*)

Slovenia
Ana Nusa Kern,
Drnovo 12,
61241 Kamnik,
Slovenia
tel: (386) 61 81 25 60/61 83 10 64
fax: (386) 61 83 21 30
(*Association in foundation*)

Spain
Asociacion del Profesorado de Geografia e
Historia,
Christina del Moral,
Santo Domingo de Silos 6,
E - 28036 Madrid
tel: (34) 1 52 13 77 5
fax: (34) 1 52 29 25 6

Feliciano Paéz-Camino,
Pilar Llarente,
c/Oltra 14,
E - 28028 Madrid

Dolors Boschi i Carrera,
Ar Diagonal 523, 15K
E - 08029 Barcelona
tel: (34) 3 439 93 64

Sweden
Historie Lärarnas Forening (HLF),
Hélène Edgren,
Finntorpsv 13,
S-13136 Nacka
tel: (56) 87 18 14 50
fax: (46) 87 18 82 98

Switzerland
Société Suisse des Professeurs d'Histoire,
Verein Schweizerischer
Geschichtslehrerinnen und
Geschichtslehrer,

Societa'svizzera delle e degli insegnanti di
storia,
Giorgio Tognola,
CH-6930 Bedano
tel: (41) 91 93 23 03

United Kingdom
The Historical Association,
59a, Kennington Park Rd,
GB-London SE 11 4JH
tel: (44) 171 735 3901
fax: (44) 171 582 4989

Wales
Grahame Nelmes,
King Henry VIII School,
Old Hereford Road,
Abergaveny,
Gwent NP7 6EP
tel: (44) 1873 852 701
fax: (44) 1873 850 430

Name Index

Subject Index